C0-ARR-813

DISCARDED

International Institutions and Multinational
Enterprises

INTERNATIONAL INSTITUTIONS AND GLOBAL GOVERNANCE

Series Editors: John-ren Chen, *Professor of Economic Theory and Econometrics, Department of Economic Theory, Policy and History, Director of the Centre for the Study of International Institutions, University of Innsbruck, Austria* and David Sapsford, *Edward Gonner Professor of Applied Economics, University of Liverpool, UK*

Titles in the series include:

The Role of International Institutions in Globalisation
The Challenges of Reform
Edited by John-ren Chen

International Institutions and Multinational Enterprises
Global Players – Global Markets
Edited by John-ren Chen

International Institutions and Multinational Enterprises

Global Players – Global Markets

Edited by

John-ren Chen

Professor of Economic Theory and Econometrics, Department of Economic Theory, Policy and History and Director, Centre for the Study of International Institutions, University of Innsbruck, Austria

INTERNATIONAL INSTITUTIONS AND GLOBAL GOVERNANCE

Edward Elgar
Cheltenham, UK • Northampton, MA, USA

© John-ren Chen, 2004

All rights reserved. No part of this publication may be reproduced, stored in a retrieval system or transmitted in any form or by any means, electronic, mechanical or photocopying, recording, or otherwise without the prior permission of the publisher.

Published by
Edward Elgar Publishing Limited
Glensanda House
Montpellier Parade
Cheltenham
Glos GL50 1UA
UK

Edward Elgar Publishing, Inc.
136 West Street
Suite 202
Northampton
Massachusetts 01060
USA

A catalogue record for this book
is available from the British Library

Library of Congress Cataloguing in Publication Data

International institutions and multinational enterprises: global players—global
    markets/edited by John-ren Chen.
        p. cm. — (International institutions and global governance)
    "The second international CSI Conference on 'Multinational Enterprises and
    International Institutions: Global Players—Global Markets' was held from 20th–
    22nd November 2002 in Innsbruck"—Preface.
        1. International business enterprises—Government policy—Congresses. 2.
    International agencies—Congresses. I. Chen, John-ren. II. Series.

    HD2755.5.I564 2004
    338.8'8—dc22

                                                                    2004047120

ISBN 1 84376 875 5

Typeset by Manton Typesetters, Louth, Lincolnshire, UK.
Printed and bound in Great Britain by MPG Books Ltd, Bodmin, Cornwall.

Physical Processing

Order Type: NTAS

		Sel ID/Seq No:

Cust/Add: 228470005/01

Cust PO No.   P0006214   JFGC   FLORIDA GULF COAST UNIVERSITY   **26240**

Cust Ord Date: 03-Feb-2005   **/258**

BBS Order No: C226386   Ln:197   Del:1   **BBS Ord Date:**   03-Feb-2005

1843768755-18683185   **Sales Qty:** 1   **#Vols:** 001

International institutions and multinational enterprises

Subtitle:global players--global markets

HARDBACK   **Pub Year:**2004   **Vol No.:**   Stmt of Resp:edited by John-ren Chen.

Ser. Title: Edition:

Edward Elgar

Acc Mat:

Tech Services Charges:
- TechPro Cataloging US   Spine Label Protector US   Barcode Label
- Security Device US   Spine Label PromptCat   PromptCat Barcode US
- Property Stamp US   Base Charge Processing   PromptCat Barcode US
- CD ROM US   Barcode Label Protector

Order Line Notes

Cust Fund Code: **Cust Location:**
Stock Category: BUS05-1000   **Cust Dept:**FGAA

Notes to Vendor   ;

400206

Blackwell's Book Services

Contents

Contributors

Professor V.N. Balasubramanyam, Professor of Development Economics, Department of Economics, Management School, University of Lancaster, UK.

Doctor Oliver Budzinski, Research Associate, Chair of Economic Policy, Philipps – University of Marburg, Germany.

Doctor Matthias Busse, Research Associate at the Hamburg Institute of International Economics – HWWA, Department of World Economy, Hamburg, Germany.

Professor John-ren Chen, Professor of Economic Theory and Econometrics, Centre for the Study of International Institutions, University of Innsbruck, Austria.

Professor Daniel Daianu, Professor of Economics, Academy of Economic Studies, Bucharest.

Professor John H. Dunning, Emeritus Professor of International Business, University of Reading, UK.

Doctor Francesca Gastaldi, Research Associate in the Department of Economics, 'La Sapienza' University of Rome, Italy.

Professor Hans H. Hinterhuber, Professor of Strategic Management, Head of the Department of Management at the University of Innsbruck, Austria.

Doctor Klaus Liebscher, Governor of the Austrian National Bank – Oesterreichische Nationalbank.

Professor Kurt Matzler, Professor of Marketing and International Management at the University of Klagenfurt, Austria.

Doctor Maria Grazia Pazienza, Research Associate in the Department of Economics, University of Florence, Italy.

Professor Harald Pechlaner, Foundation Professor of Tourism, University of Eichstätt, Germany.

Doctor Mike Peters, Assistant Professor, Centre for Tourism and Service Economics, University of Innsbruck, Austria.

Brian Portelli, Research Fellow at the Centre for Technology, Innovation and Culture, University of Oslo, Norway.

Doctor Birgit Renzl, Assistant Professor at the Department of Management, University of Innsbruck, Austria.

Professor David Sapsford, Edward Gonner Professor of Applied Economics, Chairman, Economics Division, Management School, University of Liverpool, UK.

Professor Karl Socher, Emeritus Professor of Political Economy, Centre for the Study of International Institutions, University of Innsbruck, Austria.

Professor Klaus Weiermair, Professor and Director, Centre for Tourism and Service Economics, University of Innsbruck, Austria.

Preface

International institutions have contributed a great deal to the development of a free access to global markets, giving chances for economic development and reduction of poverty, especially to developing countries and countries in the process of transformation to market economies. Multinational enterprises (MNEs) have become the most important actors in this global market of goods and capital.

Many activities of the MNEs have had positive effects on the developing and transforming countries, but some negative effects on the economy, on income distribution, other social aspects and on the environment in these countries have been observed. In some of these cases, national states are not able to control and avoid these negative effects. The question arises whether international institutions can play a role in this important task.

In this discussion there are many divergent interests of governments, bureaucrats, manager of MNEs, NGOs and special interest groups. Therefore the Centre for the Study of International Institutions at the Faculty of Social and Economic Sciences of the University of Innsbruck has tried to bring together economists doing research in this field on a scientific basis in a conference. The aim of the conference was to discuss, how far the management of MNEs takes into account negative aspects of their activities, how national states or international institutions control the activities of MNEs and how the role and strategies of international institutions could be changed to minimise the negative effects without hampering the positive effect of MNEs.

The second International CSI Conference on 'Multinational Enterprises and International Institutions – Global Players – Global Markets' was held on 20–22 November 2002 in Innsbruck. Selected contributions of this conference on international institutions are published in this book.

We are very indebted to the Oesterreichische Nationalbank for financial assistance to set up the Centre for the Study of International Institutions, which would not have been possible without this support.

We are also very grateful to the Österreichische Forschungsgemeinschaft (Austrian Research Association) who supported the second Conference on International Institutions and financed this publication.

We thank Masmedia Publishing, Graphic and Business Services of Zagreb, Croatia for granting permission to Professor Daniel Daianu to reproduce here parts of his previously published paper.

Last but not least we also want to express our deep appreciation to the Tiroler Sparkasse Bank for sponsoring the Böhm-Bawerk Lecture, to the members of the Advisory Board, especially my friends Christian Smekal, Karl Socher (both University of Innsbruck), David Sapsford (University of Lancaster) and John Toye (University of Oxford), and to Richard Hule (University of Innsbruck), Gudrun Eder (CSI/University of Innsbruck) as well as Helga Landauer for making the conference such a successful event.

John-ren Chen
Innsbruck

Introduction

Karl Socher

The creation of international institutions after the Second World War had the aim of inducing economic growth and reducing poverty in the industrialised and developing countries by freezing markets for goods, services and capital from restrictions and creating a stable international monetary system. Later, environmental protection became an important aim and, after the breakdown of planned economies in socialist countries, liberalisation, deregulation and privatisation ('Washington Consensus') were implemented in the transition economies. In this process of globalisation, multinational enterprises (MNEs) have become the most important actors in the global markets.

The aim of the second International CSI Conference was to discuss the controversial questions raised by critical economists as well as non-governmental organisations (NGOs) concerning the power and influence of today's global market players. One question was whether the activities of MNEs are in conformity with the aims of the global international institutions: economic growth, development, reduction of poverty and protection of the environment. Do their managements take into account negative effects of their activities? Another question was whether market or government failures prevent countries achieving their aims, so that global international institutions have to act and have to be adapted to eliminate these failures in order to minimise the negative effects without hampering the positive effects of the activities of MNEs.

CORPORATE GOVERNANCE OF MNES

In Chapter 1, John-ren Chen refers to the tasks of governments to correct market failures (especially by the production of public goods and by internalising externalities) and to create a framework for good corporate governance. These two tasks cannot be fulfilled by sovereign states alone, because the activities of MNEs and NGOs go beyond borders and a good corporate governance system is important for an efficient resource allocation and a stable financial architecture.

It is a task for international institutions to spread knowledge about corporate governance rules especially to developing and transition countries and to ascertain that corporate governance of MNEs accords with these rules. Chen discusses the different aspects of a good corporate governance system especially as they are incorporated in the OECD's *Principles of Corporate Governance*. He concludes that, in the dynamic global economy, corporations have to innovate and adapt their governance practices, and similarly the legal and regulatory frameworks have to be adjusted to the new needs of the community.

John H. Dunning, giving the 'Böhm-Bawerk Lecture', spoke on the moral challenge of global capitalism. He proposes a responsible global capitalism as a means towards a richer, healthier and more meaningful lifestyle and not as an end in itself. In order to move towards this inclusive and acceptable global capitalism, the organisational structures of markets, governments and international institutions needs to be reconfigured. To achieve responsible global capitalism, an acceptable moral ecology is needed underpinning the attitudes, motives and behaviour of its individuals and institutions. This ecology needs a continual reappraisal and careful nurturing by the appropriate incentives and enforcement mechanism.

The upgrading of moral attitudes and values could be reached either by a bottom-up approach (from NGOs and so on) or from a top-down approach (for instance the Global Compact approach by the UN). Both approaches could be guided by religious revelations. Dunning refers to his 1998 proposal that an annual meeting of a group of the world's religious leaders should be convened. As an alternative course of action he proposed in this lecture a UN Commission on the Moral and Ethical Implications of Globalisation.

He ends in a plea to all international business scholars to integrate the moral and ethical dimension in their analysis and seek to explain how global capitalism might work to the greater good of a larger number of people throughout the world.

Hans Hinterhuber, Kurt Matzler, Harald Pechlaner and Birgit Renzl first describe the different corporate governance systems in the USA, Great Britain, Germany and Japan. They conclude that the 'power-base' for legitimising the strategy of a corporation is larger, more complex and more political in Europe than in the USA. Therefore, in a European corporation, not only the priorities of shareholders but also those of the stakeholders, like the employees, the government and the environment, are included in the strategies. This example should be followed by MNEs in their own interest. The many rules for corporate governance systems developed by international institutions (the UN Code of Conduct, UN Global Compact, ICC Guidelines, OECD Guidelines and others) do not have much impact on the governance of MNEs, because they have only voluntary compliance and are not enforced by many governments.

However they have been useful for the codes of ethics which many firms have formulated, serving all stakeholders' interests.

MERGER CONTROL OF MNES

Oliver Budzinski discusses the problem of cross-border merger control, which has become widespread during the recent globalisation process, with mega-mergers forming large global MNEs. It needs cross-border merger governance by an international institutional arrangement to coordinate the national merger controls.

However neither centralism, in the form of a uniform global competition rule and enforcement, nor decentralism can adequately cope with the problem. Centralism inhibits learning and innovations, decentralism lacks consistency and leads to conflicts between the different national merger controls.

Budzinski proposes a multi-level system of institutions, which could probably emerge from the International Competition Network (ICN) which was founded in 2001 by an initiative from the USA and is supported by the EU against a centralised solution of the WTO.

TAXES ON MNES

Francesca Gastaldi and Maria Grazia Pazienza try to find out whether MNEs in the Italian textile and clothing sector pay fewer taxes than local enterprises. Because capital mobility has become higher and taxes on capital are different, MNEs may try to avoid high taxation by shifting profits to low-tax countries.

On the other hand, governments may try to compete with lower taxation of foreign capital to attract investments. International organisation (such as the OECD) try to restrict this tax competition, because it could lead to a beggar-my-neighbour policy. Gastaldi and Pazienza give empirical evidence that domestic firms pay higher taxes than MNEs, which have a lower profit rate, suggesting that they aim at minimising the tax burden. However, the authors do not find clear evidence for profit shifting, either by leverage or by transfer pricing practices.

MNE WAGES AND LABOUR STANDARDS

Matthias Busse challenges the conventional perception that MNEs set up in lower labour standard countries. To the contrary, he can show that the level of labour standards is positively associated with a foreign direct investment (FDI) inflow. Then he discusses the arguments for and against internationally binding rules for labour standards. He proposes not to set binding rules through international organisations, because they may be unfair to guiltless workers and firms and therefore wasteful. He considers that product labelling is a more effective approach, which allows for voluntary commitments. For international institutions like the ILO there remains the task of monitoring the observance of labour standards and its violations.

Vuduyagi Balasubramanyam and David Sapsford state some propositions about the relationship between MNEs and wages: for instance, that FDI is attracted by low-wage locations, foreign firms pay relatively higher wages than domestic firms, especially to skilled workers, and disperse production across countries, thereby fragmenting the labour market. The MNEs become monopsonists in certain sectors of the international labour market and distort the resource allocation even within the domestic economies. This monopsonistic power of MNEs cannot be controlled by the legislation of national governments.

The authors propose to create a multinational trade union and, because the transnational collective bargaining may not reach a pareto-efficient allocation, to create a Transnational Labour Court to oversee this bargaining.

MARKET ENTRY OF MNES

Brian Portelli finds that liberalisation of FDI in least developed countries introduces new economic actors, the MNEs, which are supposed to act as an engine of growth by increasing the competitiveness of indigenous resources and capabilities. But, as the author shows, this requires a major restructuring of the existing economic system to increase the absorptive capacities and the capabilities of the country. An FDI-led upgrading of the host country system needs many steps in a virtuous interactive process between MNEs and the host economic agents.

Klaus Weiermair and Mike Peters first describe the rise of MNEs in tourism and the theories which try to explain this rise. They show to what extent MNEs may be capable of outcompeting the small and medium-sized enterprises in alpine tourism in Austria, and give some indications for economic policy intervention on behalf of the small and medium enterprises: government sponsoring of education and training to correct market failures in education, a national and international competition policy against monopolistic pricing of MNEs, and development of new forms of organisations for cooperation between small and medium enterprises and sponsoring of innovations.

INTERNATIONAL FINANCIAL INSTITUTIONS AND FINANCIAL MARKET STABILITY

Daniel Daianu, in a wide-ranging discussion of temporary problems of the world economy, warns of fundamentalism in policy making and asks for more creative policies which acknowledge particular circumstances.

He cites many examples in developed, developing and transition countries. At the level of the international financial institutions, failures in development policy had been made by applying the 'Washington Consensus' rigidly, but there is not only one way or one best practice. The backlash against globalisation is a reminder of the perils of such monolithic policies. Free trade and capital flows are not in all circumstances conducive to economic growth and stability.

New theories show us the importance of multiple equilibria and undermine some constructs of neoclassical economics. Also the different institutional set-ups in transition countries make clear that there has to be a wide variety and creativity of policy making.

Klaus Liebscher, Governor of the Oesterreichische Nationalbank (Central Bank of Austria) deals with the measures used in the EU and global financial institutions to increase the stability of financial markets.

National governments and national banks cannot handle the necessary governance of world financial markets. Financial stability is a global public good. Most of the financial crises of the past decades were caused by political interferences in the supervisory process, weak regulations and lack of public sector accountability and transparency.

Liebscher discusses the measures of the European Monetary Union of Basle II and the Financial Sector Assessment Program of the IMF as good examples of international efforts at coordination and cooperation to avoid financial crises in the future. There are also private initiatives of self-regulation, for instance the International Council of Securities Associations (ICSA).

The central pillars of the international financial system (institutions, markets and the infrastructure) have been strengthened in recent times, but further progress has to be made in implementing many practices which are already recognised as desirable. This last sentence could be said to be the 'Leitmotiv' for most of the authors of this book, who discussed and proposed many initiatives for a better corporate governance of MNEs and reforms for international institutions to achieve more growth and stability and less poverty in the world economy.

1. International institutions and corporate governance

John-ren Chen[1]

THE ROLE OF INTERNATIONAL INSTITUTIONS IN THE GLOBAL COMMUNITY

The economics of international institutions is concerned with problems of international public goods and cross border externalities, such as how to provide international public goods, how to regulate market failures and how to regulate cross border externalities. A public good has two crucial properties, namely non-rivalry and non-excludability of its consumption. Both public goods and externalities can be limited geographically or not. Therefore there are local public goods (LPGs) as well as global public goods (GPGs). Those local public goods which are limited geographically within a country have been considered in the theory of the state since the beginning of economics as a discipline. A national government has the sovereignty to provide the national public goods and to regulate the failures of the national markets, but sovereign states have appeared incapable of providing global public goods efficiently or of regulating failures of global markets effectively without international cooperation. The main reason is the existence of both global players and conflicts of interest between the sovereign states. It is obvious that an individual sovereign state is incapable of regulating activities of global players effectively since the latter can switch their activities between different countries. Among the global players multinational enterprises (MNEs) and international non-governmental organisations (NGOs) are the most active in the modern global society. International institutions (IIs) and international organisations (IOs) have been able to provide a favourable infrastructure for international coordination and cooperation. In this chapter no distinction is made between IIs and IOs. Kindleberger (1986) identified the following GPGs: trading systems, international money, capital flows, consistent macroeconomic policies in a period of tranquillity and as a source of crisis management when needed. Stiglitz (1995), on the other hand, identified the following six GPGs: global security, global economic stability, knowledge, global environment, humanitarian assistance (for example for families) and global health, especially the control of contagious diseases (see also Chen, 2001).

These identifications of GPGs are neither complete nor exclusive between the different GPGs. While Kindleberger only considered those GPGs which are needed for running a sound global economy, Stiglitz also took into account those which are used for a sustainable world economic development. For a 'perfect' sustainable world development more GPGs are needed. Peace, culture and education can therefore be identified as additional GPGs. Consumption (or production) of a good generates not only benefit (or cost) to the consumer (or producer) but also to the society. Thus there are private benefits (or costs) and also public benefits (or costs) generated by consuming (producing) a good. The difference between the private and public benefits (or costs) is called an externality. A public good involves in general substantial externalities. Because of its externality a public good tends to suffer from underprovision, since it is often rational for the individual actors to let others provide the good and to enjoy it as a free rider, free of charge. This is true for an LPG as well as a GPG.

The identification of GPGs given both by Kindleberger and by Stiglitz contains very broad categories of GPGs. They are not only related but also not exclusive; for instance, global security and global economic stability are strongly complementary to each other. Knowledge is also highly complementary to both of these. Ideas and instructions for an appropriate answer to a question or solution to a problem are generally called knowledge. Mathematical theorems, computer programs, laws of chemistry and physics, and laws of economics accordingly belong to the above definition of knowledge.

Knowledge, which is central to successful development, is recognised not only as a public good but also a GPG. Non-rivalry and non-excludability are the two critical properties of a public good. Knowledge as a PG is both non-rival and non exclusive. The first property means that consumption by one individual does not detract from that by another: 'he who receives an idea from me, receives instruction himself without lessening mine' (Thomas Jefferson). Knowledge of a mathematical theorem clearly satisfies this property. This implies that there is zero marginal cost from an additional individual enjoying the benefits of the knowledge. The second property (of non-excludability) of a public good implies that no one can be excluded. In other words, the cost of excluding an individual from the enjoyment of a public good is very high. Because of these two special properties knowledge will usually be underprovided by the private sector. Recognising that knowledge is a GPG and also central to successful development, the international community has to take over a collective responsibility for creation and dissemination of knowledge for perfect sustainable development. Knowledge of a good corporate governance system (CGS) is essential for efficient global resource allocation as well as sound global financial architecture and therefore crucial for perfect sustainable global development. IIs are thus invited to provide good CGSs.

The OECD as a global international organisation has taken over a collective responsibility for the creation and dissemination of a GPG – knowledge for a sound corporate governance system: OECD, *Principles of Corporate Governance* (in the following discussion in this chapter, *Principles* is used as an abbreviation). In its Preface, the OECD underlines the character of the CGS as a GPG and encourages its widespread use:

> Because good corporate governance is a shared responsibility, the OECD welcomes and encourages the widespread use of the Principles by governments, private associations, companies, investors and other parties committed to improving corporate governance practices. The OECD looks forward to co-operating with countries …, with international organizations, regional organizations and private sector bodies in the collective effort to strengthen the fabric of corporate governance around the world.

This chapter is organised as follows: after the discussion of the role of IIs in the global community in the first section, some special characteristics of the modern world economy are presented in the second Section. In the third section a brief discussion about corporate governance (CG) and the main issues studied within the CG are given. In the fourth section the role of a CGS in global resource allocation and financial stability is discussed. In the fifth section the OECD *Principles of Corporate Government* are briefly reported. In the final section some core elements of a good CGS are proposed.

SOME SPECIAL CHARACTERISTICS OF THE MODERN WORLD ECONOMY

The following special characteristics of the modern world economy are essential in emphasising that the knowledge of good corporate governance is central to the efficiency of resource allocation and stable financial architecture. First is the separation of ownership and management in the modern business community. The thesis of the separation of ownership from control forms the basis of the new theory of capitalism, a phenomenon held to be sufficiently dissimilar from its classical forbear to possess revolutionary implications, not only in the sphere of economics, where it originated, but also in the spheres of sociology and politics (see Beed, 1966). The separation of ownership and management has been a prevailing property of the American business community for more than half a century; according to Berle and Means (1932) in most individual large companies the control is not influenced subject to or identical with the ownership to any significant degree, for ownership is so widely distributed that no one individual or small group has even a minority interest large enough to dominate the affairs of the company. Therefore, since typically within the large company there is an implicitly complete separation of ownership from control because of the wide dispersion of shareholdings, a similar situation characterises the social context, such as the direction of industry by persons other than those who have ventured their wealth. The consequence of this separation induces the so-called principal–agent problem. The owner or owners of a modern enterprise (especially a large one), in general do not have the ability or capacity to run the business, therefore managers are hired for this purpose. Managers of enterprises have their own interest, which is not identical to that of the owners. Also there exists asymmetric information between them. Since the owners (or shareholders of a company) let managers run their business they need to check whether the business is being run in their interest and whether the managers are doing their best to manage the enterprise. It is obvious that the action of managers has external effects on the owners of the enterprise.

A second characteristic concerns big and small shareholders. In a modern enterprise, especially a large publicly held share company, there are usually many shareholders consisting of small and big investors, with much more control or power over the enterprise exercised by the large shareholders. Therefore large investors are more able to protect their interest and even dominate in the control of the enterprise. Since the small shareholders have little power and because of the widely distributed ownership with minor interest to control they tend to be free-riders, and leave control of the enterprise to large shareholders. The share of ownership is quite different in different countries of the world. According to Schleifer and Vishny (1996), large shareholdings, especially majority ownership, are relatively uncommon in the USA. But in the rest of the world, large shareholdings are the norm. In Germany, large commercial banks often control over a quarter of the votes in major companies. Gortan and Schmid (1996) estimate that about 80 per cent of the large German companies have over 25 per cent non-bank shareholders. In smaller German companies, the norm is family control majority ownership, or pyramids. In Japan, large cross-holdings as well as shareholdings by major banks are the norm. In France, core investors (with cross-ownership) are common. In most of the rest of the world heavily concentrated shareholdings seem to be the rule. Because of the uneven distribution of power to the detriment of the small shareholders a good CGS has therefore to concern itself with protecting their interests against the expropriations of the big shareholders and the management of the company.

There are several ways for investors to invest their money and, similarly for firms to obtain financial product capital. Roughly speaking, there are two categories of financial contracts, debt and equity. A debt is a contract in which a borrower obtains some funds from the lender and promises a pre-specified stream of future payments to the lender. Usually the borrower promises in addition not to violate a range of covenants, such as maintaining the value of the firm's assets. An equity represents an ownership of a share of the firm's net capital. People holding equities of a firm are shareholders. Unlike lenders or creditors, shareholders are not promised any payments in return for their financial investment in the firm. They often receive dividends at the discretion of the board of directors. Unlike lenders, shareholders do not have a claim to special assets of the firm used as collateral for a debt contract, but a shareholder typically gets the right to vote for the board of directors. Even this right is not universal, since many countries have multiple classes of common stock. The voting rights for small shareholders are of limited value unless they are concentrated. But concentrated action by a large group of shareholders is required to take control via the voting mechanism, therefore most small shareholders do not even have an incentive to become informed on how to vote. Preference shares are a special financial contract with a character between a debt and an equity.

In this introduction I do not intend to discuss the details or the differences of the ways in which the suppliers of finance to corporations assure them-selves of getting a return on their investment. It is important to point out the variety of possibilities for both the corporations and the investors to make an 'optimal' decision on corporate finance and portfolio investment, respec-tively. Since the financial market is not perfect, for reasons such as asymmetrical information, moral hazard and principal–agent problems, the proposition of Modigliani-Miller is not appropriate for the real business world. Because of differences in preference with respect to risk and uncer-tainty, different optimal portfolio combinations of debt, preference equities, equities and other financial assets will be the rule for financial investors. A corporation will in general carry out its optimal use of product capital. Owing to the imperfect competition on financial markets described above, some regulations are needed, especially to enable the suppliers of finance to corpo-rations to assure themselves of getting a return on their investment.

In a modern economy not only shareholders and managers but also stakeholders are important actors. A corporation, as a producer, needs not only capital, but also labour, as an indispensable production factor, and customers, as buyers of its outputs. Theoretical propositions suggest that 'perfect' competition would force firms to minimise cost and provide an efficient resource allocation, but since in real life a lot of markets for products and also for labour are not perfectly competitive, regulations are needed to resolve the market failures. Markets for products are not perfectly competi-tive either because of the different market power, asymmetrical information between their buyers and suppliers, and also because of the long-term character of transaction contracts, especially for durable goods. On a product market suppliers usually have much higher market power and get more information about the quality of the product than the buyers. Because of the long-term character of a transaction contract, customers who buy the durable product need to be assured of its usefulness. Therefore a justification for the regulation of business to correct failures of markets was already given by the classical economist John Stuart Mill (1962, p. 227): 'trade is a social act. Whoever undertakes to sell any description of goods to the public, does what affects the interest of other persons, and of society in general, and thus his conduct, in principle, comes within the jurisdiction of the society'.

Employees have in general had weaker bargaining power over an employment contract than the employer. Furthermore, because of the high degree of specialisation in the modern economy, specific skill is needed. Skilled labour has to undergo lengthy training. This implies that the people who have invested in obtaining a specific skill need to be assured of getting the desired reward for their effort. The corporate governance mechanism should provide this assurance. Otherwise a specific skill will be underprovided. Additionally productivity of labour has played a crucial role in the good performance of an enterprise. Different measures have therefore been applied to enforce the productivity of labour. Workers' participation in management has been informally or formally implemented as a way to increase motivation of labour. In most European countries workers' participation in management is usually in the form of a legally formal mechanism which permits representatives of workers to influence organisational decisions. A corporation carries out its activities in the society through the headquarters, the plants and subsidiaries and utilises local public goods and causes environmental pollution just like other members of the society. Public goods have been provided by public or private producers, but they are generally regulated. To provide public goods both local and national authorities collect taxes. Taxation is an important example of a CGS in the modern business community. In general, a firm's audited balance sheet has been used for the purpose of assessing its tax liability. This imposes a role on the management to provide business information to shareholders, investors, banks and others in the society and to the state. Obviously there are entirely different interests for the state as collector of tax and for the shareholders as payers of tax. The single balance sheet has to serve these conflicting purposes. Because internationally there are differences in the standards of accounting and auditing systems, a single nationally audited balance sheet seems unable to fulfil this dual role of MNEs.

For the suppliers of finance and corporations the most important perspective on corporate governance (CG) is an agency perspective because of the separation of ownership and control. For the suppliers of finance the main question to be answered with respect to CGS is to know how investors get the managers to give them back their money. For the employees as stakeholders the most important question with respect to the CGS is how to ensure that their rights, which are protected by law, are respected.

In addition, as mentioned in the preface of the OECD *Principles*, the best run corporations recognise the business ethics and corporate awareness of the environmental and social interest of the communities in which they operate, because these can have an impact on the reputation and long-term perform-ance of corporations.

CORPORATE GOVERNANCE

Corporate governance in the narrow sense deals with the ways in which suppliers of finance to corporations assure themselves of getting a return on their investments. Schleifer and Vishny (1996, p. 2) identify the following questions for corporate governance. How do the suppliers of finance get managers to return some of the profits to them? How do they make sure that managers do not steal the capital they supply or invest it in bad projects? How do suppliers of finance control managers? According to the OECD, 'Corporate governance relates to the internal means by which corporations are operated and controlled' (OECD, *Principles of Corporate Governance*, 1999, p. 5). Following this definition, corporate governance deals not only with the ways in which the suppliers of finance to corporations assure them-selves of getting a return on their investment but also with the means to ensure that corporations take into account the interests of a wide ranges of constituencies, as well as of the communities within which they operate, and ensure that their boards are accountable to the company and the shareholders.

The Program Committee of the 2nd CSI Annual Conference follows the definition of the OECD *Principles*. In the second section of this the external effects of a corporation in a modern economy were explicitly presented. Thus, according to the economic theory of the states, governments have to play a central role in shaping the legal, institutional and regulatory climate within which individual corporate governance systems are developed. But in our global world economy, where there are global players (such as MNEs and non-profit-oriented NGOs), the sovereign state is not able to regulate these global players. Therefore international institutions are called on to provide a global legal, institutional and regulatory climate for developing good corpo-rate governance systems. Additionally the external effects caused even by nationally active corporations can influence other countries because of inter-national interdependence of economic activities. Therefore the role of IIs has been essential, especially in providing GPGs. Knowledge has been identified as a GPG. A good CGS can also be classified as a CPG of the category 'knowledge' which can be efficiently provided by IIs.

In the modern world economy the importance of private corporations for the welfare of individuals has increased, as market-based approaches to economic policy have been adopted in almost all countries of the global society. Private corporations have been the most important actors to create jobs, produce goods and services at reasonable prices, generate tax income and increasingly to manage our financial resources; they are also mainly responsible for our sustainable global development. Because of growing reliance worldwide on the private sector, the CG issue has similarly increased in importance. Although governments play a central role in shaping the legal, institutional climate for developing an individual CGS, the main responsibility lies with the private sector. The different legal and institutional frameworks of individual countries as well as the responsibility of the private sector have been the main reasons for there being different CGSs in the world. Among the current developed countries of the world, the United States, Germany, Japan and the United Kingdom have some of the best CGSs. The differences between them are probably small relative to their differences from other countries. In this volume Hans Hinterhuber discusses these best CGSs of the developed countries.

THE ROLE OF A CORPORATE GOVERNANCE SYSTEM IN GLOBAL RESOURCE ALLOCATION AND FINANCIAL STABILITY

The corporation has been established as a legal entity to do business as an individual would but with the added ability to assemble and use the capital of numerous individuals and can therefore undertake tasks beyond the reach of any single person. The liability of investors has been limited to the amount of their original investment. The powers and responsibilities of the managers who are charged to run the business are defined, and the investors as owners who in general do not run the business of the enterprise by themselves are assured of a vote on the significant affairs of the corporation. The MNEs have in general been transnational corporations. The separation of capital from management has significant implications for the modern global economy.

The first is managerial capitalism versus traditional capitalism. Traditional capitalism is characterised by enterprises with the classic entrepreneurs who own and run the business by themselves with the objective of profit maximisation. Managerial capitalism is characterised by corporations with separation of ownership from management. A lot of publications have identified the managerial motives as salary, security, power, status, prestige and professional excellence and have summarised the objective of the managerial decision as to realise their aims as fast as is permitted by the capital market on the one hand and by their product markets on the other (see Marris, 1963, 1964), Williamson, 1963, 1966) or to maximise the rate of growth of sales (see Baumol, 1962).

The second implication is the fast growing influence of large corporations both nationally and internationally with an increase in their market powers, which imply imperfect markets or market failures. The third implication is the need for a good CGS. With a few exceptions, such as Du Pont and, to a lesser degree, Firestone and Ford, which have participated actively in management, among the 200 largest corporations in the United States there are few in which owners exercise any important influence on decisions (see Galbraith, 1970, p. 91).

The recent corporate scandals of US corporations, the Enrons and World Coms, and the financial crises in Asia, Russia and now in Argentinia have made amply clear to other countries around the world why the issue of transparency and accountability in CG is so important for investor confidence and for overall national economic performance. The bosses of companies such as Enron and World Com violated investors' trust, brought ruin on their companies' owners and caused (national) financial turmoil as well as economic instability. The financial crises in individual countries in our global community, such as the Asian crisis, have induced contagion effects in another countries. These experiences have shown the important role of the CGS in global resource allocation and financial stability.

Making an investment is a decision with long-run effects in the returns on the investment and on the wealth of the individual investor. Because of asymmetrical information between the corporation and the investors, a CGS is essential for the suppliers of finance. A good CGS will increase the trust of investors and enable corporations to receive financial resources. Since both returns and risks are important determinants of portfolio decisions of the investors, a reduction in risk with similar returns will increase investment volume, reduce the price (expressed in interest burden of the production capital) and increase capital input and production activities. On the other hand, a bad CGS does not prevent the managers from expropriating the competitive return after the capital is sunk. In such a CGS corporations find it hard to gain the investors' trust and therefore it is not easy to raise external finance for running a business and a higher price has to be paid. In a global financial market countries with a good CGS will obtain more financial resources and reduce the cost of capital. An improvement of the CGS strengthens the confidence of domestic investors in a country's own corporations and stock markets. This in turn matters greatly to the long-term competitiveness of corporations and to the overall health and vitality of national economies and global economic development.

Empirical studies have shown that less developed countries (LDCs) in general do not have a good CGS. Thus the international community, through institutions like the World Bank or UNCTAD has a collective responsibility for the creation and dissemination of knowledge for development, including a good CGS. The OECD recognised that good CG is a GPG and developed a set of standards and guidelines for good CG. It tries to cooperate with countries within and beyond OECD membership, with IOs such as the World Bank and the IMF in the collective effort to strengthen the fabric of CG around the world. Countries whose CGS is bad can increase their access to global financial resources and make a crucial contribution to creating a sound financial structure. LDCs in general have low saving rates and need financial resources from the international capital market to support their economic development. But, because of their 'bad' CGS, the LDCs have found it more difficult to reap the benefits of the global capital market. If they are to attract financial resources especially long-term financial capital from outside, their corporate governance arrangement must be credible. Therefore improving the CGS in LDCs can reduce the international difference in interest rates and enable an integration of the international financial market. In this way an improvement in efficiency of resource allocation can be expected.

THE OECD *PRINCIPLES OF CORPORATE GOVERNANCE*[2]

Acknowledging the importance of a CGS for the overall national and international economic performance, the OECD, in conjunction with national governments, other relevant IOs and the private sector, developed a set of corporate governance standards and guidelines in 1998 and published the *Principles of Corporate Governance* in 1999 (hereafter the *Principles*).

The *Principles* consist of a preamble and five sections which represent the rights of shareholders, the equitable treatment of shareholders, the role of stakeholders in corporate governance, disclosure and transparency and the responsibilities of the board, respectively. Part of the Preamble reads as follows:

> The Principles are intended to assist member and non-member governments in their efforts to evaluate and improve the legal, institutional and regulatory framework for corporate governance in their countries, and to provide guidance and suggestions for stock exchanges, investors, corporations, and other parties that have a role in the process of developing good corporate governance. The Principles focus is on publicly traded companies. However, to the extent they are

deemed applicable, they might also be a useful tool to improve corporate governance in non-trades companies, for example, privately held and state-owned enterprises.

Increasingly, the OECD and its Member governments have recognised the synergy between macroeconomic and structural policies. One key element in improving economic efficiency is corporate governance, which involves a set of relationships between a company's management, its board, its shareholders and other stakeholders. Corporate governance also provides the structure through which the objectives of the company are set, and the means of attaining those objectives and monitoring performance are determined. Good corporate governance should provide proper incentives for the board and management to pursue objectives that are in the interests of the company and shareholders and should facilitate effective monitoring, thereby encouraging firms to use resources more efficiently.

The Principles focus on governance problems that result from the separation of ownership and control. Some other issues relevant to a company's decision-making processes, such as environmental of ethical concerns, are taken into account ...

The degree to which corporations observe basic principles of good corporate governance is an increasingly important factor for investment decisions. Of particular relevance is the relation between corporate governance practices and the increasingly international character of investment. International flows of capital enable companies to access financing from a much larger pool of investors. If countries are to reap the full benefits of the global capital market, and if they are to attract long-term 'patient' capital, corporate governance arrangements must be credible and well understood across borders.

The *Principles* acknowledge that 'There is no single model of good corporate governance. At the same time, work carried out in Member countries and within the OECD has identified some common elements that underlie good corporate governance. The Principles build on these common elements and are formulated to embrace the different models that exist.'

The *Principles* comprise the following:

1. The rights of shareholders: the corporate governance framework should protect shareholders' rights.
2. The equitable treatment of shareholders: the corporate governance framework should ensure the equitable treatment of all shareholders, including minority and foreign shareholders. All shareholders should have the opportunity to obtain effective redress for violation of their rights.
3. The roles of stakeholders in corporate governance: the corporate governance framework should recognise the rights of stakeholders as established by law and encourage active cooperation between corporations and stakeholders in creating wealth, jobs and the sustainability of financially sound enterprises.
4. Disclosure and transparency: the corporate governance framework should

ensure that timely and accurate disclosure is made on all material matters regarding the corporation, including the financial situation, performance, ownership and governance of the company.

5. The responsibility of the board: the corporate governance framework should ensure the strategic guidance of the company, the effective monitoring of management by the board and the board's accountability to the company and the shareholders.

SUMMARY REMARKS

Summarising the above discussion, a good CGS for a modern enterprise has to take a number of points into consideration. First, the private sector has to take initiatives to develop best practice in CG to realise its objectives of running businesses.

Second, the problems of CG have resulted from the separation of ownership and control of finance. Managers of a modern enterprise not only have more information than their owners, but in addition they make business decisions and actually run the business. Because of the different interests of management and ownership, especially in large companies usually characterised by the separation of ownership and management, a good CGS has to be able to assure the investors of getting a return on their investment.

Third, because of external effects and asymmetrical information, regulations are needed to correct market failures and to improve efficiency of resource allocation. Policy makers have to develop legal and regulatory frameworks for CG.

Thus IIs, governments and the private sector are responsible for good CG, especially for MNEs which in general are characterised by the separation of ownership from management. While IIs provide favourable infrastructure for cooperation of national governments who have to play a central role in shaping the legal, institutional and regulatory climate within which individual CGSs are developed, the main responsibility lies with the private sector.

Since government has to reflect its own economic, social, legal and cultural circumstances in developing its legal and regulatory framework for CG, and the private sector has to develop its own practice for CG, there is no single good CG. A legal and regulatory framework for CG has to provide sufficient flexibility to allow markets to function effectively and to respond to expectations of shareholders and other stakeholders. In a dynamic global economy, corporations must innovate and adapt their CG practices so that they can meet new demands and grasp new opportunities. Similarly the legal and regulatory frameworks have to be adjusted to the needs of the new development of the community. Therefore, in the study of CG, both theoretical and empirical contributions have been able to make important contributions to create new knowledge for the GPG.

NOTES

1. I am indebted to Dr Richard Hule for his valuable comments.
2. The OECD is going to revise the *Principles of Corporate Governance* discussed in this section because of several scandals of multinational enterprises in recent years. The focus of the revision is how to improve the transparency in corporate governance. A process of 'peer review' should contribute to a progressive improvement of the rules proposed by the OECD *Principles of Corporate Governance* in individual countries.

REFERENCES

Baumol, W.J. (1962), 'On the theory of expansion of the firm', *American Economic Review*, **52**, 1078–87.

Beed, C.S. (1966), 'The separation of ownership from control', *Journal of Economic Studies*, 29–46

Berle, A.A. and G. Means (1932), *The Modern Corporation and Private Property*, London: Macmillan.

Chen, John-ren (2001), 'Global market, national sovereignty and international institution' inaugural speech to the first CSI Conference, in Chen, John-ren (2003), *The Role of International Institutions in Globalisation*, Cheltenham: Edward Elgar.

Galbraith, J.K. (1970), *The New Industrial State*, Harmondsworth: Penguin Books.

Gortan, Gary and Frank Schmid (1996), 'Universal banking and the performance of German firms', National Bureau of Economic Research working paper 5453, Cambridge, MA.

Kindleberger, Charles (1986), 'Presidential Address', *American Economic Rreview*, 8.

Marris, R.L. (1963), 'A model of the managerial enterprise', *Quarterly Journal of Economics*, **77**, 185–209.

Marris, R.L. (1964), *The Economics Theory of 'Managerial' Capitalism*, London: Macmillan.

Mill, John Stuart (1962), 'On Liberty', *Utilitarianism and other Essays*, London: Fontana.

OECD (1999), *Principles of Corporate Governance*, Paris: OECD.

Schleifer, Andrei and Robert W. Vishny (1996), 'A survey of corporate governance', National Bureau of Economic Research working paper 5554.

Stiglitz, J.E. (1995), 'The theory of international public goods and architecture of international organization', United Nations background paper 7, Department for Economic and Social Information and Policy Analysis, July.

Stiglitz, J.E. (1999), 'Knowledge as a global public good', in I. Kaul, I. Grunberg and M.A. Stern (eds), *Global Public Goods, International Cooperation in the 21st Century*, Oxford: Oxford University Press, 308–25.

Williamson, O.E. (1963), 'Managerial discretion and business behavior', *American Economic Review*, **53**, 1032–57.

Williamson, O.E. (1966), 'Profit, growth and sales maximization', *Economica*, **33**, 1–16.

2.   Global capitalism: the moral challenge

John H. Dunning[1]

INTRODUCTION

It is just over 14 years since the fall of the Berlin Wall, and the burgeoning of the Internet and e-commerce. These events, the one political and the other technological, coupled with the extensive liberalisation of cross-border markets, and the advent of several new players on the world economic stage, heralded a new era for the global community. In the last decade, a plethora of scholarly and popular monographs and articles have explored the implications of this phenomenon, popularly referred to as 'globalisation'. In the beginning, there was nothing but praise for it; then, in the mid-1990s, its downsides began to be highlighted. More recently there has been a 'backlash' against the 'backlash', fuelled in part by the tragic events of 11 September 2001 and their aftermath. My reading of the latest contributions on the subject by such analysts as George Soros (1998, 2002), Thomas Friedman (2000) Paul Streeten (2001) and Joseph Stiglitz (2002), is that they are showing a much more realistic and balanced appreciation of the constraints and challenges of globalisation. I sense that there is a growing feeling that if we can 'get it right' (and 'right' includes the right way to globalise), global capitalism, as it is now emerging, can help achieve many of the economic and social aspirations which most people hold dear, better than any other alternative currently (and I stress currently) on offer. (Dunning, 2000; Friedman, 2000; Fukuyama, 1999; Sen, 1999).

If we get it right. 'If' is clearly the critical word. What, then, needs to be done to devise and monitor a global economic architecture which is efficient, morally acceptable, geographically inclusive and sustainable over time?[2] In what follows I will try and identify a few of the more important conditions which, I believe, need to be put in place if this is to be accomplished. Several of these, particularly the economic prerequisites, have already been well aired elsewhere.[3] Because of this, my thoughts and views will focus on (what I perceive to be) the essential moral foundations of the global architecture if it is to meet the demands likely to be made of it.

More particularly, I propose to explore, and base my observations on, three propositions:

1. Responsible global capitalism (RGC) (and I will define what I mean by this later) should not be considered as an end in itself, but rather a means towards providing a richer, healthier and more meaningful life style for individuals and their families; and of advancing the economic objectives and the social transformation of societies.
2. In order to move towards a more inclusive and acceptable global capitalism, the organisational structures and strategies of each of its participating organisations and institutions (markets, civil society, governments and supranational agencies) need to be reconfigured and strengthened.
3. RGC can only be achieved and sustained if there is a strong and generally acceptable moral ecology underpinning the attitudes, motives and behaviour of its constituent individuals and organisations; in a transforming global society, this ecology needs continual reappraisal and careful nurturing by the appropriate incentives and enforcement mechanisms.

GLOBALISATION, GLOBAL MARKETS AND GLOBAL CAPITALISM

Let me now briefly define the main global concepts I shall deal with in this presentation. These are globalisation itself, the global market place and global capitalism. Each has its own distinctive meaning, although, all too often, they are treated as if they were one and the same. By globalisation, I mean the connectivity of individuals and institutions across the globe, or at least, over most of it. Such connectivity may be shallow or deep, short or long-lasting. It may be geared to advancing personal or institutional interests and economic, cultural or ideological goals. There are many channels of cross-border connectivity, but the Internet is the quintessential vehicle of modern interpersonal and intercorporate communications. Globalisation is a morally neutral concept. In itself, it is neither good nor bad, but it may be motivated for good or bad reasons, and used to bring about good or bad results.

The 'global market place' refers more specifically to the flow of goods, services and assets across national boundaries which are mediated through the market place, the price, quantity and quality of which is determined by the participants in the market. All of us, directly or indirectly, participate in global markets; look, if you will, at the labels of origin on the goods each of us buys at our local supermarkets. As workers, too, many of us are helping to supply goods and services for sale in export markets, or are employed by foreign-owned firms. In our leisure pursuits, we may travel abroad, look at foreign TV and purchase the services of foreign airlines, hotels and ethnic restaurants. All of us like to get the best deal we can out of the market; indeed the market system is designed on the premise that the self seeking of its participants yields socially beneficial results.

The concept of 'global capitalism' (GC) is more difficult to get a handle on. There is really no such thing as a global capitalist system today in the same way as there is a global firm. For this to be so there would have to be a single and centralised system of global governance. Instead, what we have is a large number of distinctive national (or regional) capitalist systems each of which are connected through a network of cross-border economic relationships, and particularly through the free or relatively free movement of goods, services, capital and information across the globe (Hall and Soskice, 2001). I use the word 'system' advisedly. GC, as a social system, embraces much more than global markets. It includes a set of non-market organisations within which the market is embedded and which, together, characterise a global society (Hamlin, 1995). Inter alia it is the task of these institutions to set the rules and monitor the behaviour of markets, to engage in a variety of market-facilitating and/or regulatory activities, and to produce public goods and services, which, left unaided, the market is unable or unwilling to produce.[4]

GC, then, is a system made up of individuals, private commercial corporations, civil society, governments and supranational agencies. Each has a unique and critical role to play in advancing and sustaining the goals of GC;[5] and it is on GC rather than globalisation or the global market place that I propose to focus my thoughts. More especially I shall be asserting that if RGC is to achieve its goals (and I will describe these more fully a little later) there has to be a set of ethical ground rules to which all its constituents must adhere. It is not enough for the organisations of RGC to perform efficiently; they have to do so in a way which conforms to certain ethical standards. For, at the end of the day, the answers to the questions of 'what goods and services should be produced', 'how and where best to produce them' and 'how the resulting benefits be distributed – the three tasks which RGC must seek to address – critically depend on the values and virtues of the individuals and institutions participating in the system. Unless these values and virtues, including those which are not easily translated into a monetary value, are factored into the workings of RGC, then its economic benefits are unlikely to be either fully realised or sustainable.

The interaction between the moral obligations of the participants in the RGC system – be they individuals or organisations – is a complex and changing one. It has long been acknowledged that, if the market system is to be both efficient and equitable, the transacting participants must behave in a socially responsible manner. But some commentators[6] take this a step further and assert that there are certain endogenous features of the market which ensure the required standards of honesty, truth, reciprocity and integrity.[7]

However, this claim may be questioned whenever markets are intrinsically imperfect, uncertain or volatile, or where its participants behave in a non-competitive way. And it is these features of global markets on which those who are the most critical of them tend to focus.[8]

Similarly it is generally accepted that good government does not just mean that national administrations should perform their tasks efficiently, but that they should do so without corruption, dishonesty or nepotism, and with a commitment to transparency, accountability and the pursuit of social justice. History, indeed, is replete with examples of private enterprises, labour unions, governments and NGOs eroding the benefits of societal capitalism by their unacceptable moral codes and behaviour.

At the same time, the ethical content of RGC must also reflect the wider social and cultural mores of society. These are likely to be highly contextual over time and space. Thus societies with a Confucian tradition are likely to interpret the ideal conduct of their capitalistic organisations differently from those steeped in a Christian or Jewish tradition, while the strong emphasis currently placed on individual freedom by Western societies is likely to generate mind sets and behaviour (for example, towards education, innovation and entrepreneurship, and to the idea of social safety nets) very differently than the erstwhile Communist countries or Islamic communities. The questions then arise, 'Should today's RGC be modified to reflect these different attitudes and virtues?' and 'Does its emergence demand that, as, when and where appropriate, these mores, or their prioritisation, be harmonised?'

THE TASKS OF RGC

I have suggested that the success of RGC is best judged by its ability to deliver economically efficient and socially acceptable answers to three questions: 'what to produce', 'how to produce' and 'how to distribute the benefits' arising from global economic activity. I have further averred that each answer must rest on both the capabilities and the intentions of each of the participating institutions, and on the moral outcomes of their actions. Let me now explain what I mean by evaluating the current status of RGC.

The Goals of RGC: the 'What Should be Produced?' Question

Until quite recently, the efficacy of alternative economic systems was largely measured by the market value of the individual goods and services produced. The aggregate of these individual values was the gross national (or domestic) product per capita. Not surprisingly, then, the main goal of capitalism was perceived to be that of increasing GNP (or GDP) per head.

Such a measure is increasingly viewed as only a partial reflection of economic and social wellbeing, though sages of yesteryear were no less critical of the benefits of material wealth per se.[9] This is partly because it is recognised that money prices, even when markets work well, do not necessarily reflect real economic welfare (a dollar allocated to reducing such 'bads' as AIDS, or crime prevention, is counted the same as that spent on housing and food). Moreover such an index excludes those goods and services which are not transacted in the market place, or those to which it is difficult to attach a price tag, such as the protection of the environment, road safety, a fair judicial system and reducing hospital waiting lists, not to mention such intangible benefits as reputation, sovereignty and, most of all, freedom of choice. Several attempts have been made to devise more acceptable measures of living standards. The United Nations Development Program, for example, has compiled a human development index (HDI) which adds to GNP per head such variables as life expectancy and educational attainment (UNDP 2000).[10]

However, the point I wish to emphasise is that, in evaluating the efficacy of RGC, we first need to establish the criteria by which we are to judge it. Exactly what are the objectives and aspirations of society which, if they are to be met, involve the use of scarce resources? Such goals and aspirations, it should be observed, are not static; new goods and services are continually entering the salad bowl of economic welfare, and many of these either are not marketed or take the form of public goods, that is goods we share with other people. At the same time, consumer preferences are often highly contextual. Compare, for example, the contents of a desirable living standard of a modern English or Canadian family with those of its counterpart a century ago; or those of an average Japanese with an average Nigerian family today.

What of the specific impact of global capitalism on societal objectives? The main impact is surely twofold. First, thanks to modern travel, TV and information channels, there is an increasing awareness of the desires and preferences of people throughout the world. This is leading to both a convergence and a divergence of consumer wants and expectations. Demand is converging for such global products as Nike shoes, mass-produced cars, musical and sporting events, five star hotels, some TV programmes and financial services. But, there is also divergence to cater for localised needs and tastes: ethnic food, indigenous tourist attractions, and intangible assets such as ethnic culture are examples. Second, I sense that part of the awareness is a growing recognition that 'man does not live by bread alone', and that values such as reputation, personal security, adequate health provision, minimum labour standards and environmental protection must be reprioritised and addressed by the institutions of RGC. And I repeat that these values, some of which have a high moral content, are germane to our discussion whenever and wherever their attainment involves the use of the world's scarce resources.

Production and RGC: the 'How and Where Best to Produce Question'

The second task of RGC is to produce the type, quantity and quality of goods and services that global society wants in the most efficient and socially acceptable way. Again most economists accept there are some goods and services best provided by the market, some by non-market organisations (e.g. by governments or NGOs) and some jointly by the private and public sector. The costs and benefits of production are also likely to vary according to the location of that production. In the textbook case of perfect competition, the market is fully up to meeting these objectives. But, increasingly, in an uncertain, unstable and innovation driven global economy, and one in which international public goods are being increasingly valued, this ideal state of affairs is far removed from reality.

More often than not, markets – be they product, finance, technology or labour markets – are structurally or intrinsically imperfect and, in many, but not all, instances globalisation has exacerbated these imperfections. In particular, cross-border movements of corporate and financial capital tend to be much more volatile than their domestic equivalents. An innovation-led economy is, almost by definition, an economy of change and creative destruction. Global markets today are frequently dominated by a few large firms or interest groups which, because of their size and geographical scope, can exploit such market failures as information asymmetries, moral hazards and monopoly power to their own advantage; and in so doing they may be tempted to behave in an unacceptable way.[11] Some factor inputs e.g. unskilled or semi-skilled labour and some kinds of activity are location-bound, and cannot easily respond to global market signals. Attempts to regulate the conduct of market participants and to help producers and workers to adapt to changing market needs have been around since the mid-nineteenth century. But, the impact of recent technological advances and globalisation has added a new, and more urgent, dimension to the debate. At the same time, demands by consumers for more transparency and accountability, and a closer monitoring of the behaviour of producers in sensitive markets, are becoming more vocal.

In short the standards expected from the value-adding activities of the organisations of RGC are being continually upgraded, while the moral underpinning of these activities is becoming a more integral part of their success. This is particularly seen in two directions. The first is in the dramatic increase in the number of cooperative ventures concluded between firms (including many across national boundaries) which, themselves, are reactions to the demands of the global market place and knowledge-based economy. It is here where the virtues of relational assets such as trust, reciprocity and forbearance are the *sine qua non* of business success.[12]

The second direction relates to the growing ease with which companies can tap global markets for their inputs, either by way of trade or by foreign direct investment (FDI). The ability to engage in both the horizontal and the vertical division of labour by MNEs has dramatically increased as transport costs and tariff barriers have declined. But one ethical challenge arising from the shifts in the 'where' of production, demanded on efficiency grounds, has been the growth of sweat shops and the use of child labour in several poorer developing countries, notably in East Asia. As I shall demonstrate later, there are several parallels between such downsides of global capitalism and the 'dark satanic mills' of nineteenth-century Britain, so vividly portrayed by William Blake.

RGC and the Distribution of Income: the 'Who Gets What' Question

It is often said that capitalism is a better instrument for the creation of wealth than it is for the equitable distribution of its benefits. Indeed some would go as far as to say that this latter task is the responsibility of governments rather than that of markets. Certainly it is widely acknowledged that the market economy, left to itself, is likely to result in an uneven distribution of income. Economists usually explain this in terms of the differential productivity of the factors of production, and the ability of some individuals and institutions to command large economic rents for goods and services which are absolutely scarce, or where they have the power to prevent or eradicate competition. Whatever one's conception of a fair wage or salary, it is a fact of life that there is only one Bill Gates, one Michael Jordan, and one David Beckham, while it is also human nature to charge what the market will bear for one's services. At the same time, it seems to me somewhat incongruous that, while deploring enormous income differentials between individuals and the excessive profits of some firms, we, as consumers, are often all too ready to pay large sums of money to buy the goods or services they provide.

Again there is nothing new in this attribute of free markets. It has always rewarded success (as judged by its own criteria) and penalised failure. However it is worth remembering that success can be both short-lived (as in the sporting world), unpredictable (as in the world of business) and fickle (as in the world of entertainment) and that high rewards may have taken much investment in time and money to achieve. And, I repeat, it has always been accepted by capitalist societies that it is the responsibility of non-market institutions, and particularly governments, to put right any perceived injustices of the market place.

So why is this issue of equity and social justice such a central part of the agenda of those critical of GC; and why are so many of us schizophrenic in our attitudes to wealth creation and wealth distribution? I would suggest three reasons. First, globalisation – and all the features associated with it – have exposed us as never before to the huge resource and income gaps both between countries and within countries. For example, it is estimated that 90 per cent of the world's innovatory capacity resides in the Triad nations which account for only 10 per cent of the world's population (UNDP, 2000). How-ever, of greater moral concern, perhaps, is the fact that over a billion people, or one-quarter of the world's population, live on less than one dollar a day (World Bank, 1999/2001), while the 100 or so richest *individuals* in the world (probably more than half of whom live in some of the poorer countries) have amassed fortunes worth more than this combined income.

Second, I perceive there is a heightened sense of awareness by the man in the street in the richer nations about the extreme economic deprivation of those in the poorest regions of the world. However, when this comes to taking action which might redound to their disadvantage, there is a good deal of ambivalence and hesitancy.[13] At a governmental level (as seen by the reaction to appeals to millennium debt cancellation and to the boosting of aid), there is an anxiousness to avoid upsetting the workings of the free market, or offending future voters by an unacceptable reprioritising of objectives. Third, and, perhaps, most importantly, there is currently no supranational form of governance which can correct or lessen any eco-nomic or social inter-country inequities arising from the global market place, in the same way as national governments can, and do, help to miti-gate the effects of intra country inequities. Nor is it clear that there is, or could be, common consensus on the contents of global social justice. Be-cause of this, I do not foresee any easy or comprehensive answer to this particular moral dilemma of RGC, but, as I shall explain later, I believe the teachings of the leading religions of the world offer a useful – and a global – basis for such a consensus.

CAN WE LEARN FROM HISTORY?

I have already alluded to the fact that much of the debate over the content and performance of RGC is but a rehearsal, albeit an extended and more complex rehearsal, of that which was sparked off by the emergence of industrial capitalism two centuries ago. I think it may be instructive to pause for a moment and consider how our Victorian forefathers dealt with the challenges of this new phenomenon at the time, and what, if any, lessons we might draw from their actions.

A recitation of the challenges posed by nineteenth-century capitalism would contain almost all those posed by its modern counterpart, except that its geographical ambit rarely extended beyond national boundaries. Such social downsides as child labour, prostitution, the absence of safety nets, the lack of an appropriate legal and social infrastructure, limited property rights, inadequate hygiene or safety regulations, harsh working conditions, financial fraud, unemployment, widespread poverty and an increase in serious crime all ran alongside the unprecedented increases in material welfare (Searle, 1998).

Of course, not all these social ills could, or should, be attributed to *laissez faire* capitalism. Many, indeed, were inherited from the libertarianism of the pre-Victorian era, and the results of the Napoleonic wars; but, certainly, most were exacerbated by the new industrial age. What then was the response to these challenges? There were many and varied, but I will pinpoint just one or two which are of particular relevance to our present interests.

First, successive governments stepped in by enacting a variety of laws and regulations, starting with the Factory Act of 1833, to improve working conditions, and initiating a series of major reforms with respect to health, sanitation and housing (Himmelfarb, 1995). No less important, they widened the franchise of the electorate (the 1832 Reform Act saw the true beginnings of inclusive democracy) and pioneered compulsory and free education. The introduction of limited liability and legislation to protect property rights followed. Both local and central governments helped provide and finance public utilities and new means of transport. Successive administrations, not to mention the Queen herself, did much to set and support (but not to enforce by legislation) a moral ecology for Victorian society.[14] In particular, stress was placed on the importance of family life, self-discipline, prudence and social responsibility, virtues which Max Weber (1930) so much admired in his study of the Protestant ethic and the spirit of capitalism.

Secondly, the nineteenth century saw a spectacular rise in the role of civil society, in the guise of religious organisations, friendly societies and philanthropic agencies. These early NGOs took upon themselves the task of ameliorating the worst social effects of a new industrial age, including those arising from unrestrained urbanisation. There was a strong humanitarian motive behind this movement, which was as much in evidence in the USA as in the UK (De Tocqueville, 1981).

The third response, and this occurred more abruptly across the English Channel, was to replace, partly or wholly, capitalism with socialism or social democracy. Here the argument was that, however much capitalism may have pushed out the boundaries of material wealth, it had failed dismally to ensure the social wellbeing of the majority of people. It was, de facto, an exclusive economic system, and governments were either unable or unwilling to intervene in the workings of the market to foster more inclusiveness. Those espousing a socialist economic cause believed it to be a morally superior system, as it was based on the philosophy of 'to each according to his needs, from each according to his ability'.

Fourth, and interacting with each of the first three responses, there was a concerted and vigorous effort by Victorian novelists such as Charles Dickens and Charles Kingsley, and reformers and commentators such as Elizabeth Fry and Herbert Spencer to expose some of the social and moral downsides of industrial capitalism and to encourage more humane, prudent and responsible behaviour on the part of both firms and the UK government. At the same time, the preaching of the Protestant ethic by clerics and Christian moralists such as Thomas Chalmers and F.D. Maurice, the moralising by such writers as Samuel Smiles and the example set by Queen Victoria and her household not only helped inculcate large swathes of the population with such virtues as thrift, temperance, self-discipline and duty, but also strengthened the hand of the non-market institutions of the day. Prominent examples include the emergence of a clutch of charitable enterprises and socially responsible firms, such as Rowntrees and Cadburys, and of several philanthropic, civic and educational institutions, such as Toynbee Hall.[15]

So what now of the modern stage of capitalism? Like its predecessor, it is heralding a new phase of economic organisation. Like its predecessor, it is being fuelled by a succession of new ideas, dramatic technological breakthroughs and a widening and deepening of cross-border commerce. Such events are challenging established values, economic structures, organisational modes and life styles by their speed, scope and intensity and, in so doing, are creating a host of social disruptions and moral challenges. But they are also occurring at a time when the cult of individualism is reaching new heights, and the legitimacy of such concepts as solidarity and community is being vigorously questioned.

At the same time, there are some unique features of the globalising economy that offer their own particular challenges. First, and most obviously, the geographical radius of the market place, through such means as commerce, travel and the Internet, is now embracing institutions from more diverse ideologies, social structures and cultures than ever before. Secondly, the critical engine of modern wealth creation is human capital. Such an asset is the main source not only of innovation, entrepreneurship and the upgrading of managerial and organisational expertise, but of ideals and moral values as well.[16]

Third, we are entering an age of global alliances, where, to better advance their own economic objectives, individuals, enterprises, governments and other non-market organisations need to cooperate in a wide variety of ways. As evidence of this, we see a huge explosion in all forms of cross-border inter-firm coalitions and inter-government agreements over the past two decades (UNCTAD, 2000). Fourth, today we live in a multicultural global village, and one in which (notwithstanding the burgeoning of fundamentalism) the religious source and underpinning of values, at least in Western societies, plays a less influential role than it did a century or more ago. This, as I shall explain later, has considerable implications for the extent to which, and the ways in which, society's stock of moral capital can be upgraded.

These four aspects of the modern global society present both problems and opportunities to the institutions of RGC. On the one hand, we have far more knowledge and experience than we had in the past on how to deal with the challenges and imperfections of the global market place; and there are far more non-government agencies seeking solutions to these challenges and imperfections than ever before. On the other hand, modern capitalism comprises more uncertain and volatile characteristics than those of its predecessors, while some of the nineteenth-century reactions to its less desirable effects are not as readily available today. In particular (for the moment at least) religious revelation as a mentor to moral behaviour is not as strong or pervasive as it once was. At the same time, even some of the most vocal critics of RGC concede that socialism, at least the nineteenth and twentieth-century variety, is not currently a feasible alternative economic system.[17] Neither is a return to the traditional society of the pre-industrial age. But, as I shall suggest later, there remain elements of both forms of organisation which, if redesigned and updated, could well help fashion sustainable RGC of the twenty-first century and, not least, of the moral standards underpinning it.

THE MORAL DIMENSION

In taking my thoughts a step further, I want now to briefly look at the concept of morality itself. Here, I am going to eschew any philosophical debate, and take a pragmatic approach. In this context, I shall interpret moral behaviour, first, in a negative sense, as the absence of immoral behaviour (which is generally more easily identifiable); and, second, as behaviour which is perceived to be 'right', not just by the persons or institutions engaging in it, but by the wider community of which they are part. In this sense, moral behaviour is a step removed from amoral behaviour. I shall also define moral capital as the accumulated stock of virtues and values which determine or influence moral behaviour.

Now, of course, this begs the question of what is 'right' and takes us to the heart of the debate about absolute and relative moral values. To what extent, and in what circumstances, is the 'right' moral behaviour transcendent of persons or institutions, and of time and space; and to what extent is it culturally or otherwise contextual? This latter view – the 'when in Rome do as the Romans do' view – is currently the dominant one of the libertarian ideology of much of Western society. Moral and ethical relativism appears to reign supreme, but not, I might add, among Eastern societies and particular interest groups. Yet, in practice, in all societies, there are 'no-go' areas and there are patterns of behaviour which, except in extreme cases, or by minority groups such as terrorists, are thought to be fundamentally wrong.

For myself, I am fully taken with the idea of a pyramid of morals. At its apex there are a limited number of universally, or near universally, accepted moral absolutes. The philosophy behind these cardinal values is a 'do as you would be done by' philosophy[18] which the Dalai Lama (1999) has chosen to embrace under the twin desires of 'happiness' and 'avoidance of suffering'. Tom Donaldson (1996) identifies three of these absolutes: respect for human dignity, acknowledgment of basic rights and good citizenship, the latter being defined as 'the need of members of a community to work together to support and improve the institutions on which the community depends' (p. 54).

Further down the pyramid we can identify other values which, to a greater or lesser extent, and depending on how near to the apex they are, veer towards the absolute or the relative. Thus, as examples of the former (and some cultures would regard these as fundamental) are such virtues as truthfulness, reciprocity, honesty and justice. At a slightly lower level are such virtues as trust, solidarity, reliability and loyalty, while most culturally relative of all are likely to be those such as as duty, prudence, forbearance, diligence and a sense of guilt or shame.

So, let us accept, as all great sages and religions in history have accepted, that it is possible to identify a set of globally accepted moral values, while there are others which are specific to particular societies, institutions and individuals; and which may also change over time.

What now of the implications of RGC for moral standards? Capitalism has always set a high premium on certain virtues, although in some instances in its wake it has fostered some unvirtuous characteristics, such as greed, acquisitiveness, corruption and insensitivity. But today's RGC, if it is to be sustained, has its own unique moral imperatives. Not only do some behavioural mores need to be upgraded, and be more generally practised in a global community, but globalisation itself is a compelling reappraisal of the content and significance of particular virtues. In one of my earlier contributions (Dunning, 2000) I identified three of these, which I named the three Cs: creativity, cooperation and compassion.

First consider *creativity*. In today's knowledge-based economy it is critical to encourage the moral virtues which promote human resource development, innovation, initiative and entrepreneurship. These include, at the level of the individual, the desire for self-betterment, diligence and perseverance and, at a societal level, the actions by governments to promote the intellectual, emotional and spiritual potential of all its constituents (the opposite of the 'cog in the wheel' syndrome.)

Secondly, there is *cooperation*. For reasons alluded to earlier, we are moving out of an age of hierarchical capitalism into one of alliance capitalism. This is placing a premium on the moral virtues needed for fruitful and sustainable coalitions and partnerships, whether within or between organisations, such as trust, reciprocity and due diligence, not to mention mutually acceptable ethical standards. In addition to their self-generated stock of technical and organisational competence, firms will increasingly need to draw upon the entrepreneurship, capabilities and associations of other organisations, and, to do this successfully, they need to build up their relational assets, in essence, which comprise the motivation and capabilities of both managers and workers to get the most out of collaborative agreements (Dunning, 2002).

Such alliance capitalism, then, demands a reordering and reprioritisation of moral values, and an attitude of mind which Michael Novak has called solidarity, and which he defines as 'the upgrading of personal responsibility, initiative and fulfilment which results from cooperation and communion with others' (Novak, 1991). The question now arises, do the institutions of RGC currently have the necessary stock of moral capital to make this work? Will trust be upgraded as a moral virtue, and will its radius be extended to distant places?

Of course the unique nature of RGC is precisely that it exposes cross-border economic and social activity to a mosaic of cultural mores. Here the question arises as to whether there is, or should be, an ideal or dominant moral ecology to which individuals and organisations throughout the globe might ascribe, which, at the same time, acknowledges and respects the more sensitive components of cultural diversity. This surely is an area where the combination of the virtues of moral suasion and emotional intelligence needs to be fostered.

The moral absolutes versus moral relatives debate is not the only one relevant to our current interest. One other worth mentioning, although I do not have the space to dwell on it at length, is the distinction between the kind of socially responsible behaviour which, in the end, benefits the individual or organisation practising it (what Charles Handy, 1998, has called 'proper selfishness' and that which has no expectation of gain, that is, pure unselfish behaviour. The latter kind of behaviour is, in fact, quite widespread. It is obviously practised within families, but, also among many NGOs, such as the Red Cross (founded in 1864), philanthropic and religious organisations and disaster relief agencies.

What are the implications of RGC for the two kinds of virtue? Here, as an example, I come to the third of my C virtues, *compassion*. Compassion I take to incorporate such virtues as benevolence, fairness, justice and empathy towards others' suffering, be it material or social. One of the attributes of RGC is that it challenges each of us to widen our 'radius of compassion', but to what extent is this a necessary ingredient for its sustainability? Let me put the question another way around. What are the likely consequences of the *absence* of compassionate behaviour, namely indifference or even hostility towards those who, through no fault of their own, are currently ill-served by GC or are excluded from its benefits? I think, in the long run at least, as history has demonstrated time and time again, they could be extremely serious, and cut at the very heart of Western civilisation as we know it today.

This, then, suggests the need for the richer countries (and particularly those which have benefited from globalisation) as a matter of virtuous self-interest, if nothing else, to help upgrade the economic capabilities and social welfare of their poorer neighbours, to lower or remove import barriers on their products and, wherever possible, to relieve their debt burden.[19]

This, of course, is not to deny that even the poorest developing countries can do much to help themselves. Corruption, for example, is endemic in many regimes. It is also an unpalatable fact that no fewer than 28 of the 40 poorest nations of the world are currently in the midst of armed conflict or have recently emerged from it (HMSO, 2000, para. 78). In several developing and some transition economies, a considerable part of private savings (40 per cent in the case of sub-Saharan Africa), is held abroad rather than being directed to domestic economic development.[20] Moreover, if nothing else, the East Asian economic crisis of the late 1990s exposed the imperfections and fragility of the financial and institutional architecture of several countries in the region.

HOW BEST TO PROMOTE AND UPGRADE MORAL BEHAVIOUR

I now come to the central part of my presentation. Assuming that improving the moral standards of the institutions of RGC, and those of their participants, is necessary to broaden and deepen its inclusiveness, and to sustain it in a socially acceptable way, how can this best be achieved in a world made up of countries with many distinctive cultures, ideologies and types of government regimes, and at different stages of economic development?

I want to suggest we should take a dual approach to answering this question. One is a 'top-down' approach and the other is a 'bottom-up approach'.[21] The former approach is one in which moral attitudes and standards are encouraged (e.g. by means of example or suasion) or enforced (e.g. by means of laws and regulations) on one group of individuals and organisations, by another group of individuals or organisations, at a higher level of governance. Examples include, at a macro level, the legal prohibition of the possession of hard drugs, and anti-monopoly legislation and, at a micro level, school authorities disallowing or discouraging anti-social behaviour among their students. The 'bottom up' approach implies the spontaneous or internalised upgrading of moral values and conduct by individuals, firms or interest groups, which may act as a ground swell affecting the values and conduct of the organisations of higher governance. We have seen that many of the nineteenth-century, social, educational and health reforms arose in this way. Today individuals and NGOs are among the most vocal activist groups pleading, for example, for the abolition of human rights abuses, racial discrimination, unsafe goods and the employment of child labour; and, more positively, for upgrading environmental, health and labour standards. Again one can use this approach to see how each of the three tasks of RGC may be upgraded, and also how the particular institutions involved may prefer to adopt, or be influenced by, one or other approach. Let me give just a couple of examples of what I mean.

Take first societal goals and the means of better achieving these goals by a bottom-up approach. Where the present system is perceived to be deficient in delivering these, consumers, both individually and collectively, can use their purchasing power to exert a powerful influence both on supermarkets not to stock certain products, and on corporations not to engage in, or to buy from suppliers that engage in, unacceptable business practices.[22] Consumer activism is, in fact, very much alive. A Gallup poll in Britain in the mid-1990s found that three out of five UK consumers were prepared to boycott stores or products because they were concerned about the ethical standards of the suppliers. A survey in the USA, at about the same time, revealed that 75 per cent of Americans would not buy from stores selling goods produced in sweat shops, while a more recent UK poll showed that three-quarters of respondents made their choice of products on a green or ethical basis (Hertz, 2000, pp. 119–20). Corporations, too, such as The Body Shop and Benetton, have quite spontaneously tried to incorporate these values in their product and production profiles.[23] Though this frequently takes the form of 'proper' selfishness, it can still exert a positive influence on the goals and quality of RGC.

These are examples of a bottom-up approach, which is now being further abetted by the Internet. Though not without its downsides, I believe that e-commerce could well inject a further element of my third C, compassion, into the value chain and further buttress the sustainability of RGC. I also like the idea of shareholder activism, which has been, at least partly, responsible for the launch of a series of ethical funds in several stock markets and, in London, of an ethical share index (FTSE 4 GOOD) comprising 283 publicly quoted companies (each of which has to meet certain environmental, human rights and social standards to merit inclusion).

I cannot, at this point, resist a comment about the role of NGOs in the global economy. NGOs, as a twenty-first-century version of civil society of the nineteenth century, can perform an essential and valuable function. They can, and do, prick the social conscience of the other organisations of RGC; and they can, and do, engage in a variety of value-adding activities which neither markets nor governments are able or willing to undertake.

NGOs are, of course, a highly heterogeneous group of organisations ranging from philanthropic societies through religious, educational and arts-based institutions to political activists and consumer pressure groups. Each has its own particular agenda. Sometimes this is central to the issues addressed by RGC, and sometimes not at all. But certainly there is little doubt that, as a result of their activism, issues such as debt relief, human rights, the environment and safety standards (to name but a few) have been raised much higher on the agenda of world leaders and international fora than they would otherwise have been.

Where I think the NGOs go awry, or are in danger of going awry, is first in associating themselves with the kind of violent (and anti-democratic) demonstrations we have seen in Seattle, Genoa and elsewhere; but secondly, and more importantly, in attacking the capitalist system *in toto*, rather than particular issues or the unwillingness (or inability) of its organisations or organisations to properly get to grips with their concerns. It is rarely that globalisation per se is the cause of such disquiet. As much as anything, it is technological advance, the concentration of economic power and the inability or unwillingness of some (but not all) of the organisations of capitalism to deal adequately with the phenomena of global connectivity.[24] I also believe that NGOs tend to underestimate the progress which has been made towards RGC (on the part of both MNEs and governments) and the role RGC itself could play to meet their own needs and aspirations. Indeed I believe that the smart civil activists are those who acknowledge that RGC can help them to achieve their objectives, and know how to use it, rather than destroy it.

What of the top-down approach? This is essentially to do with law making, regulatory and other enforcement mechanisms. Let me concentrate on the role of national governments. While (as I have already said) I do not believe that governments should determine the ethical mores of society, it is their job to provide an infrastructure and a safety net, which encourages the kind of virtues which make up an acceptable moral ecology. This is exactly what corporate, civil and criminal law, backed by appropriate policies, example and suasion, seeks to do. And it is the quality of these ingredients of capitalism which separates the thriving economies in the world from the rest, and which sustains the former in times of social upheaval better than the latter.

A case in point is the reintroduction of capitalism into the Russian Federation in the early 1990s. When the erstwhile communist country was opened up, the IMF and World Bank stepped in to aid its transition to a market-based economy. But almost the entire focus of the guidance given by these two institutions was directed to removing the technical barriers to free markets, and to do so according to the principles of the Washington Consensus. Yet what was no less needed from the West was its help in establishing a modern, transparent and corruption-free political, legal and banking system, and to provide the moral underpinnings for free markets, characteristics which had been absent in Russia for the past three generations.

As a result, the aftermath of the Cold War saw little effort being made to reform the Federation's institutional framework, or to encourage the renaissance of civil society which had been dormant for so long. To this extent, the West failed the erstwhile Soviet Union; it offered the key to a new materialism without the social and moral capital necessary to support and sustain it. As a result, over the last decade, there has been a huge increase in crime and kleptocracy,[25] and in income inequality, while the real economy has shrunk by up to a third (Stiglitz, 1998). Should we not be surprised, then, that, in a recent poll, four out of five Russians indicated they would support a reinstatement of the old communist state? All too late, the protagonists of free global markets have begun to realise that, without the right institutional infrastructure and moral ecology, the profit motive, particularly when combined with full capital market liberalisation, rather than offering the right incentives for wealth creation is likely to set in motion a drive to strip assets, and ship the proceeds abroad.

A more positive example of the top-down approach is the role the UN has played, over the years, in promoting a constructive dialogue among the constituents of global capitalism. The most recent initiative, which is now involving several hundred firms and an impressive array of NGOs and governments, is that of a 'Global Compact' launched in 1999 at Davos by Kofi Annan (Kell and Ruggie, 1999). Its task is primarily to encourage businesses, and especially MNEs, not only to behave in an ethically responsible way, but to make a compact with the UN to do just this, and to work with governments who do so. It is based on nine moral and social principles grouped into three headings: human rights, labour standards and environmental protection.

Whether this will be a major influence in advancing or sustaining global capitalism remains to be seen, but I think it is a step, among many others I might add, in the right direction.

THE DRIVING FORCES OF MORAL BEHAVIOUR

What then drives (or should drive) the individuals and institutions shaping RGC to behave as they do? What is the source of their moral standards and what influences them to upgrade these standards? I shall eschew the 'nature' versus 'nurture' debate and, instead, draw upon Brian Griffiths's threefold categorisation of the sources of moral values influencing business conduct, which he made in a perceptive contribution three years ago (Griffiths, 1999).

The first source is one to which we have already referred, and what Griffiths terms 'enlightened self-interest'. This philosophy acknowledges few moral absolutes and is fully consistent with the current cult of self-centred and secular individualism. But, because of its particularity, its subjectivity and its unpredictability, both Griffiths and I would aver it is too insecure a foundation on which to build RGC, although, as I have already acknowledged, a 'when in Rome' type cultural relativism may be appropriate at the lower end of the moral pyramid.

The second source is adherence to a global ethic based upon a universal consensus on 'particular human values, criteria and basic attitudes' (Kung, 1998). This ethic is particularly associated with the German theologian, Professor Hans Kung, although other analysts such as Amitai Etzioni, George Soros and Francis Fukuyama come near to endorsing it. It was first promulgated at an inaugural meeting of the Council of the Parliament of the World's Religions in Chicago in 1993. It is based very much on a 'do as you would be done by' credo which emphasises the need for a broad consensus among the different institutions of global capitalism. At the top of its moral pyramid it identifies such basic virtues as respect for human dignity and reciprocity; and at the next layer, the core values of non-violence, solidarity, justice and truthfulness. It then seeks to encompass these values in a series of overlapping circles which embrace the main institutions of global capitalism.

The strength of this particular approach, as Lord Griffiths observes, is in its acceptance of both religious pluralism and secularism, its inclusive geographical coverage and the fact that it 'carries with it no baggage from the past'. At the same time, it recognises that the quality of global society cannot be enhanced without 'the consciousness of individuals' – and that is the rub. Exactly how is this done? If there is a concern I have with this concept, it is that it tends to be 'all things to all men', and it is left to each individual to find his or her moral salvation. Nevertheless it is a huge advance in helping us to formulate and better understand the moral prerequisites for sustainable RGC.

The third source of moral standards identified by Griffiths is the revealed monotheistic faiths of Christianity, Islam and Judaism, though I would extend these to embrace at least some of the Eastern religions. It is my understanding that the difference between this approach and that of a global ethic is that the former believes it to be an absolute necessity for there to be some kind of external (that is, beyond self) revelation or inspiration which prompts and guides the spontaneous moral behaviour of individuals and organisations. In other words, it is not enough to identify a number of commonly accepted virtues as set out, for example, by the Parliament of the World's Religions which must be embraced by any global consensus. What is also required is a belief in a supreme being (or the principles enumerated by the disciples of a supreme being), which guides and inspires one's conduct,[26] in a morally uplifting way.

Now clearly, in this post-modern age, for the time being at least, a morality based on religious *belief*, as opposed to religious *teachings*, is unlikely to appeal to the majority of individuals, especially in the West; and certainly Professor Kung's more eclectic approach seems to offer more realistic promise. Yet the impact of this third way should not be underestimated. Not only do the majority of the people in the world claim allegiance to one or other of the religious persuasions and seek to live their lives by the moral precepts laid down by them; no less relevant is the fact that each of the monotheistic persuasions is globally oriented and inclusive. 'Go into the world and preach the gospel' was the command of Jesus Christ.[27]

Indeed, in many respects, we already have the makings of a global moral architecture to meet the responsibilities of global capitalism, and far more so than we have any consensus about the appropriate global economic or potential governance systems. At the same time I believe that the religious persuasions are currently having a bad press and that indeed, to make their message heard more clearly and persuasively, they need to put their own houses in order. With this in mind, in 1998, I put forward a proposal that an annual or biannual meeting of a group of the world's religious and spiritual leaders – rather like that of the Group of 8 in the economic domain – should be convened. The brief of the group would be to identify, promote and monitor a set of common ground rules and enforcement mechanisms for upgrading the moral content of GC and to provide information about, and undertake research into, the interaction between moral and ethical values, cultural diversity and the content and consequences of GC. An alternative course of action might be for the UN to set up a high-level Commission of Eminent Religious (and other?) Persons on this subject. Again the commission might be supported by a secretariat which would collect information, undertake research and give advice, e.g. via publications, conferences and media presentations to both religious institutions and to the participants in GC. One model for such an entity might be that of the Commission on Transnational Corporations set up by the Economic and Social Council in 1972 (UN, 1974).

How much common ground is there between the major religions as to the moral challenges of GC? What are the differences? How fundamental are they? How far can these be resolved or the dignity of those holding them be preserved? What part does – indeed should – religion play today in identifying and prescribing moral virtues and patterns of ethical conduct? Are the challenges of globalisation demanding a reappraisal or adaptation of the role of religion as a moral stimulant? Can (or should) religious precepts and teaching play a more important role in upgrading the quality of cooperative and (particularly) covenantal relationships? What of the interaction between the religious teaching and practice and that of the beliefs and actions of civil society? These are just a few questions which deserve more serious scholarly attention than they currently receive.

While it is understandable that the practicability or effectiveness of this kind of proposal should be treated with some scepticism, it is worth recording that history provides many examples of an upsurge or reconfiguration in religious beliefs and practices which have helped enhance the moral attitudes and values of individuals, and through them the ethical conduct of institutions. It is also to be observed that, frequently in the past, the influence of religion has been most strongly felt in times of political turmoil or economic crisis, or when religious beliefs and customs were themselves under threat. Such events provided a sense of immediacy to reappraise both the value of particular virtues and their likely impact on the social content and consequences of economic activity. The question of interest is whether we are in such times today.

SUMMARY AND CONCLUSIONS

The time has come to sum up the main points of my presentation. I started with the proposition that, at its best, global capitalism (as I defined it) is, in our present state of knowledge, the most efficient economic system for creating and sustaining wealth. But I quickly went on to say that its efficacy must be judged in relation to its willingness and capabilities to meet the broader economic and social goals of society. In this, as things stand today, it is currently found wanting for three reasons. The first is that its institutions, and particularly the market, are less well designed for the production and exchange of public or social goods and services than private goods and services, and that the former are becoming a rising component of our daily welfare. The second is that there are a series of "technical" failures in each of its organisations judged by their ability to meet the demands of the majority of the world's people. The third is that the moral underpinning of these same organisations needs reconfiguring and upgrading.

I suggested that, up to now, the attention of scholars has been primarily directed at reducing these imperfections which range from specific distortions, such as monopoly power, to the instability of international financial markets at a time of volatility, uncertainty and the ease with which capital and technology can move across national boundaries. Rather differently, however, my focus has been to identify and evaluate the kind of current moral deficiencies of the institutions of global capitalism, which constrain not only the willingness and capability of the system to operate efficiently and equitably, but also the content and quality of societal values as a whole.

I then went on to distinguish between absolute and relative moral values and argued that globalisation was leading to a convergence of the former, but a divergence of the latter. This, in and of itself, called for the virtues of tolerance and patience. In identifying the virtues especially needed to upgrade and sustain RGC, I focused on those embodied in the 3 Cs: creativity, cooperation and compassion. I then went on to indicate how a top down (or externally imposed or influenced) approach, and a bottom-up (a spontaneous or internally generated) approach to upgrading moral attitudes and values were complementary routes, although, I suggested, the balance of choice between these two options was likely to vary between interest groups and societies over time and according to the particular aspect of RGC being considered.

I finally tackled (albeit somewhat tentatively) two related questions. From where do our moral values come and what must be done to promote those most relevant to RGC? I explored three possibilities. The first was a nurturing of such values primarily through the stick (punishment of bad behaviour) and carrot (praise of good behaviour), in order to steer self-interest in the right direction. Second, I examined the value of a global ethic; third, I looked at the role of the religious revelation, which might guide both top-down and bottom-up approaches. Here I suggested that, in addition to a reasoned acceptance of the need for an upgraded moral ecology, there was an additional, external, source of authority, and that all monotheistic faiths believed in this, although they differed in their emphasis on, or prioritisation of, particular virtues.[28] I argued that this put a huge responsibility on the part of the religious leaders to present a vociferous, reasoned but conciliatory, united front on this issue – without, I might add, straying too much into the methodological territory of economics and politics. Can we not conceive of a group of five, six or seven (or whatever number) of religious leaders to perform a similar task in the *moral* domain to that of the Group of 8 in the economic and political domain? Is this such a pipe dream?

Finally I would like to think that all of us engaged in the teaching and research of international business (IB) will grasp the cudgel in exploring the relevance of morally related issues to the functioning of global capitalism and the global market place. It is too important a subject to be neglected. Of course, for a long time, IB scholars have identified the importance of culture in influencing the success of firms, and countries; and some economists, notably the Nobel Prize winner Amartya Sen, have argued for moral issues to be more widely embraced by economists. Sen's recent book on *Development as Freedom* is a brilliant exposition of the fact that the transformation of societies through economic development cannot be successfully achieved without a simultaneous reappraisal and upgrading of moral standards. My plea is for mainstream IB scholars to integrate the moral dimension in their analysis and thinking, as they seek to explain how global capitalism might both benefit and be made more acceptable to a much larger number of people across the planet; and for each of its organisations to work in a holistic and cooperative manner to achieve this goal.

NOTES

1. I am indebted to Jack Behrman, Peter Buckley, Mark Casson, Tony Corley, Peter Hart, Robert Heilbronner and Steve Kobrin for the helpful comments they made on an earlier draft of this chapter. This chapter also contains material which was published in a volume edited by J.H. Dunning (2003), *The Moral Challenges of Global Capitalism*, published by Oxford University Press. I am indebted to the Templeton and Carnegie Bosch Foundations for financial support in the preparation of this chapter.
2. See especially Friedman (2000), Gray (1998), Hertz (2000), HMSO (2000), Soros (1998), Stiglitz (1998) and the World Bank (2000).
3. As reviewed and identified, for example, in Dunning (2000), Dicken (2000), Hirst and Thompson (1999), HMSO (2000) and Svetlicic (2000).
4. Amartya Sen (1995) reminds us that the production of public and/or not for profit goods and services are part of the capitalist economic system and that non-market institutions are frequently in a better position to supply these goods and services. Many years earlier, Fred Hirsch (1976) argued that, in post-industrial economies, social goods and services (health, safety, pollution control, parks and so on) were assuming an increasing role in the GDP of countries.
5. In 1991, the Pope gave his definition of responsible capitalism 'as an economic system which recognises the fundamental and positive role of business, the market and private property and the resulting responsibility for the means of production, as well as the free human creativity in the economic sector' (as quoted by Sirocco, 1994, p. 18).
6. See, e.g., the writings of Smith (1776), Hirschman (1982), Gray (1992), Barry (1995).
7. Albert Hirschman has called this the 'doux-commerce' or civilising force of markets (Hirschman, 1982).
8. Much of the defence of the market as a moral system rests on the assumption that markets are ideally competitive (or perfect in the economists' sense). But, as Soros (1998, p. 197) has pointed out, if this is so, such markets de facto exempt participants from a moral choice *as long as they abide by its rules*. Only when markets are less than perfect (as indeed is usually the case) does the issue of choice enter the picture. And, in such a situation, there is absolutely no reason to suppose that there is something inherent in the market which will force all of its participants to behave with moral responsibility.
9. To quote from Aristotle, for example, 'Wealth obviously is not the good we seek, for the sole purpose it serves is to provide the means of getting something else. So far as it goes the ends we have already mentioned (pleasure, virtue and honour) would have a better title to be considered the good, for they are to be desired for their own account.' (Quoted by Handy, 1998, p. 15.)
10. More generally several studies have questioned the idea that economic welfare (as nor-

mally measured) buys happiness. A report compiled by Robert Worcester in 1998 for Demos found that there was little correlation between GNP per head and people's 'perception' of their own contentment or happiness; another more recent study (Cooper et al., 2001) has shown that, while real incomes and consumption have more than trebled in the UK, Italy and Germany over the past 30 years, reported happiness levels in those countries have declined. By contrast, other surveys have suggested there is quite a significant correlation between economic freedom and economic prosperity (Johnson *et al.*, 1999).

11.   Such behaviour includes corruption, the bypassing of safety or hygiene regulations, and questionable labour practices (as in the case of some sweat shops and child labour). Of course, these are not new concerns, nor are they specific to globalisation. But they have been exacerbated and brought to the public awareness as a result of globalisation.

12.   As set out in some detail in Buckley and Casson (1988), Dunning (2002).

13.   There are, however, outstanding exceptions to this statement. It has been estimated, for example, that private charitable contributions by US individuals and private institutions to the betterment of living standards in developing countries exceed those of the Federal government by more than six times (Cowley, 2002).

14.   Victorian moralists believed in a strictly limited view of the state. T.H. Green, for example, was opposed to paternal government. He wrote, 'The State should promote morality by strengthening the moral disposition of the individual, not by subjecting the individual to any kind of moral tutelage' (Green, 1941, quoted in Himmelfarb, 1995). Wise words, and highly relevant to today's debate.

15.   Set up as a microcosm of civil society in 1884 by the Rev. Samuel Barnett, Vicar of St. Judes in London, Toynbee Hall was not a charitable institution. Instead of providing economic relief, it dispensed learning culture and social amenities, and it did so in Whitechapel, the poorest district of London. The Hall was dedicated to the memory of Arnold Toynbee, who believed the Victorian middle classes had a duty both to set an example and to educate the working classes in the concept of citizenship (Himmelfarb, 1995).

16.   To quote from Michael Novak, 'Human capital includes moral labels, such as hard work, cooperativeness, social trust, alertness, honesty and social habits such as respect for the rule of law (Novak, 1999).

17.   At the same time, as one observer (Rothkopf 2002) has put it, 'Somewhere in the world today walks the next Marx ... we may not know from which region he will hail or his particular approach. But we can be sure that someone, somewhere will offer an alternative vision' (page 2).

18.   From time immemorial, most, if not all, major faiths and moral philosophies accept this as one, if not *the*, universal moral value. Each religion and philosophy has its particular manner of expressing it. In the Christian faith, for example, it is essentially contained in Christ's injunction 'Thou shalt love thy neighbour as thyself.'

19.   HMSO (2000).

20.   Such a flight of sorely needed capital can be reversed. In Uganda, for example, following domestic economic reform, and a crackdown on corruption, net private capital more than doubled as a percentage of GNP in the 1990s (HMSO, 2000, para. 153).

21.   See also the incisive comments made on an earlier contribution of mine (Dunning, 2000) by Buckley and Casson (2001).

22.   Noreen Hertz, in her discussion of this issue, quotes the words of two CEOs of leading brand name corporations. One told her, 'What we fear most is not legislation' and the other, 'If people think corporations are powerful they haven't been in a corporation ... Consumer choice does not allow us to have unfettered power' (Hertz, 2000, p. 126).

23.   In 1999, following a series of exposures of the use of child labour and sweat shops by some of the leading US apparel manufacturers and clothing retailers, a group of these corporations joined with human rights and labour representatives to establish a Fair Labour Association. Inter alia, the association would formally accredit auditors to certify companies as complying with an agreed code of conduct relating to minimum wages and working conditions including restrictions on child labour and working hours. This was followed by a Workers Rights Consortium, a body comprising university students and

officials and labour and human rights campaigners (Friedman 2000, p. 206; Hertz, 2000, p. 138). At the same time, as mainstream economists frequently point out, in the past, the first stage of economic development of industrialising countries has always taken the form of something akin to sweat shops. The question which moralists and others have to address is not so much 'whether' but 'what kind of' sweatshops.

24. For a recent examination of the panoply of NGOs and popular transnational movements, see, e.g., Sinnar (1995/6), Scholtz *et al.* (1999), Ostry (1998), Vakil (1997) and Wilson and Whitmore (1998).
25. Thomas Friedman (2000, p. 146) defines kleptocracy as a situation in which many, or all, of the functions of the state system, from tax collection to customs, to privatisation to regulation, have become so infected by corruption that legal transactions become the exception rather than the norm.
26. The ultimate is the Christian belief that the spirit of a living Christ may motivate and guide a person's attitudes and behaviour.
27. Matthew 28: 19.
28. For example, Islam places great stress on social justice as a primary virtue; Judaism lays particular emphasis on duty and tradition; Christianity places love and compassion at the top of the pyramid of its virtues.

REFERENCES

Barry, N. (1995), 'What moral constraints for business?', in S. Brittan and A. Hamlin (eds), *Market Capitalism and Moral Values*, Aldershot, UK and Brookfield, US: Edward Elgar, pp. 57–78.

Buckley, P.J. and M. Casson (1988), 'A theory of cooperation in international business' in F.J. Contractor and P. Lorange (eds), *Cooperative Strategies in International Business*, Lexington: D.C. Heath and Co., pp. 31–53.

Buckley, P.J. and M. Casson (2001), 'The moral basis of global capitalism: beyond the eclectic theory', *International Journal of the Economics of Business*, **8**(2), 303–27.

Church of England (2000), *Faith in a Global Economy*, GS Misc. 538, London: General Synod of the Church of England.

Cooper, B., C. Garcia-Penolosa and P. Funk (2001), 'Status effects and negative utility growth', *Economic Journal*, **111**(473), 642–65.

Cowley, G. (2002), 'Bill's biggest bet yet', *Newsweek*, 4 February, 45–52.

Dahrendorf, R. (2000), *'Politics and Society'*, mimeo, lecture presented at Reading University, November.

Dalai Lama (1999), *Ethics for the New Millennium*, New York: Riverhead Books.

Davies, J. (ed.) (1995), *God and the Market Place*, Health and Welfare Unit, Choice in Welfare, no. 14, Institute of Economic Affairs, London.

De Tocqueville (1981), *Democracy in America* (abridged with an introduction by Thomas Bender), New York: The Modern Library.

Dicken, P. (2000), *Global Shift*, 4th edn, New York: The Guilford Press.

Donaldson, T. (1996), 'Values in tension: ethics away from home', *Harvard Business Review*, Sept./Oct., 48–62.

Dunning, J.H. (2000), *Global Capitalism at Bay?*, London and New York: Routledge.

Dunning, J.H. (2002), 'Relational assets, networks and international business activity', in F. Contractor and P. Lorange (eds), *Cooperation Strategies and Alliances*, Oxford: Elsevier Science, pp. 569–93.

Elazar, D. (1989), *People and Polity: The Organizational Dynamics of World Jewry*, Detroit: Wayne State University Press.

Etzioni, A. (1996), *The New Golden Rule: Community and Morality in a Democratic Society*, New York: Basic Books.

Etzioni, A. (1998), *The Moral Dimension: Towards a New Economics*, New York: Free Press.

Falk, R. (1998), 'Global civil society: perspectives, initiatives, movements', *Oxford Development Studies*, **26**(1), 99–110.

Flemming, J.S. (1995), 'The ethics of unemployment and Mafia capitalism', in S. Brittan and A. Hamlin (eds), *Market Capitalism and Moral Values*, Aldershot, UK and Brookfield, US: Edward Elgar.

Friedman, T.L. (2000), *The Lexus and the Olive Tree*, New York: Anchor Books.

Fukuyama, F. (1999), *The Great Disruption*, London: Profile Books.

Gray, J. (1998), *False Dawn*, New York: The New Press.

Gray, J. (1992), 'The moral foundations of market institutions', Health and Welfare Unit, Choice in Welfare, no. 10, Institute of Economic Affairs, London.

Green, D. (1993), '*Reinventing civil society*', Health and Welfare Unit, Choice in Welfare, 17, Institute of Economic Affairs, London.

Green, T.H. ([1882]1941), *Lectures on the Principles of Political Obligation*, London.

Griffiths, B. (1996), '*The business of values*', inaugural Hansen-Wessner Memorial Lecture, US Service Master Company.

Griffiths, B. (1999), '*The role of the business corporation as a moral community*', the Hansen-Wessner Memorial Lecture, Oxford.

Hall, P.A. and Soskice, D. (2001), *Varieties of Capitalism*, Oxford: Oxford University Press.

Hamlin, A. (1995), 'The morality of the market', in S. Brittan and A. Hamlin (eds), *Market Capitalism and Moral Values*, Aldershot, UK and Brookfield, US: Edward Elgar, pp. 137–50.

Hamlin, A., H. Giersch and A. Norton (1996), 'Markets, morals and community', Centre for Independent Studies, St. Leonards, Australia.

Handy, C. (1998), *The Hungry Spirit*, London: Arrow Books.

Harrison, L.E. and S.P. Huntington (eds) (2000), *Culture Matters: How Values Shape Human Progress*, New York: Basic Books.

Heilbroner, R. (1992), *21st Century Capitalism*, London: University College Press.

Henderson, D. (1998), 'The changing fortunes of economic liberalism', Institute of Economic Affairs, London.

Hertz, N. (2000), *The Silent Takeover: Global Capitalism and the Death of Democracy*, London: William Heinemann.

Himmelfarb, G. (1995), 'The Demoralization of Society: From Victorian Virtues to Modern Values', Health and Welfare Unit, Institute of Economic Affairs, London.

Hirsch, F. (1976), *Social Limits to Growth*, Cambridge, MA: Harvard University Press.

Hirschman, A. (1977), *The Passions and the Interests: Political Arguments for Capitalism Before its Triumph*, Princeton, NJ: Princeton University Press.

Hirschman, A. (1982), 'Rival interpretations of market society: civilizing, destructive or feeble', *Journal of Economic Literature*, **XX**(December), 1463–84.

Hirst, P. and G. Thompson (1999), *Globalisation in Question?*, 2nd edn, Cambridge: Polity Press.

HMSO (2000), *Eliminating World Poverty: Making Globalisation Work for the Poor*, London: HMSO, Cm. 5006.

Johnson, B.R., K.R. Holmes and M. Kirkpatrick (1999), 'The 1999 Index of Economic Freedom', The Heritage Foundation/Wall Street Journal, New York.

Kell, G. and G. Ruggie (1999), 'Global markets and social legitimacy: the case of the "Global Compact"', *Transnational Corporation*, **9**(3), 101–20.

Kennedy, P. (1993), *Preparing for the Twenty First Century*, New York: Vintage Books.

Kung, H. (1998), *A Global Ethic for Global Politics and Economics*, Oxford: Oxford University Press.

Kung, H. (2001), '*Globale Markwirtschaft und Ethische Rahmenordnu*', mimeo, Tübingen, Germany.

Lal, D. (1998), *Unintended Consequences*, Cambridge, MA: MIT Press.

Landes, D. (1998), *The Wealth and Poverty of Nations*, New York, W.W. Norton.

Lewis, C.S. (1978), *The Abolition of Man*, London: Collins.

Mandeville, B. (1729), *The Fable of the Bees*, ed. F.B. Kaye, reprinted 1924, Oxford: Clarendon Press.

North, D.C. (1999), '*Understanding the process of economic change*' (The Wincott Lecture, 1998), Institute of Economic Affairs, London.

Novak, M. (1991), *The Spirit of Democratic Capitalism*, Lanham MD: Madison Books.

Novak, M. (1999), 'Solidarity in a time of globalization', lecture given at the University of Notre Dame, Notre Dame, Indiana, 11 October, mimeo, University of Notre Dame.

Novak, M. and R. Preston (1994), '*Christian capitalism or Christian socialism?*', Health and Welfare Unit, Institute of Economic Affairs, London.

Olson, M. (1982), *The Rise and Fall of Nations*, New Haven and London: Yale University Press.

Ostry, S. (1998), 'Convergence and sovereignty: policy scope for compromise', momeo, Carleton University, Ottawa.

Presbyterian Church (1984), *Christian Faith and Economic Justice*, Atlanta, GA: Office of the General Assembly.

Preston, R.H. (1993), *Religion and the Ambiguities of Capitalism*, Cleveland, OH: The Pilgrim Press.

Putnam, R.D. (1995), 'Bowling alone: America's declining social capital', *Journal of Democracy*, **6**, 65–78.

Rawls, J. (1972), *A Theory of Justice*, Oxford: Clarendon Press.

Reed, C. (ed.) (2001), *Development Matters. Christian Perspectives on Globalization*, London: Church House Publishing.

Rifkin, J. (2000), *The Age of Access*, London: Penguin Books.

Rothkopf, D.J. (2002), 'The failures of capitalism', *Washington Post National; Weekly Edition*, 28 Jan.–3 Feb., p. 2.

Russell, B. (1962), *A History of Western Philosophy*, London: George Allen and Unwin.

Sacks, J. (1999), '*Morals and markets*', Institute of Economic Affairs, London.

Salamon, L.M. (1994), 'The rise of the non-profit sector', *Foreign Affairs*, **73**(4), 109–22.

Scholtz, J.A., R. O'Brien and M. Williams (1999), 'The WTO and civil society', *Journal of World Trade*, **33**(1), 107–23.

Searle, G.R. (1998), *Morality and the Market in Victorian Britain*, Oxford: Clarendon Press.

Sen, A. (1995), 'Moral codes and economic success', in S. Brittan and A. Hamlin (eds), *Market Capitalism and Moral Values*, Aldershot, UK and Brookfield, US: Edward Elgar.

Sen, A. (1999), *Development as Freedom*, Oxford: Oxford University Press.

Sinnar, S. (1995/6), 'Mixed blessing: the growing influence of NGOs', *Harvard International Review*, **18**(1), 54–7, 79, 80.

Sirocco, R.A. (1994), '*A moral basis for liberty*', Health and Welfare Unit, Religion and Liberty Series, 2, Institute of Economic Affairs, London.

Smith, A. (1776), *An Inquiry into the Nature and Causes of the Wealth of Nations*, reprinted 1937, ed. Edwin Cannon, London: Modern Library.

Soros, G. (1998), *The Crisis of Global Capitalism*, London: Little, Brown and Company.

Soros, G. (2002), *On Globalization*, Oxford: Public Affairs.

Stiglitz, J.E. (1998), '*Towards a new paradigm of development*', 9th Raul Prebisch Lecture, UNCTAD, Geneva.

Stiglitz, J.E. (2002), *Globalization and its Discontents*, London: Penguin Books.

Streeten, P. (2001), *Globalization: Threat or Opportunity*, Copenhagen: Copenhagen Business Press.

Svetlicic, M. (2000), 'Globalisation: neither hell nor paradise', *Journal of International Relations and Development*, **3**(4), 369–94.

Tawney, R. (1926), *Religion and the Rise of Capitalism*, London: John Murray.

Tillich, P. (1971), 'Political Expectations', in J.L. Adams (ed.), New York: Harper and Row, p. 51.

UN (1974), *The Impact of Multinational Corporations on Development and International Relations*, New York: United Nations, E/55/Rev I.

UNCTAD (2000), *World Investment Report 2000: Cross Border Mergers and Acquisitions*, New York and Geneva: UN.

UNDP (2000), *Human Development Report 2000*, Oxford: Oxford University Press.

Vakil, A.C. (1997), 'Confronting the classification problem: towards a taxonomy of NGOs', *World Development*, **25**(12), 2057–70.

Weber, M. (1930), *The Protestant Ethic and the Spirit of Capitalism*, London: George Allen and Unwin.

Wilson, M.G. and E. Whitmore (1998), 'The transnationalization of popular movements: social policy making from below', *Canadian Journal of Development Studies*, **XIXIX**(1), 7–36.

Worcester, R. (1998), 'More than money', in I. Christie and L. Nash (eds), *The Good Life*, London: Demos.

World Bank (2000), *Attacking Poverty: World Development Report 2000–2001*, Oxford: Oxford University Press.

3. Corporate governance in multinational companies

Hans H. Hinterhuber, Kurt Matzler, Harald Pechlaner and Birgit Renzl

INTRODUCTION

In the last two decades the international business environment has become increasingly competitive, complex and sophisticated. Two basic forces lead companies to internationalise their operations: digitisation of technologies and deregulation of economies (Barkema *et al.*, 2002). Figure 3.1 shows these two forces driving globalisation and identifies the key management challenges that result for multinational companies.

Digitisation lowers radically the cost of information storage and transmission and increases dramatically the speed of information transmission; this allows carrying out the different stages of the value chain in low-cost countries or highly effective regional environments. Firms in developing countries manufacture and assemble components as subcontractors of complex products or provide business services for multinational companies. The deregulation of economies together with the privatisation of firms opens new markets; the opening of new and the globalisation of existing markets is compounded by the digitisation of technologies. Both forces give rise (a) to global small and medium-sized enterprises (SMEs), (b) to global networks between existing and new companies along their value chains, and (c) to large, focused global firms. The competitive dynamics becoming more and more intense requires all companies not only to learn and to innovate, but to do so better and faster than its competitors.

Digitization of technologies and deregulation of markets address new challenges for multinational companies. All competitive advantages erode over time. The performance of multinational firms depends on their ability to synchronise the requirements of their value chains in different countries, to develop new technologies for new and better products and services and continually to review their competencies, thus avoiding the risk of competency traps. To cope, multinational companies have continually to review

47

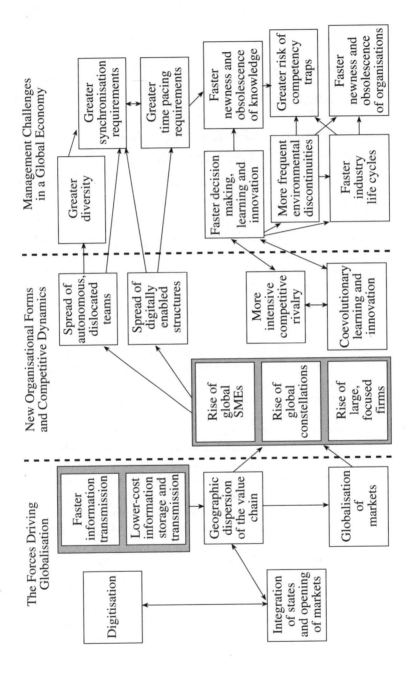

Source: Barkema *et al.* (2002).

Figure 3.1   The forces driving globalisation and the management challenges in a global economy

their structures, to focus on their core business, to outsource value chain activities to firms in developing countries and to cooperate even with competitors in order to compete in symbiotic networks that pool complementary assets. Multinational companies are becoming orchestrators of geographically dispersed value chains (Hinterhuber, 2003).

In order to achieve competitive advantages in global markets, companies need to pursue three objectives simultaneously (Bartlett *et al.*, 2000): global efficiency, multinational flexibility and worldwide learning. The pursuit of these three objectives requires a company to exploit differences in sourcing and market potential across countries, benefit from economies of scale and take advantage of economies of scope. Table 3.1 gives a brief overview on the way a multinational company can build the sources of competitive advantages to achieve the strategic objectives.

Research in strategic management, however, reveals that a company's ability to formulate and implement global strategies is greatly influenced and constrained by 'existing asset configurations, its historical definition of management responsibilities, and the ingrained organizational norms' (Bartlett and Ghoshal, 2000). These factors constitute a company's 'administrative heritage'. Porter (1990) emphasises the importance of ownership structure and corporate governance in determining corporate strategy:

> Company goals are most strongly determined by ownership structure, the motivation of owners and holders of debt, the nature of corporate governance and the incentive processes that shape the motivation of senior managers. The goals of publicly held corporations reflect the characteristics of that nation's capital markets. (1990, p. 110)

The ability of multinational companies to compete thus depends on time and history. Resources and dynamic capabilities built up in the past cannot be easily competed away (Barkema *et al.*, 2002).

CORPORATE GOVERNANCE SYSTEMS IN DIFFERENT COUNTRIES

Corporate governance covers the way of organising ownership, management and control of a corporation (Feddersen *et al.* 1996; Keasey and Thompson, 1997; Shleifer and Vishny, 1997; Witt, 2000). The prevailing corporate governance system influences the corporation regarding overall strategy, that is, the recognition of stakeholder interests, especially, the interest of customers, shareholders, banks, institutional investors, financial community, management and employees. It is necessary to balance the varying interests among the parties involved and the existing asymmetries in information consequently

Table 3.1   Global competitive advantage: goals and means

Strategic objectives	Sources of Competitive Advantage		
	National differences	Economies of scale	Economies of scope
Global efficiency	Benefiting from differences in factor costs: wages and cost of capital	Expanding and exploiting potential scale economies in each activity	Sharing of investments and costs across markets and businesses
Multinational flexibility	Managing different kinds of risks arising from market- or policy-induced changes in comparative advantages of different countries	Balancing scale with strategic and operational flexibility	Portfolio diversification of risks and creation of options and side-bets
Worldwide learning	Learning from societal differences in organisational and managerial processes and systems	Benefiting from experience: cost reduction and innovation	Shared learning across organisational components in different products, markets or businesses

Source: Bartlett *et al.* (2004).

(Witt, 2000, p. 159). However the mechanisms of balancing these interests vary across different countries.

A number of studies found significant differences in the institutional contexts in which corporate governance relationships are embedded (Heinrich, 2002). The literature identifies two general systems of corporate governance. The United States and the United Kingdom are characterised by relatively passive shareholders, boards of directors that are not always independent of managers, and active markets for corporate control. The system found in Continental Europe and Japan is associated with coalitions of active shareholders (other companies or banks), boards of directors that are more independent of management and limited markets for corporate control. These differences are thought to influence greatly the goals and performance of companies. Indeed Gedajlovic and Shapiro's (1998) findings indicate significant differences across countries due to different corporate governance mechanisms. One of the key differences lies in the orientation towards the shareholder value perspective or the stakeholder value perspective.

Japan, however, does not seem to fit perfectly into these two systems, hence it is frequently suggested that the countries be divided into three groups (Yoshimori, 1995) with either monistic, dualistic or pluralistic concepts. The monistic concept with the corporate board as the centre of power and control of the corporation is highly shareholder-oriented. The corporation is regarded as the private property of its owners. The primary focus is on shareholder value creation: Cost of capital is decreasing since equity can be raised more easily and with the increase in the value of the firm and its creditworthiness the cost of debts is decreasing. Lower cost of capital symbolises the central argument in favour of this capital market-oriented approach towards corporate governance, which is prevalent in the United States and the United Kingdom.

However, stock prices do not necessarily equal the actual value created in the firm and thus the primacy of the shareholder value is questioned. In the stakeholder value approach the balancing of interests of the varying stakeholders (shareholders, employees, banks and so on) is of primary importance (the shareholder versus stakeholder approach will be outlined below in more detail). The stakeholder approach is part of the dualistic system of corporate governance. The dualistic system is widely used in Germany, where the corporate governance concept differentiates between the group of people who are leading the firm (executive board) on the one hand and on the other hand the group of people who exercise control (supervisory board). In this dualistic system power and control are split between those two groups in order to be able to serve better all stakeholders' interests.

Another characteristic of the dualistic system prevalent in Germany is the principle of cooperative decision making within the board of directors, whereas, in countries like the United States and the United Kingdom, with a monistic system, the principle of directorship dominates, based on the authority of the CEO. The CEO is held responsible and thus his performance is crucial. This principle of directorship is in line with the market-oriented corporate governance approach.

The principle of directorship in the monistic system is also evident in terms of remuneration of the top management. Especially in European companies, stock options are considered with increasing suspicion. This form of remuneration is considered to represent an incentive for increasing corporate value. However, by using remuneration through stock options it is assumed that stock prices reflect the actual value created. In the United States, management is usually remunerated to a large extent by stock options. According to a recent survey (see Mintzberg *et al.*, 2002) CEO pay rose by 570 per cent during the 1990s, whereas profits rose by 114 per cent. In 1999, CEO direct compensation rose by 10.8 per cent, while shareholder returns fell by 3.9 per cent. These figures call into question the effectiveness of such incentive schemes. In the dualistic system of corporate governance, remuneration of top management is less capital market-oriented. In Germany, for instance, remuneration usually contains a fixed payment plus a dividend-based amount.

In discussing the advantages and disadvantages of the monistic concept over the dualistic there has to be considered a third system, the pluralistic concept. The pluralistic system of corporate governance is prevalent in Japan. The assumption behind the pluralistic approach is that the corporation belongs to all the stakeholders, with primary focus on the employees' interests. This system is specific to Japan, where long-term relationships dominate business practices, for instance the Keiretsu including various stakeholders such as the main banks, major suppliers, subcontractors and distributors. In this pluralistic approach power and control are exercised by numerous interest groups. The governance concept is based on the principles of seniority and its long-term relationships. Thus, in terms of management payments, incentives are not directed towards sharing of profits. A comparison of the three systems of corporate governance outlined above is shown in Table 3.2.

Table 3.2 shows that one key difference in corporate governance lies in the orientation towards the creation of shareholder value or stakeholder value. Since this topic is crucial in terms of corporate governance mechanisms, a comparison of the stakeholder model and the shareholder model is discussed in the following section.

Table 3.2   Comparison of three corporate governance systems

	Germany	USA	Japan
Purpose	Corporate interests 'Stakeholder value'	'Shareholder value'	Corporate interests 'Stakeholder value'
Governance principles	Cooperative with dividend-based remuneration	Directorship with stock options	Seniority and little sharing of profits
Governance practice	Dualistic, dominated by institutions and banks	Monistic, capital market-oriented	Pluralistic, dominated by institutions and banks
Participation of stakeholder	Firm as a social institution (of employees, banks, politicians and so on)		Banks and Keiretsu partner

Source: Witt (2000), p. 160; Yoshimori (1995).

The Stakeholder Model versus the Shareholder Model

Two models of corporate governance describe the business landscape of today (Halal, 1996): the stakeholder model and the shareholder model of the corporation. The stakeholder model (see Figure 3.2) views the corporation as a socioeconomic system composed of various constituencies: customers, employees, shareholders and the financial community, the public and its government representatives. The stakeholders have obligations to the firm as well as rights. The performance of the corporation depends on receiving the support of all key stakeholders. The corporation does not privilege one group of stakeholders: all stakeholders are equally important to the success of the corporation.

The shareholder model (see Figure 3.2) focuses on serving the interest of those owning the capital. The interests of the other stakeholders – customers, employees, the public, and so on – are considered to be means for or constraints on maximising the economic value of the firm.

> Corporate managers are dependent on stakeholders because the economic role of the firm is to combine as effectively as possible the unique resources each stakeholder contributes: the risk capital of investors; the talents, training and

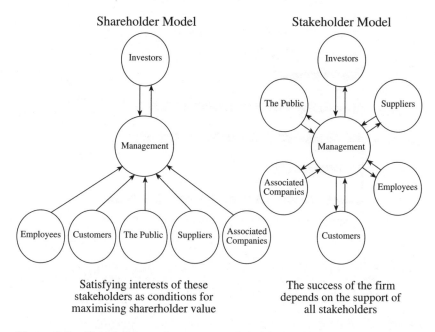

Satisfying interests of these
stakeholders as conditions for
maximising sharerholder value

The success of the firm
depends on the support of
all stakeholders

Figure 3.2   Shareholder value versus stakeholder value

efforts of employees; the continued patronage of customers; the capabilities of business partners; and the economic infrastructure provided by government. The need for capital is essential, of course, but the contributions of other stakeholders are no less essential. Because companies are socioeconomic systems, these functions are all essential as the diverse organs of a body. (Halal, 1996)

Professor Mirow (2002), the former chief strategic planner at Siemens, summarises the point of German entrepreneurs and senior executives this way: 'The overall objective of a company is not shareholder value. Increasing the value of the investment for the shareholder is a condition necessary for the long-term survival of the corporation as are customer satisfaction, employee engagement, and so on. The overall objective of a corporation is sustainability/viability for its long-term development and growth'. Europeans have never fully adopted the simplistic approach of Milton Freeman, who claims that the only social responsibility of business is to make money (Calori and De Woot, 1994).

The categorisation of corporate governance in the shareholder value and the stakeholder model is supported by findings of an empirical study with executives in France, Germany, the United Kingdom, the United States and

Question: under which of the following assumptions is a large company in your country managed? 1. Shareholder interest should be given the first priority. 2. A firm exists for the interest of all stakeholders.

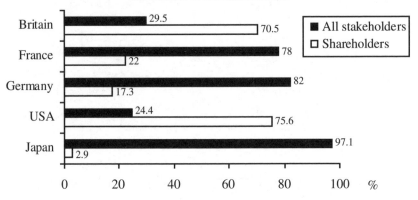

Source: Reprinted from M. Yoshimori (1995), 'Whose company is it? The concept of the corporation in Japan and the West', *Long Range Planning*, **28**(4), 33–44. Copyright (1995) with permission from Elsevier.

Figure 3.3   Shareholder versus stakeholder orientation in different countries

Japan conducted by Yoshimori (Yoshimori, 1995). Figure 3.3 shows that in Britain and in the USA the first priority is given to the shareholders' interests; in Japan corporations exist for the beneft of all stakeholders; France and Germany are somewhere in between.

Implications of the different approaches towards corporate governance in the countries mentioned can be seen in Figure 3.3. Considering the Japanese concept of the corporation, the president of the company is the representative of both the employees and the other stakeholders. His primary role is to defend job security of the employees rather than to maintain dividends. In this system employees and the other stakeholders symbolise the most important power base for the head of the corporation. To the contrary, in the monistic system of the United States or the United Kingdom, with primacy of the shareholders' interests, maintaining dividends is considered more important, as can be seen in Figure 3.4.

Question: suppose a CEO must choose either to maintain dividends or to lay off a number of employees. In your country which of these alternatives would be chosen?

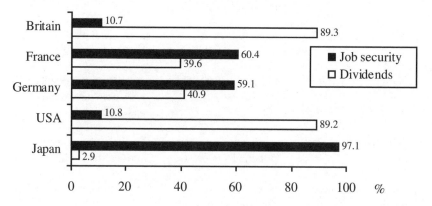

Source: Adapted from M. Yoshimori (1995), 'Whose company is it? The concept of the corporation in Japan and the West', *Long Range Planning*, **28**(4), 33–44. Copyright (1995) with permission from Elsevier.

Figure 3.4   Job security and dividends in the countries studied

Table 3.3 summarizes the key differences between the shareholder value perspective and the stakeholder value perspective.

THE SOCIAL RESPONSIBILITY OF MULTINATIONAL CORPORATIONS (MNCS)

A Real-life Situation

Consider being sent as product manager of an MNC in a developing country. You are responsible for a dietary supplement product for children. The product is very attractive for poor countries, where the agricultural production is not sufficient to feed the population in a balanced way. The product is cheaper than a balanced diet, the monthly consumption of a child, however, absorbs about 25% of the

Table 3.3   Shareholder value versus stakeholder value

	Shareholder value perspective	Stakeholder value perspective
Emphasis on	profitability over responsibility	responsibility over profitability
Organisations seen as	means to maximise profits	socioeconomic system
Organisational purpose	to serve owners	to serve all parties involved
Long-term objectives	maximise shareholder value	sustainability/viability of long-term development and survival
Major difficulty	getting agent to pursue principal's interests	balancing interests of various stakeholders
Corporate governance through	independent outside directors with shares	stakeholder representation
Stakeholder management	means	end and means
Social responsibility	individual, not organisational matter	both individual and organisational
Society best served by	Pursuing self-interest (economic efficiency)	Pursuing joint interests (economic symbiosis)

Source: De Wit and Meyer (1998), p. 811.

average monthly salary of a worker. As in many developing countries, the families have from six to eight children.

The demand is great. You know that the product achieves a gross margin of well over 50%. Your company needs this gross margin in order to develop new products. The competitors are developing products substituting your product. When they enter the market, there will be a dramatic reduction of prices. You ask yourself whether the high price is justified in the developing country. You know that the present profit and the profit expected for the future play a decisive role not only for the survival of your company, but also for sustaining the local organization which employs about 300 local workers.

What strategy would you pursue? You are responsible for the decision; the decision, however, has to be justified to the headquarters of your company (translated from Cullen, 2002).

The social responsibility ranges from one extreme (the only responsibility of a business, according to Milton Friedman, is to make a profit, within the confines of the law, in order to produce goods and services and to serve its shareholders' interests) to the other extreme (companies should play an active role in handling worldwide social and economic problems and they should at least be concerned with host-country welfare (Deresky, 2000).

Carroll's classic model (Carroll, 1979) shows the relationship between (a) the philosophy of responsiveness of the MNC (proactive, accommodating, defensive or reactive) (b) the social responsibility categories (discretionary, ethical, legal and economic) and (c) the social issues involved (consumerism, environment, discrimination, occupational safety, shareholders, and so on). An MNC with a proactive philosophy, for example, will put in the extra effort to fulfil discretionary responsibilities, whereas a company with a defensive philosophy will not be concerned beyond its legal responsibilities. (See Figure 3.5.)

The social responsibility that a company should take in its international operations, however, is much more complex. The subsidiary has to consider additional stakeholders – the local economy, the community, the consumers, employees and so on – and balance their rights against the rights of domestic stakeholders.

THE IMPACT OF INTERNATIONAL INSTITUTIONS ON CORPORATE GOVERNANCE SYSTEMS

The following international institutions have provided rules for guiding the behaviour of multinational companies (Cullen, 2002):

- The UN Universal Declaration of Human Rights,
- The UN Convention on the Right of the Child,

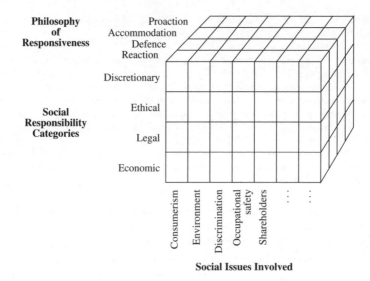

Source: Adapted from Carroll (1979).

Figure 3.5 The social responsibilities of MNCs

- The UN Code of Conduct on Transnational Corporations,
- The UN Global Compact,
- The ICC Guidelines for Multinational Enterprises,
- The ICC Business Charter for Sustainable Development,
- The ILO Tripartite Declarations of Principles Concerning Multinational Enterprises and Social Policy,
- The OECD Guidelines for Multinational Enterprises,
- The OECD Convention to Counteract Corruption.

These rules specify the duties of multinational companies regarding the local economy:

- payment of fair taxes,
- reinvestment of profits in the local economy,
- transfer of technology to the host country,
- environmental protection,
- health and safety standards for employees,
- employment practices,
- training opportunities,
- prohibition of bribes and other improper payments.

The impact of these rules on corporate governance of multinational companies is limited; the reasons are that the rules have only voluntary compliance; the agreements are between governments and not the multinational companies themselves; and not all governments subscribe to the agreements or, if party to the agreements, they may choose to ignore them.

'It as an illusion,' said Peter Brabeck-Lemathè, CEO of Nestlé, 'to think to be able to create a secure institution with rules and thus to protect it against human failures; what is needed, are solid principles and not legally elaborated and detailed rules.' Corporate governance, indeed, is a question of principles, respect for and correct execution of which depend on the personal integrity of the management of a company.

A corporate governance mechanism is a framework of principles and guidelines for entrepreneurial action. Peter Brabeck-Lemathè says, 'complex rules do not prevent abuse, they occupy mainly lawyers and risk to undermine the basic principles for effective decision making'.

Without an international enforcement agency, it is impossible to expect multinational companies to follow rigorous rules of conduct. The problem with the rules of conduct is that, if they are too rigorous, the multinational companies will ignore them; if, on the other hand, they are too general, they are of no use.

Although the rules are not enforceable, they are useful and can serve as a moral guide to the executives of multinational companies (Cullen, 2002; Deresky, 2000). International institutions are challenged to cooperate with governments in order (a) to insert the rules into the corporate governance systems of the multinational company's home country, (b) to make the rules enforceable and (c) to adapt them continually to the changing environment. Many corporations have formulated formal codes of ethics: Fiat, General Electric, Nestlé, Shell and Unilever are examples among global firms. According to one survey, 93 per cent of Fortune 1000 firms, 71 per cent of UK firms and 30 per cent of continental European firms reported having a code of ethics (Parker, 1998).

> Ethical codes do not ensure success, but they may prevent failures. Their existence makes it less likely that leaders or managers will unwittingly guide the firm into an ethical morass, or that individuals will bring their own ethics to bear when acting on behalf of the firm. This is particularly important at a global level because cultural differences in beliefs and values do lead to cross-cultural differences in behaviour. (Parker, 1998)

A global code of business ethics is the Caux Round Table (CRT) Principles for Business launched in 1994 by leaders of global businesses and translated into many languages. The limitation of this code of conduct as well as of other global codes of business ethics lies in that fact that they are developed

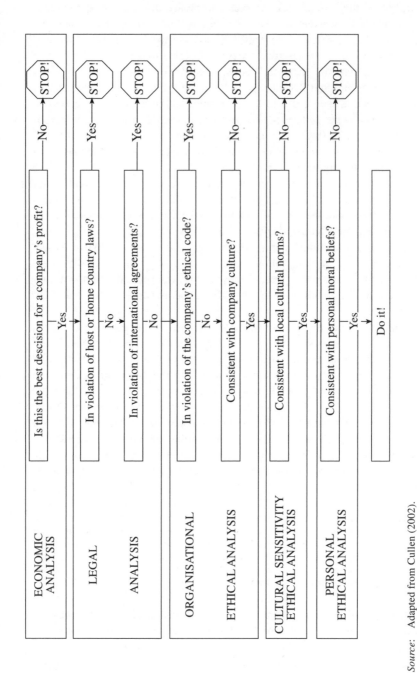

Source: Adapted from Cullen (2002).

Figure 3.6   A model for ethical decision making in multinational companies

in Western countries and do not reflect sufficiently cultural differences. Figure 3.6 presents a summary of the decision-making process in multinational companies.

CONCLUDING REMARKS

The specific function of the firm which can be fulfilled only by the firm itself and which differentiates it from other institutions can be expressed in terms of economic and technological creativity (Bloom *et al.*, 1994). The firm does not only produce goods and services, it is renewing itself continuously, it is creating new and better products and services through institutionalised innovative processes.

In order to finalise this function of the firm, to foster economic and technological progress, the following questions have to be answered regarding technological and economic progress: How, for whom and why? In our research we found that this function can be implemented successfully by (a) developing the leadership capabilities and the sense of social corporate responsibility not only of their executives, but of all the people involved in the corporation; and (b) creating in all people involved a perspective of common good which goes beyond the corporation.

'Corporations are economic entities, to be sure, but they are also social institutions that must justify their existence by their overall contribution to society. Specifically, they must serve a balanced set of stakeholders' (Mintzberg *et al.*, 2002). If we have learned something from the past, it is that leadership processes in MNCs are highly complex. 'Most serious researchers in the area agree that leadership is an interaction between the leader and the leadership situation, but this principle still has to be translated into practice' (Fiedler, 1996).

Leaders, chief executive officers and senior executives need a power base to be legitimate. In the United States the main source of the legitimacy of a top team is the shareholders' assembly. In Europe, the top team has to be accepted not only by the shareholders, but also by the employees and their unions, by the politicians, by the parties, by the central and/or regional government, by public opinion, and so on. Entrepreneurs and/or senior executives have to deal with all these stakeholders.

The power base in Europe is larger, more complex and more political than the power base in the United States. Therefore priorities in satisfying key stakeholders must be established. The more transparent the process is and the better an 'argumentative discourse' can be established between leaders and key stakeholders, the more effectively the company will be able to increase its viability for long-term development and growth. Thus leadership is not limited to creating short-term value for the shareholders, but involves taking into consideration the logic and the feelings of all stakeholders; in this way the long-term economic value of the firm for the shareholders can be maximised.

We wish to conclude with a statement by the German philosopher and scientist Georg Christoph Lichtenberg: 'I cannot say if things get better when they will be different. However, I can say, definitely, that things must be different if they are going to be good.'

REFERENCES

Barkema, H.G., J.A. Baum and E.A. Mannix (2002), 'Management challenges in a new time', *Academy of Management Journal*, **45**, 916–30.

Bartlett, C.A., S. Ghoshal and J. Birkinshaw (2004), *Transnational Management. Text, Cases and Readings*, 4th edn, Boston: McGraw-Hill.

Bloom, H., R. Calori and Ph. de Woot (1994), *Euro Management. A New Style for the Global Market*, London: Kogan Page.

Calori, R. and P. De Woot (eds) (1994), *A European Management Model. Beyond Diversity*, New York: Prentice-Hall.

Carroll, A.B. (1979), 'A three-dimensional conceptual model of corporate performance', *Academy of Management Review*, **4**, 497–505.

Cullen, J.B. (2002), *Multinational Management. A Strategic Approach*, 2nd edn, Cincinnati, Ohio: South-Western College Publishing.

De Wit, B. and R. Meyer (1998), *Strategy, Process, Content, Context*, 2nd edn, London: ITP Press.

Deresky, H. (2000), *International Management. Managing Across Borders and Cultures*, 3rd edn, Upper Saddle River: Prentice-Hall.

Feddersen, D., P. Hommelhoff and U.H. Schneider (eds) (1996), *Corporate Governance*, Cologne: Westdeutsche, Verlag.

Fiedler, F.E. (1996), 'Research on leadership selection and training: one view of the future', *Administrative Science Quarterly*, **41**, 241–50.

Gedajlovic, E.R. and D.M. Shapiro (1998), 'Management and ownership effects: evidence from five countries', *Strategic Management Journal*, **19**, 533–53.

Halal, W.E. (1996), *The New Management. Democracy and Enterprise are Transforming Organizations*, San Francisco: Berret-Koehler Publishers.

Heinrich, R.P. (2002), *Complementarities in Corporate Governance*, Heidelberg: Springer Verlag.

Hinterhuber, A. (2002), 'Value chain orchestration in action and the case of the global agrochemical industry', *Long Range Planning*, **35**(6), 615–35.

Keasey, K. and S. Thompson (1997), *Corporate Governance*, Oxford: Oxford University Press.

Mintzberg, H., R. Simons and K. Basu (2002), 'Beyond selfishness', *MIT Sloan Management Review*, Fall, 67–74.

Mirow, M. (2002), 'Chancen und Risiken globalisierter Unternehmen im Spannungsfeld zwischen Kooperation und Wettbewerb', in M.J. Oesterle (ed.), *Risiken im unternehmerischen Handeln durch Individualisierung und Globalisierung*, Bremen: Aschenbeck, pp. 50–61.

Parker, B. (1998), *Globalization and Business Practice*, London: Sage.

Porter, M. (1990), *The Competitive Advantage of Nations*, New York: The Free Press.

Shleifer, A. and R.W. Vishny (1997), 'A survey of corporate governance', *Journal of Finance*, **LII**(2).

Witt, P. (2000), 'Corporate governance im Wandel', *Zeitschrift für Führung und Organisation*, **69**(3), 159–63.

Yip, G.S. (1995), *Total Global Strategy*, Englewood Cliffs, NJ: Prentice-Hall.

Yoshimori, M. (1995), 'Whose company is it? The concept of the corporation in Japan and the West', *Long Range Planning*, **28**(4), 33–44.

4. The international competition network as an international merger control institution

Oliver Budzinski

INTERNATIONAL MERGERS AND COMPETITION POLICY[1]

The second half of the 1990s was strongly characterised by a massive wave of cross-border mergers which caused an intensive academic and political discussion.[2] Although there have been other important and extensive merger waves before (see Figure 4.1) and Table 4.1,[3] this one was distinctive in a number of ways:

1. With its peak in the year 2000, the 1990s' merger wave exceeded the last merger wave by approximately five times (see Figure 4.2).
2. Different from all the historic merger waves, it consisted of a unique volume of cross-border mergers (see Figure 4.3). This is true not only in regard to the origin of the merging companies, but even more so concerning the regional distribution of the affected markets.
3. Not only did the total value of mergers reach an all-time peak, but the average transaction volume also significantly exceeded previous mergers. For instance, the transaction values of *Vodafone Airtouch/Mannesmann* (190 billion US$ in 2000) and *AOL/Time Warner* (166 billion US$ in 2000) more than doubled the biggest merger[4] so far and exceeded the GDP of middle-sized industrial countries like Portugal (about 120 billion US$).
4. While mergers traditionally are characterised by the acquisition of a smaller company by a bigger one, the 1990s' merger wave consisted of a distinct increase in mergers between equally-sized companies (see Table 4.2).
5. This megamerger wave encompasses virtually every industry and, contrary to the other merger waves, especially service and innovative industries.[5]

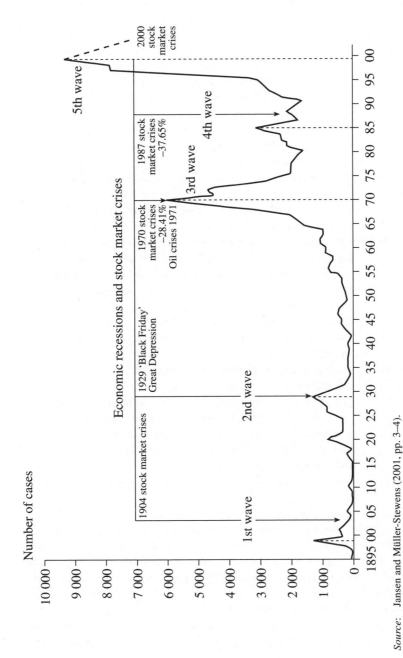

Source: Jansen and Müller-Stewens (2001, pp. 3–4).

Figure 4.1 Historical merger waves

Table 4.1   The five merger waves

Period	Special features
1897–1904 *1st wave*	'Industrialisation' and cartel prohibitions (USA, Canada) induce massive horizontal integration; mergers with monopolies and trusts with the intention of market dominance; high percentage of market-wide mergers including five or more companies
1916–1929 *2nd wave*	Predominantly vertical integration; striving for control over the whole production chain; reaction to new antitrust laws which hamper horizontal mergers (USA)
1965–1969 *3rd wave*	The 'conglomerate era', but also horizontal and vertical integration; diversification and portfolio theory as dominant strategies (predominantly USA); economies of scale and industrial mass production
1984–1990 *4th wave*	Strategic mergers to gain short-run profits; development of mergers and acquisition (M&A) markets and specialised M&A enterprises ('merger mania'); in the beginning many conglomerate mergers (economies of scope, especially Europe), later increasingly horizontal and vertical integration; other driving forces: liberalisation and deregulation of markets, globalisation of business and especially financial markets
1993–2000 *5th wave*	High percentage of cross-border mergers; increasing transaction volumes (megamergers); mergers of equals; predominantly horizontal integration due to core-competence strategy and shareholder value orientation; other driving forces: globalisation of business, European market integration, trade liberalisation, deregulation of network industries, 'new economy'

Following recessive tendencies of the relevant stock markets as well as the cooling of the world economy, cross-border merger activity significantly decreased in 2001 and 2002. However, starting in the second half of 2003, signals of a new acceleration of cross-border merger announcements can be observed.[6] Driving-forces for cross-border mergers include the accelerating process of liberalisation and deregulation through the 1990s. Markets internationalised and sometimes even globalised[7] and, thus, the playing field of the enterprises grew across national borders. This international market enlargement increases the competitive pressure on national enterprises and

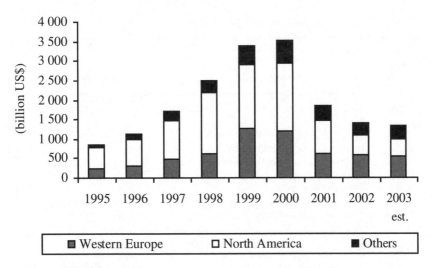

Source: www.m-and-a.de.

Figure 4.2 Total value of announced worldwide transactions

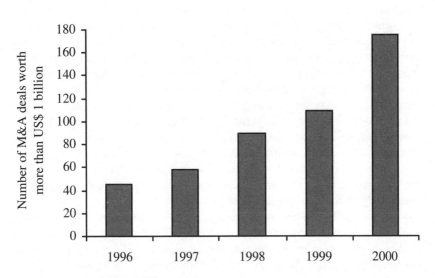

Source: Evenett (2003, p. 31).

Figure 4.3 The growing number of billion dollar-plus M&A deals

Table 4.2   Cross-border megamergers, 1998–2001

Volume in billion US$	Merging Companies (country of origin)	Industry	Year
190	Vodafone Airtouch (GB) & Mannesmann (D)	Telecommunications	2000
166	AOL (USA) & Time Warner (USA)	Internet, media	2000
87	Exxon (USA) & Mobil (USA)	Energy	1998
66	Vodafone Group (GB) & AirTouch (USA)	Telecommunications	1999
66	Glaxo Wellcome (GB) & Smithkline (GB)	Pharmaceutics	2000
55	BP (GB) & Amoco (USA)	Energy	1998
46	France Telecom (F) & Orange (GB)	Telecommunications	2000
45	Deutsche Telekom (D) & Voicestream Wireless (USA)	Telecommunications	2000
41	Daimler Benz (D) & Chrysler (USA)	Automobiles	1998
41	Chevron (USA) & Texaco (USA)	Energy	2000
40	Vivendi (F) & Seagram (CDN)	Water supply, media	2000
13	Repsol (E) / YPF (ARG)	Energy	1999
13	Citigroup (USA) & Benacci (MEX)	Commercial banks	2001
12	BHP (AUS) & Billiton (GB)	Steel, metals	2001

Sources: Evenett (2003, pp. 42–52); Budzinski and Kerber (2003, p. 16); www.m-and-a.de.

challenges market dominant positions (as well as national cartels or cartel surrogates), thereby inducing a process of reorganisation of business structures. Enterprises intending to maintain (or reconquer) their positions as market leaders must expand to compete on the larger international market. In doing so, the acquisition of a foreign enterprise (with its distinctive knowledge of special regional conditions, supply and sales chains and so on) can simplify things in terms of pace and costs in comparison to internal growth. An additional effect stems from the switch of the dominant business strategy from diversification (until the 1980s) to the strengthening of core competences (Prahalad and Hamel, 1990). Instead of conglomerate mergers, the 1990s wave focused on horizontal mergers. This fuelled cross-border mergers because companies with similar core competences in foreign countries represent particularly 'fitting' targets for acquisitions.

From a competition economics perspective, the cross-border megamerger wave has procompetitive and anticompetitive effects, calling for a differentiated assessment. On the one hand, liberalisation and deregulation increase competition by the enlargement of markets, opening up sclerotic national market structures. Although the mergers of the 1990s were gigantic, they did not necessarily cause antitrust concerns since international market enlargement increases both the actual number of competitors and the contestability of the relevant markets. On the other hand, merger dynamics can overcompensate market enlargement and cause market dominance on a global scale. This would be particularly severe if markets were globalised. There could be no further liberalisation, as well as no horizontal competitors from abroad. Therefore, the disciplining threat of easy market entry by companies that produce similar products on foreign markets is not available anymore to break up sclerotic markets.[8] Both the Boeing–Airbus duopoly on the world market for large jet aircrafts, a consequence of the 1997 Boeing–McDonnell Douglas merger (and many other mergers over the past five decades) and the worldwide market dominance of Microsoft on a couple of software markets represent striking examples.

The domination of the core-competence approach raises additional problems since horizontal mergers are much more critical from a competition policy point of view than vertical or even conglomerate mergers. Altogether, and in spite of the procompetitive effects of market globalisation, there is a case for an international competition policy system which is able to control cross-border mergers and prohibits such with anticompetitive effects, or demands modifications, respectively. This is especially true since the current decline of cross-border merger activity is probably a short-run phenomenon. International merger dynamics will speed up again as soon as the world economy and the stock markets enter the next boom period because the process of adjustment of the business structures to international markets is definitely far from being completed.

THE INTERNATIONAL COMPETITION NETWORK AND ITS MERGER CONTROL INSTITUTIONS

The Road towards the ICN

The idea of establishing supranational merger control institutions is not a new one. As far back as 1948, the proposal for an International Trade Organisation (ITO, outlined in the Havana Charta) was designed to introduce supranational governance of both public restraints of trade (realised through the GATT) and private restrictions on competition. However, the proposal failed to be ratified by a considerable number of nations during the 1950s and eventually was abandoned.

In the absence of promising multilateral arrangements and initiatives, the effects doctrine has governed international competition policy over the last five decades. According to the effects doctrine, which successively became (more or less) accepted by all major competition policy jurisdictions, every country and every competition authority claims jurisdiction on a merger if it affects the domestic market of the country or the authority, irrespective of the location of the merger. This kind of extraterritorial enforcement allows competition policy regimes to protect domestic competition against foreign anticompetitive mergers but also against competitive pressure from abroad (strategic competition policy),[9] since the protection of international competition is not usually one of the goals of national competition laws and policies. Moreover independent and non-coordinated extraterritorial merger policy generates jurisdictional conflicts (Klodt, 2001), multijurisdictional review of cross-border mergers, with the consequence of increasing transaction costs (ICN, 2002),[10] and power asymmetries between countries.[11]

To reduce these deficiencies, a number of bilateral arrangements on mutual notification and consultation emerged, especially during the 1980s (Fullerton and Mazard, 2001). However, many of them exclude either merger control altogether or effectively reduce more ambitious arrangements like the introduction of comity principles to the prosecution of hardcore cartels. Moreover non-industrialised countries predominantly were not included in such arrangements (Jenny, 2003).

In the face of the parallel globalisation of competition, cross-border mergers and anticompetitive practices, the European Union, in the mid-1990s, revived the idea of an international competition governance regime which not only addresses anticompetitive state action but also possesses competencies to prevent private restrictions of competition (Brittan and Van Miert, 1995). With the foundation of the World Trade Organization (WTO, 1995) as the successor of GATT (and, implicitly, the successor of the failed ITO), the 'natural' organisational forum for international merger control seemed to be born. In 1996, the Singapore Conference adopted this initiative and created the WTO Working Group on the Interaction of Trade and Competition. The agenda of the working group encompassed the preparation of negotiations on a WTO competition code but, in the following years, it had to face increasing opposition, especially from the USA and a number of developing countries. Nevertheless the 2001 Doha Conference took the next step and, in the Doha Declaration, negotiations were announced, although still without a binding time schedule. However, in the light of the failure of the 2003 Cancún Conference, the prospective progress of the process towards WTO competition and merger control rules seems insecure and doubtful.[12]

Establishment and General Features

On 25 October 2001, a new epoque in international competition policy started with the creation of the International Competition Network (ICN).[13] The proposal was launched by the USA and closely followed the recommendations of the International Competition Policy Advisory Committee (ICPAC,

2000) which was established by the US Department of Justice, Antitrust Division. Considering the background of an elaborated critique of the WTO as the forum for an international competition and, particularly, merger control regime (ibid., pp. 259–77), an alternative forum with governance modes that strongly deviate from the idea of binding supranational rules or binding international agreement was outlined. The ICN represents an informal network of national and multinational competition agencies, not codified in any international treaty and not establishing international law. Instead the participating agencies fuel the network with their own staff and financial resources. A Steering Group consisting of leading antitrust officials and their offices is managing it, since September 2003 chaired by Fernando Sanchez Ugarte, of the Mexican Federal Competition Commission.[14] Up to November 2003, more than 70 national and multinational competition agencies from over 60 countries had joined the ICN.

The purpose of the ICN is to facilitate international cooperation on competition issues, to promote procedural and substantive convergence among competition jurisdictions concerning cross-border cases, and to advance knowledge about best practices on competition matters of common interest. As a matter of principle, all its proposals are non-binding and compliance is completely voluntary. The ICN has established six working groups (WG) in which consensus-based proposals about best practices for competition policy issues will be generated (see Figure 4.4).

ICN Merger Control Institutions

The WG on the Merger Control Process in the Multi-jurisdictional Context is led by the US Department of Justice and aims to promote the adoption of best practices in the design of merger review governance. As a result, the effectiveness of the jurisdictional merger reviews shall be enhanced, jurisdictional conflicts reduced, procedural and substantive convergence facilitated and transaction costs reduced. The relevant practical problems of multijurisdictional merger control are addressed in detail by three subgroups (SG).

1. The SG on Merger Notification and Review Procedures is chaired by the US Federal Trade Commission. It has developed eight general guiding principles for merger review regimes: (i) sovereignty, (ii) transparency, (iii) non-discrimination (on the basis of nationality), (iv) procedural fairness, (v) efficient, timely and effective review, (vi) coordination, (vii) convergence, and (viii) protection of confidential information. They are intended to serve as guidelines for the development of best practices in regard to (i) notification thresholds, (ii) the timing of notification and review periods, (iii) requirements for initial notification, (iv) the appro-

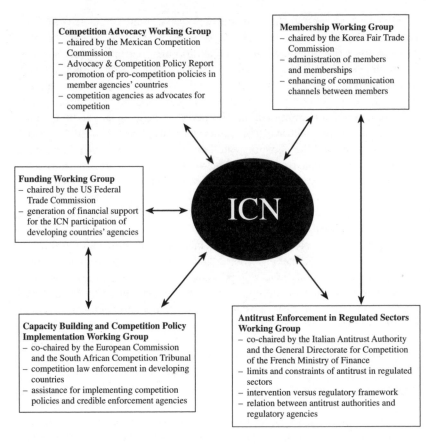

Figure 4.4   Non-merger working group of the ICN

priate nexus between a transaction's effects and the reviewing jurisdiction, and (v) continual reviews of merger control procedures with periodical evaluations of the state of convergence towards ICN best practices (ICN, 2003a).

2. The SG on the Analytical Review Framework is chaired by the UK Office of Fair Trading. One of its main goals is to provide model merger guidelines. In doing this, the SG has presented an interim report (ICN, 2003b) which reviews existing merger guidelines of member countries, compiling information about their common features and main differences in regard to (i) market definition, (ii) unilateral effects, (iii) coordinated effects, (iv) barriers to entry, and (v) the consideration of efficiencies. Furthermore it attempts to lead a best-practice discussion on the substantive standards for prohibiting anticompetitive mergers, namely

'substantial lessening of competition', versus 'creation or strengthening of dominant market positions' versus 'public interest'.

3. The SG on Investigative Techniques is chaired by the Israel Antitrust Authority and aims to develop best practices for investigating mergers, including methods for gathering reliable information and for coordinating inter-agency information sharing, including the protection of confidential business data. It has published a comprehensive compendium on the current practices of the member agencies (ICN, 2003c) which shall serve as the basic source for the upcoming process of evaluation. Additionally the fashionable discussion on the role of theoretical economic analysis in merger control procedures will be addressed.

The spectrum of problems that are picked up by the Merger WG is quite impressive. On the one hand, it covers rather practical and technical problems of merger control procedures such as the convergence and eventual standardisation of notification forms. Although such issues may not breathe the spirit of exploring scientific frontiers, their meaning both for the daily work of the competition agencies and for the costs and troubles of the filing enterprises should not be underestimated. However the working programme also encompasses far more ambitious projects such as model merger guidelines, discussions on substantive standards or dealing with confidential business information. These issues include most important and rather difficult theoretical and ideological questions and exceed administrative problems by touching on important political, social and also scientific decisions and controversies. Although the ICN merger control is still in its early stages and many of the current topics seem more or less inoffensive, the complete agenda indicates that this is – or could be – the process of the genesis of a fully-fledged international institution and, maybe, even organisation.

A CRITICAL ANALYSIS OF THE ICN MERGER GOVERNANCE

Institutions and Governance between Coherence and Diversity

In economics, institutions are sharply distinguished from organisations.[15] 'Institutions are generally known systems of interpersonal rules which order repetitive interactions of individual actors and are followed by a majority of them' (Budzinski, 2003a, p. 218), whereas organisations are 'groups of individuals bound by some common purpose to achieve objectives' (North, 1990, p. 5). Thus organisations perform as agents in the competitive market process and, therefore, belong to the players and not to the rules of the 'game'.

Economic examples are the European Central Bank or the Federal Cartel Office of Germany (Bundeskartellamt) for organisations, and the standing facilities of the ECB or the Clayton Act for institutions.

Taking an institutional–economic perspective, the problem of international merger governance is one of the design of an appropriate international institutional arrangement. The main difficulty arises from a problem that is very common to the general field of international institution building: the necessity to combine decentralised and centralised features and to balance them. As the discussion about cross-border mergers has clearly demonstrated, some kind of an international institutional arrangement is needed to solve the problems and deficiencies resulting from the non-coordinated application of the effects doctrine. In other words, the current cacophony of multiple merger control regimes (all claiming jurisdiction on cross-border mergers) lacks any *coherence* and, instead, produces inconsistent, contradictory and cumulative assessments of trans-border mergers and acquisitions, thereby generating conflicts between antitrust authorities and their governments and producing considerable deficiencies both for the merging parties (increasing transaction costs) and the competition agencies (unnecessary duplication of review procedures). Consequently a *demand for coherence* can be derived as the first requirement for an appropriate institutional arrangement for the governance of cross-border mergers. However, and as in many other fields of international institution building, a centralised solution with a monolithic global merger control institution, which would clearly provide a high degree of coherence, is not available. Currently, and for the foreseeable future, national interests do not allow the transfer of extensive merger control competencies from the national agencies to an international authority – at least, as long as substantive competencies are concerned. The history of failures and resistance from the Havana Charta to Cancún offers illustrative proof. This alone justifies the postulation of the second requirement for an appropriate institutional design of an international merger control: the *demand for diversity*. However, I will present some theoretical arguments in favour of decentralised solutions, preserving diversity on pages 80–82.

Combining coherence and diversity represents a challenging task for the design of international institutions and global governance. Because of the increasing importance and urgency of this task, a couple of governance concepts have been developed recently which are intended to cope with the integration of coherence and diversity.[16] Notably the concepts of network governance, open method of coordination, participatory governance or virtual organisations try to fill this gap of (not only economic) governance theory for international institutions.[17] Regarding international competition policy, such kinds of informal governance modes have been suggested by several authors, notably Tarullo (2000; regulatory-convergence approach),

Maher (2002; regime-building competition policy networks), O'Connor (2002; enforcement networks and case law evolution) and First (2003; mapping of antitrust networks). The ICN represents the first attempt to design a rather informal global institutional arrangement for the governance of cross-border mergers which relies upon related governance approaches.

The Governance Approach of the ICN: Prospects, Limits and Shortcomings

The governance approach concerning international mergers of the ICN can be characterised by two basic elements: *cognitive convergence* and *best practice proposals*. Permanent interaction between the leading competition policy officials of the member agencies and the corresponding systematic exchange of views, data, facts and interpretations in regard to cross-border mergers shall lead to a process of cognitive convergence. Many inconsistencies in the assessments of the (anti-) competitive impact of specific mergers cannot be traced back to substantial divergences in competition laws but, instead, rely on different views and theories as well as differing evaluations of the facts of the case – and sometimes even on a differing availability of facts.[18] Systematic interaction of the responsible officials can make their views more congruent and the emergence of some kind of a common competition culture may be the result.

The development and publication of best practices for all relevant fields of merger control shall cause peer pressure on the member agencies to adopt these practices. Thereby a process of incremental procedural and (subsequent) substantial harmonisation shall be induced, reinforced through the publication of state-of-convergence evaluations (WG Merger Control, SG I). Member agencies who refuse to adopt consensually proposed best practices will probably face a loss of reputation both within the network and among the public.

While the case for the preserving of diversity lies in the rejection of any binding arrangements and in the renunciation of organisation building, cognitive convergence and peer pressured best practice harmonisation shall strengthen the degree of coherence. The ICN only acts through its members and it does not generate outcomes which are not consensually approved by its members. At first sight, it seems rather improbable that such a constellation would yield a coherent merger control regime (as a complex institutional system). However, there is some theoretical support for the ICN approach in Experimental Institutional Economics. The extremely repetitive character of the intra-network interaction leads to the stabilisation of mutual expectations and to the emergence of substantial trust, reputation and cognitive convergence, thereby reinforcing the stability of cooperation.[19] In the face of (i) a high probability of detection and (ii) future dependence on the voluntary cooperation of other network members, defecting behaviour is not the dominating strategy of rational agents. The economics of reciprocity and fairness show that conflict reduction is a likely outcome of network structures like the ICN. However, this does not imply that conflicts can be totally excluded. Cognitive convergence represents a hurdle to defecting behaviour which can be overridden if conflicting interests are severe enough.

Since most of the participating agencies are not independent of their home governments, the latter could introduce non-competition interests into the ICN. Governments and other political authorities can ignore the ICN outcomes or influence their competition agencies to achieve 'consensual' outcomes that favour the jurisdiction's discriminating interests. It is not difficult to imagine that the latter can occur via bargaining processes and will probably discriminate against smaller network members. A decisive factor for the bargaining power of a jurisdiction within the ICN is the importance of the jurisdiction's domestic market for foreign and international enterprises. Almost no country can afford to ignore threats by the USA or the EU to (re-)engage in discriminatory extraterritorial merger law enforcement in order to achieve compliance with their ideas and interests. Things look very different in regard to nations like Uzbekistan or Kenya (both being ICN members). However, since defection is costly, rational governments will defect from the ICN only if serious jurisdictional interests occur. Merger cases, though, have a higher probability of representing such serious national interests as, for example, cartels.[20] Thus there is some danger that the ICN can only solve minor conflicting cases.

Although maybe limited to cases which do not touch national interests too deeply, the process of cognitive convergence is beneficial nonetheless. The facilitation of procedural convergence not only contributes to the reduction of inter-agency conflict (in minor conflicting cases) but also significantly reduces the transaction costs for merging companies (even though not to zero). Even if no substantial convergence occurred and, thus, no transaction-cost minimum was achieved, the efficiency of cross-border merger control would be significantly increased compared to the current kaleidoscope of non-coordinated reviews. Moreover, if it is true that deviating assessments of mergers by different competition authorities are often not rooted in substantive rule conflicts but in deviating interpretations of the facts of the respective cases, conflict reduction will also cover cases of apparently substantive divergence. Altogether, the ICN as an international merger control institution offers potentials for an improvement of the coherence in the international merger control system, although it seems doubtful whether some kind of optimum can be reached.

Cognitive convergence alone cannot help in cases where the national merger control rules are incompatible with each other and the discretionary scope of the competition agencies involved is not sufficient to avoid an inconsistent treatment of a cross-border case. Thus the best practice approach can further improve the demand for coherence. The effectiveness of the governance of cross-border mergers by the respective ICN WGs relies on the enlargement and diffusion of knowledge about best practices and in peer pressure to adopt them. If best practices for notification and review procedures (SG I), for merger guidelines and substantive standards (SG II) and for investigative techniques (SG III) are – reliably and consensually – detected and published, then a competition agency (and the corresponding legislative unit) will probably have difficulties in explaining why it refuses to adopt these benchmarks. However informal, this might represent an effective enforcement mechanism. In modern institutional economics, it is common knowledge that the sanction and enforcement mechanisms of informal institutions can be effective as, for example, the enforcement of informal moral rules, conventions and manners demonstrates. However, the requirement of a consensus for the paraphrasing of a best practice proposal might prove to be the relevant hurdle. Until now, the ICN members have consensually agreed upon standards like transparency or procedural fairness (see pages 71–3) which are either almost not conflicting at all (who wants to argue against transparency?) or rather vague (what exactly is meant by fairness?). It will be very interesting to observe the continuing ICN process when more difficult issues come onto the agenda. The task of generating consensual best practices concerning the appropriate nexus between a transaction's effects and the reviewing jurisdiction or in regard to substantive standards for the prohibition of anticompetitive mergers (see pages 71–2) is much more ambitious than the (beneficial) convergence of merger control procedures in regard to notification forms, time schedules and the rest.

If the peer pressure and best practice proposal prove to be powerful instruments (which is not yet clear), coherence might be improved at the expense of diversity and, thus, the balance of centralism and decentralism violated. At first sight, diversity seems to play an indispensable role in the ICN governance mode. The existing national and supranational merger control agencies retain their full autonomy and no jurisdiction is formally forced to let their merger control institutions and practices converge to the ICN proposals. Furthermore the genesis of best practices inevitably relies on the existence of a multitude of different solutions in the ICN member countries. It is the process of reviewing and evaluating these existing practices that represents the key mechanism to generate best practice proposals. This systematic and evaluative review of the merger control policies of the member agencies (and the publication of the results) creates a high transparency about the diversity of institutional solutions and their relative performance. Thereby the institutional yardstick competition between the ICN members becomes boosted.

Addressing the suitability of institutional competition of merger control regimes, such a yardstick competition proves to be the most important type of institutional competition, since locational competition and free choice of law cannot (or to a much lesser extent) be expected to yield acceptable outcomes.[21] While institutional yardstick competition is often hampered by information deficits and asymmetries, the ICN, in regard to merger control institutions, serves as an information intermediation institution, creating transparency so that the yardsticks (or benchmarks) can be identified and subsequently adopted by the ICN members. This should boost the process of mutual learning.

However, taking a closer look, doubts arise over whether diversity plays any *sustainable* role within the ICN framework. The existing diversity of institutions and practices is 'only' used to identify the best of them and, subsequently, to harmonise on the level of these superior institutional arrangements. Institutional yardstick competition, thus, is reduced to an instrument of harmonisation or, in other words, to an efficient path towards harmonisation. This corresponds to the view that diversity and decentralised institutions are only required because of a lack of willingness by the sovereign nations of the member agencies to engage in harmonised solutions and to transfer own competencies to an international merger control institution. According to this view, there are no original, independent merits of decentralised and diversity-promoting solutions. However, there is an inconsistency in the best practice–harmonisation approach. If diversity is viewed to be indispensable to generate best practices in some kind of bottom-up process, why should this only be true for the present and not for the future? If it is more efficient to generate best practices through a process of evaluating decentralised emerged institutions and practices than through (centralised) academic or political design (top-down process), why should we waive this efficiency in the future? There can be no doubt that the environment in which merger control has to act is an evolutionary one. Markets will keep changing, new technologies will enter the economy, and business will develop new strategies, some of them procompetitive but some of them anticompetitive. It seems rather improbable that the best practices of today will also be the best ones to cope with tomorrow's innovative anticompetitive practices.[22] Altogether the ICN does promote a beneficial yardstick competition for the best merger control institutions and practices, but only to stop (and discard) this competition if the currently 'best' ones are found (or declared). It remains vague which role institutional diversity, regional agencies and decentralised institutions will play in the long run.

APPROACHING AN EXTENDED ECONOMIC FRAMEWORK FOR THE ANALYSIS OF COHERENCE AND DIVERSITY IN MULTI-LEVEL SYSTEMS OF INSTITUTIONS: A RESEARCH PROGRAMME OUTLINE

In the last section of this chapter, I want to outline elements of a theory that can deepen our understanding of the complex relationship between institutional coherence and diversity. The key concept is to model international institutional arrangements as *multi-level systems of institutions*. In a multi-level system of institutions, an international institution does not supersede the prevailing national/supranational ones (multi-level). At the same time, the different levels become interconnected to form a coherent regime (system). Thus the concept of institutional multi-level systems represents an appropriate framework for the analysis of the integration of coherence and diversity. Balancing centralising and decentralising forces within the system is the core problem. If centralism on the top level dominates, the internal dynamics of the system will lead to uniformity and to the erosion of diversity. On the other hand, a dominance of decentralising forces on lower levels will drive the system to decay, thereby eroding coherence.

It is possible to describe the two most important merger control regimes of the world in terms of multi-level systems. In the EU system of competition policies, the top level is represented by the common merger control institutions (Council Regulation (EEC) No. 4064/89 'Merger Regulation') that are enforced by the European Commission, DG Competition.[23] The second level consists of the merger control institutions and agencies of the member countries, which still have considerable scope for the application of the national laws. On this level, there are also numerous industry-specific regulatory agencies with (direct or more often indirect) competencies in merger control, such as in the media, telecommunications, banking, energy services and so on. In some states, there are additionally competition policy competences on regional levels but they usually do not encompass merger control issues but rather focus on unfair practices.[24] Thus there is a two-level system of merger control within the EU. The US merger control system even consists of (at least) three interrelated levels.[25] On the top level there are the federal merger institutions (Sherman Act, Clayton Act, Merger Guidelines and so on) and the federal agencies (the US Department of Justice (Antitrust Division) and the Federal Trade Commission (FTC) as general competition authorities as well as several industry-specific regulatory agencies like the Securities and Exchange Commission (SEC), the Federal Energy Regulatory Commission, or the Federal Communication Commission (FCC),[26] with largely overlapping competencies concerning merger control). The second level is represented by the states (namely the state attorneys general) and their merger control institutions. Additionally a third level is constituted by private litigation, meaning that both consumers and competitors of merging companies also have standing to pursue antitrust cases.

In both systems, the prevailing balance of decentralising and centralising forces is under fire. In the USA, there is a vital discussion on whether the competencies of states should be reduced and, thus, whether a process of centralisation should be initiated.[27] In the EU, the discussion is much more complex. The current modernisation process includes elements of centralisation as well as elements of decentralisation. As a general tendency, the enforcement of EU competition institutions becomes decentralised whereas the rule-making competency centralises. As a consequence, the meaning of the national merger control rules diminishes, whilst the meaning of the national agencies is maintained, but they increasingly have to decide according to EU rules (instead of according to the national rules).[28]

In economic terms, the problem of balancing centralising and decentralising forces to allow for an integrative relation of coherence and diversity is one of the allocation of competencies. In multi-level systems of institutions, competence allocation is twofold: it includes (i) the assignment of competencies and (ii) the design of the interfaces between the different competence carriers. The latter aspect is indispensable as soon as complex institutional arrangements are addressed because, there, a completely unequivocal allocation of competencies without any concurrent powers is practically impossible (Budzinski, 2002). In institutional multi-level systems, such interfaces occur (i) between different levels (*vertical institutional interfaces*) and (ii) between different institutions and agencies on the same level (*horizontal institutional interfaces*). Neither dimension of competence allocation is yet well enough understood in the literature and, in this chapter, I can only outline a systematic treatment of the first dimension (assignment of competencies). Further research is necessary to address adequately the second dimension of competence allocation in institutional multi-level systems.

Whether a specific merger control competency should be assigned to an upstream level (and thus be centralised) or to a downstream level (and thus be decentralised) can be analysed by scrutinising the following economic criteria.[29]

Externalities and Spillovers

Jurisdiction over a merger case should be allocated to the institutional level which has the highest degree of congruency with the territorial or geographical scope of the mergers, for instance in terms of affected markets. Otherwise, negative externalities provide incentives for the engagement in welfare-reducing strategies like selective merger control (non-)enforcement to create 'national global players' or to keep foreign corporate control out. Positive externalities, on the other hand, reduce the incentive to provide the related policies. Examples include merger decisions which take into account anticompetitive effects on the domestic market *and* on foreign markets (thus providing a public good). Since such a world welfare-oriented national merger control agency does get any reward for its engagement if others insist on their 'national markets only' view, rational agencies or jurisdictions will be reluctant to provide positive externalities. Therefore these arguments point towards an upward allocation of competencies if mergers affect several markets in different downward jurisdictions or international markets. However, there is also an argument for downward allocation if mergers predominantly affect regional markets.

Transaction Costs and Economies of Scale

A centralisation of rule-making and enforcement competencies on the top level can reduce transaction costs that otherwise result from the necessity to notify cross-border mergers in a multitude of jurisdictions (enterprise costs)[30] and the parallel review procedures of one and the same case by these jurisdictions (competition authority costs). Furthermore centralisation of law allows for economies of scale (implying an upward allocation of competencies). While the fixed costs of merger control like the drafting and implementation of laws, the decision processes of the legislators, the building up of specific human capital (legal scholars, lawyers, judges and so on) and the staff of competition authorities and courts are rather high, the variable costs of applying the merger control are comparatively small, leading to decreasing marginal costs. Moreover, in a dynamic perspective, the quality of legal institutions improves with the number of cases that have been decided on its basis (cumulating experience and knowledge, higher predictability because of reference cases, stabilisation of expectations and so on).[31]

Preference Orientation

The goals of merger control policy as well as competition cultures differ among jurisdictions (Trebilcock, 1996; Ullrich, 1998). This is rooted in different preferences of the citizens regarding the role of competition, concentration and mergers. Internationally differing preferences demand a decentralisation of competencies (downward allocation of competencies). Obviously any uniform merger control on the global level cannot cope with differing (heterogeneous) preferences about supplier concentration of the lower-level jurisdictions and their citizens. More ambivalent is the problem of rent-seeking activities. On the one hand, decentralised competencies may increase the ability of the citizens to control rent-seeking influences on their agents. On the other hand, it might be more difficult for interest groups to capture a supranational agency with centralised competencies than decentralised agencies that are focused on the location in which the interest group predominantly acts.

Institutional Evolution

A merger control regime has to be flexible and capable of evolving in response to its environment if it is to be capable of coping with future challenges. This can be derived from the fact (discussed above) that merger control deals with creative enterprises which can innovate on anticompetitive arrangements (evolutionary character of competition). However, I would like to stress also another aspect which reveals an additional theoretical argument in favour of decentralised institutions. A uniform merger control on the global level is not preferable since there is considerable pluralism in competition economics in regard to the effects (on welfare, efficiency, innovation and so on) and the desirability of mergers.[32] Following a static perspective, it is not possible to identify one 'right' merger theory and to derive an 'ultimate' merger control programme, at least not from a non-ideological point of view. A dynamic perspective points to the sustainability of theory pluralism since scientific knowledge on merger effects will keep evolving, that is, the evaluation of existing theories will be revised and new theories will be developed.[33] This represents an argument in favour of a downward allocation of competencies since a diversity of (decentralised) merger control institutions offers a higher permeability for institutional innovation and evolution.[34] Mutual learning can be improved if parallel experimentation with different institutional arrangements is introduced and sustainably maintained within the multi-level system.[35]

As the analysis on pages 75–9 has demonstrated, the ICN offers opportunities to economise on transaction costs and use economies of scale, albeit in an incomplete way. The problem of externalities is addressed by the discussion about the appropriate nexus between a transaction's effects and the reviewing jurisdiction (Merger WG, SG I). However, it remains more than speculative whether there will be any solution at all, and, if there was a best practice proposal, whether this would refer to the geographic scope of a merger as the decisive criterion for the allocation of jurisdiction. Apparently the ICN aims at a high preference orientation since sovereignty and voluntariness play major roles. Thus merger control agencies only have to comply with ICN proposals if this corresponds to the preferences of the citizens of their jurisdiction.[36] Concerning rent seeking and lobbyism, no major influences can be identified at the moment, but this is a very preliminary assessment since, to date, most of the ICN proposals are not too explosive. Although the

ICN draws strongly on the existing diversity of merger control institutions, the analysis on pages 75–9 has also demonstrated that there is no clear sustainable role for diversity within the ICN. This shortcoming may not be too important in the early years of the network in which the struggle for an increase in coherence (in comparison to the non-coordinated effects doctrine 'system') is dominant. However, if the ICN governance modes cognitive convergence and best practice harmonisation work, a process of self-reinforcing centralising forces might speed up and might not be easily slowed down again. Therefore it is important to care about the preservation (and appropriate designs) of institutional diversity.

CONCLUSION: ON THE ROAD TOWARDS AN APPROPRIATE INTERNATIONAL MERGER CONTROL INSTITUTION?

Cross-border mergers represent a problem that (i) is empirically relevant (and, despite the setbacks during the last three years, will probably be so in the future) and (ii) cannot be governed adequately without an international institution. However, it is both unlikely and undesirable that such an international merger control institution can be a monolithic construct, something like a gigantic world competition agency, a worldwide monster bureaucracy for merging companies. Thus, and as in so many other areas, international governance has to rely on complex institutional arrangements which provide a coherent framework without eroding the meaning and independence of national institutions.

In the field of merger control, the International Competition Network represents an attempt to introduce a concept of international governance and an institutional arrangement that provides coherence by preserving diversity. Although improvements in regard to both demands have to be conceded, serious shortcomings allow for doubts concerning the appropriateness of the ICN. The induced process of cognitive convergence might reduce a significant number of inconsistencies and conflicts concerning national merger control decisions on international mergers. However, the rare cases which really cause trouble and lead to serious conflicts are characterised by severe national interests (many of them discriminatory in nature). Precisely these cases are the ones with which the ICN will probably have difficulties dealing because cognitive convergence of the competition agency officials does not prevent national governments exerting their discriminatory/protectionist interests if public choice effects (rent seeking, maximisation of votes) are strong enough. Only independent competition agencies, which are very rare internationally, would make a difference.

From today's perspective, it is difficult to estimate the centralising force of the ICN best practice harmonisation. If the members fail to agree upon consensual best practices in regard to hardcore problems of cross-border merger governance, such as the appropriate nexus of jurisdiction and economic effect of a merger or substantive standards for the prohibition of mergers, no significant centralisation will occur. It has to be emphasised that, even then, the ICN can have beneficial overall effects if the minor conflicting procedural issues become more congruent. However, a failure to achieve consensus on hardcore issues might also erode the improvements in other areas and drive the network to decay.

If the peer pressure to adopt best practice proposals is high enough to initiate substantive harmonisation, the long-term preservation of institutional diversity seems doubtful. Apparent paper tigers can develop a strong momentum and powerful self-reinforcing dynamics over the course of time, as the example of the European competition policy demonstrates. Therefore it is a shortcoming of the ICN not to define a sustainable role for institutional diversity, although, in the short run, the more serious problem seems to be the improvement of coherence.

However, a clear and convincing evaluation of the appropriateness of the ICN as an international merger control institution is complicated by shortcomings of the scientific knowledge about complex institutional arrangements and corresponding governance concepts in general, and about ways to combine coherence with diversity in particular. With this chapter, I suggest the concept of multi-level systems of institutions as a starting point for the development of a general theory of (governance in) complex international institutions. This framework is particularly adequate both for descriptive modelling of existing multi-level systems of merger control institutions (USA, EU, ICN) and for an economic analysis of the allocation of competencies within such systems. However, this contribution only outlines the avenue of further research and cannot yet present an elaborated theoretical framework.

NOTES

1. This contribution is part of the refereed research project 'International Competition Policy – A Decentralised System of International Merger Control' funded by the Volkswagen Foundation, priority area 'Global Structures and Governance'. For helpful comments on earlier drafts of the paper I would like to thank Harry First, Richard Hule, Wolfgang Kerber and Karl Socher, as well as all participants in the 2002 CSI conference.
2. See Bundeskartellamt (2000), Andrade *et al.* (2001), Pryor (2001), Karpoff and Wessels (2002), Kleinert and Klodt (2002), Budzinski and Kerber (2003) and Evenett (2003).
3. See also Carroll (2002) and Kleinert and Klodt (2002).
4. Exxon and Mobil (86.4 billion US$ in 1998). At the beginning of the fifth merger wave,

the Time/Warner merger with a transaction volume of 14 billion US$ was the all-time leader.

5. See Andrade *et al.* (2001) and Evenett (2003).

6. Prominent examples include the acquisition of AT&T wireless by Cingular as well as the bids of Safoni to take over Aventis and Comcast to merge with Disney – all taking place in the first two months of 2004.

7. In fact, most of the so-called globalisation is internationalisation between industrialised or nearly-industrialised countries.

8. Helfat and Lieberman (2002) argue against the background of empirical evidence that companies which produce similar products on different geographical markets and/or use similar resources and modes of production compared to the ones within the respective industry have a significantly higher likelihood to enter the respective market than other companies.

9. Examples include the creation of 'national champions', 'domestic global players' or the promotion of a 'defence concentration' to keep foreign companies out of the market. The instrument is a permissive and discriminating merger control policy which selectively enforces or does not enforce the domestic competition law. See, for more details, Budzinski (2002) and Kerber and Budzinski (2004).

10. Merging companies often have to comply with more than a dozen different merger control procedures and requirements. Thereby significant costs and burdens for both merging enterprises and the involved jurisdictions are generated.

11. The USA and the EU are probably able to protect domestic competition against multinational companies because free access to these markets is indispensable for them. However, smaller countries and especially developing countries often do not dispose of sufficient power to enforce their antitrust policy against multinational enterprises. See Jacquemin (1995) and Fox (2000).

12. See, on the pre-Cancún perspective of WTO competition rules, the very elaborate and detailed analysis by Clarke and Evenett (2003).

13. For descriptions 'from within', see Devellennes and Kiriazis (2002), Todino (2003) and von Finckenstein (2003).

14. He succeeds Canadian Konrad von Finckenstein. The Canadian Bureau of Competition remains responsible for secretarial duties of the Steering Group.

15. For comprehensive surveys on the New Institutional Economics, see, for example, Langlois (1986), Williamson (2000) and Kasper and Streit (1999).

16. Or, as Forrester (2003) terms it, the cohabitation of coherence and diversity.

17. See generally Marin and Mayntz (1991), Ladeur (1997), Young (1999), Régent (2002), and the chapters in Héritier (2002) as well as, for corporate governance, Davidow and Malone (1992). Fields of international institution building and evolution which discuss issues of global governance along these lines include labour standards, social security, environmental protection, intellectual property and so on.

18. A considerable number of experts (see, among others, Böge and Müller, 2002) argue that there are only minor substantial differences between the European standard to prohibit mergers (market dominance) and its US pendant (substantial lessening of competition – SLC). Prominent conflicting cases would probably not have been evaluated differently if the two authorities had exchanged their standards. The European Commission's prohibition of the GE/Honeywell merger (2001) relied on a very specific evaluation of vertical integration and product bundling which is not codified in the competition rules and, thus, would most probably not have changed if the SLC test had been applied. And, vice versa, the US antitrust authorities, using different economic theories, would surely not have prohibited the merger on these grounds even if they had applied the market dominance test. Instead of incompatibilities in substantial competition rules, the conflict was caused by divergences in the evaluation of the facts.

19. See Güth and Kliemt (1994), Gächter *et al.* (1996), Güth *et al.* (1997) and Fehr and Gächter (2000).

20. If one considers the Boeing/MDD case, it seems doubtful that the ICN would have been able to prevent the massive jurisdictional conflict, given the severe industrial interests

both of the US government (reorganisation of the US armaments industry) and the EU member states (competitiveness of the highly subsidised Airbus company). See, for example, Fox (1998).

21. For more details, see Kerber and Budzinski (2004).
22. Moreover it is doubtful whether there is *one* best practice at all if countries are heterogeneous, as with industrialised versus developing countries.
23. See, for example, Bellamy and Child (2001), Van den Bergh and Camesasca (2001, pp. 136–65) and, with special focus on the EU merger control system, Cook and Kerse (2000). Currently there is no regulatory agency with merger control competencies on the EU level. However, this might change in the future. See generally Hewitt (1999).
24. However, in Germany, State Cartel Offices ('Landeskartellämter') have some competencies in the area of merger control.
25. See the analyses by Kovacic (1992, 1996) and Ginsburg and Angstreich (2000), as well as the overviews by Hovenkamp (1999, pp. 721–45) and Sullivan and Grimes (2000, pp. 536–56, 887–967).
26. For example, the FCC generally has to prohibit mergers in telecommunications if the buying company comes from abroad and is state-owned (more than 25 per cent of the shares). It also has the discretionary power to allow exemptions. For overviews on the interrelation of antitrust and regulatory institutions, agencies and policies in the USA, see Kaserman and Mayo (1995, pp. 441–8), Hovenkamp (1999, pp. 698–720) and Sullivan and Grimes (2000, pp. 697–798).
27. See the two extreme positions by Posner (2004), demanding a cutback in antitrust federalism, and Grimes (2003), highlighting the beneficial role of state antitrust policy in terms of preventing an ideological monoculture.
28. See, among others, Schaub (2002), Gerber (2003) and Berg and Ostendorf (2003).
29. See, on (parts of) these arguments, Van den Bergh (1996, 2000), Van den Bergh and Camesasca (2001, pp. 127–36) and Kerber (2003). A related analysis addressing contract laws is provided by Grundmann and Kerber (2002).
30. This includes information costs due to the necessity to accumulate knowledge about different rules and proceedings in different legal systems (or to engage specialists). Additionally, the pure fact that a cross-border merger has to pass a multitude of merger control procedures increases legal uncertainty, which represents another category of transaction costs.
31. However, one must take into account that path dependencies can lead to lock-ins and, thus, persistent inefficient paths might result. See Heine and Kerber (2002).
32. Merger control paradigms which are largely incompatible with each other can be derived from the Harvard School (theory of workable competition), the Chicago School, the Freiburg School (Ordoliberalism), the Austrian School and so on.
33. See, on the whole line of thought, in more detail, Budzinski (2003b).
34. To a certain degree, a sufficient permeability for external injections of ideas and theories can be provided by horizontal enforcement diversity. See the analysis of different antitrust systems in this regard elaborated by Budzinski (2003b).
35. On the advantages of parallel experimentation in comparison to sequential experimentation see Vanberg and Kerber (1994), Budzinski (2002), Kerber (2003) and Kerber and Budzinski (2004). Parallel experimentation can also take place between vertically related levels. Therefore this argument does promote competencies on downward levels but it does not exclude competencies on upward levels as long as they are non-exclusive.
36. Of course, principal–agent problems can distort or disturb the transmission mechanism from citizen preferences to agency action.

REFERENCES

Andrade, Gregor, Mark Mitchell and Erik Stafford (2001), 'New evidence and perspectives on mergers', *Journal of Economic Perspectives*, **15**(2), 103–20.

Bellamy, Christopher and Graham Child (2001), *European Community Law of Competition*, 5th edn, London: Sweet & Maxwell.

Berg, Werner and Patrick Ostendorf (2003), 'The reform of EC merger control: substance and impact of the proposed new procedural rules', *European Competition Law Review*, **24**(11), 594–603.

Böge, Ulf and Edith Müller (2002), 'From the market dominance test to the SLC test: are there any reasons for a change?', *European Competition Law Review*, **23**(10), 495–8.

Brittan, Leon and Karel van Miert (1996), 'Towards an international framework of competition rules', *International Business Lawyer*, **24**(10), 454–7.

Budzinski, Oliver (2002), 'Institutional aspects of complex international competition policy arrangements', in Clemens Esser and Michael H. Stierle (eds), *Current Issues in Competition Theory and Policy*, Berlin: VWF, pp. 109–32.

Budzinski, Oliver (2003a), 'Cognitive rules, institutions, and competition', *Constitutional Political Economy*, **14**(3), 213–33.

Budzinski, Oliver (2003b), 'Pluralism of competition policy paradigms and the call for regulatory diversity', Philipps-University of Marburg Volkswirtschaftliche Beiträge no. 14/2003, http://ssrn.com/abstract=452900.

Budzinski, Oliver and Wolfgang Kerber (2003), *Megafusionen, Wettbewerb und Globalisierung*, Stuttgart: Lucius & Lucius.

Bundeskartellamt (ed.) (2000), 'Mega-mergers – a new challenge for antitrust laws', *Proceedings the 9th International Conference on Competition*, ed. Knud Hansen, Bonn.

Carroll, Carolyn A. (2002), 'A century of mergers and acquisitions', in Benton E. Gup (ed.), *Megamergers in a Global Economy – Causes and Consequences*, Westport, Ct, Quorum Books, pp. 19–43.

Clarke, Julian L. and Simon J. Evenett (2003), 'A multilateral framework for competition policy?', in State Secretariat of Economic Affairs and Simon J. Evenett (eds), *The Singapore Issues and the World Trading System: The Road to Cancún and Beyond*, Berne, pp. 77–168.

Cook, C. John and Christopher S. Kerse (2000), E.C. Merger Control, 3rd edn, London: Sweet & Maxwell.

Davidow, William H. and Michael S. Malone (1992), *The Virtual Corporation*, New York: Harper Collins.

Devellennes, Yves and Georgios Kiriazis (2002), 'The creation of an international competition network', *Competition Policy Newsletter*, Number 1, February, pp. 25–6.

European Commission (2001), 'Case NoComp/M.220 – General Electric/Honeywell', Regulation (EEC) No4064/89 Merger Procedure, Brussels.

Evenett, Simon J. (2003), 'The cross border mergers and acquisitions wave of the late 1990s', NBER working paper no. w9655.

Fehr, Ernst and Simon Gächter (2000), 'Fairness and retaliation – the economics of reciprocity', *Journal of Economic Perspectives*, **14**(3), 159–81.

First, Harry (2003), 'Evolving toward what? The development of international antitrust', in Josef Drexl (ed.), *The Future of Transnational Antitrust – From*

Comparative to Common Competition Law, Berne: Staempfli Publishers, pp. 23–51.

Forrester, Ian (2003), 'Diversity and consistency: can they cohabit?', in Claus-Dieter Ehlermann and Isabela Atanasiu (eds), *Constructing the EU Network of Competition Authorities*, Oxford: Hart Publishing.

Fox, Eleanor M. (1998), 'Antitrust regulation across national borders – the United States of Boeing versus the European Union of Airbus', *The Brookings Review*, **16** (1), 30–32.

Fox, Eleanor M. (2000), 'Antitrust and regulatory federalism: races up, down, and sideways', *New York University Law Review*, **75**(6), 1781–1807.

Fullerton, Larry and Camelia C. Mazard (2001), 'International antitrust cooperation agreements', *World Competition*, **24**(3), 405–23.

Gächter, Simon, Ernst Fehr and Christiane Kment (1996), 'Does social exchange increase voluntary cooperation?', *Kyklos*, **49**(4), 541–54.

Gerber, David J. (2003), 'The evolution of a European competition law network', in Claus-Dieter Ehlermann and Isabela Atanasiu (eds), *Constructing the EU Network of Competition Authorities*, Oxford: Hart Publishing.

Ginsburg, Douglas H. and Scott H. Angstreich (2000), 'Multinational merger review: lessons from our federalism', *Antitrust Law Journal*, 68 (1), 219–37.

Grimes, Warren S. (2003), 'The Microsoft litigation and federalism in US antitrust enforcement: implications for international competition law', in Josef Drexl (ed.), *The Future of Transnational Antitrust – From Comparative to Common Competition Law*, Bern: Staempfli Publishers, pp. 237–58.

Grundmann, Stefan and Wolfgang Kerber (2002), 'European system of contract laws – a map for combining the advantages of centralised and decentralised rule-making', in S. Grundmann and J. Stuyck (eds), *An Academic Greenpaper on European Contract Law*, Dordrecht: Kluwer Law International, pp. 295–342.

Güth, Werner and Hartmut Kliemt (1994), 'Competition or cooperation: on the evolutionary economics of trust, exploitation and moral attitudes', *Metroeconomica*, **45**(2), 155–87.

Güth, Werner, Peter Ockenfels and Markus Wendel (1997), 'Cooperation based on trust: an experimental investigation', *Journal of Economic Psychology*, **18**(1), 15–43.

Heine, Klaus and Wolfgang Kerber (2002), 'European corporate laws, regulatory competition and path dependence', *European Journal of Law and Economics*, **13**(1), 47–71.

Helfat, Constance E. and Marvin B. Lieberman (2002), 'The birth of capabilities: market entry and the importance of pre-history', *Industrial and Corporate Change*, **11**(4), 725–60.

Héritier, Adrienne (ed.) (2002), *Common Goods: Reinventing European and International Governance*, London: Rowman & Littlefield.

Hewitt, Gary (1999), 'The relationship between competition and regulatory authorities', *OECD Journal of Competition Law and Policy*, **1**(3), 177–219.

Hovenkamp, Herbert (1999), *Federal Antitrust Policy – The Law of Competition and its Practice*, 2nd edn, St. Paul, MN: West Group.

ICN (2002), 'Report on the costs and burdens of multijurisdictional merger review, Naples (http://www.internationalcompetitionnetwork.org/costburd.doc).

ICN (2003a), 'Recommended practices for merger notification procedures', Merida (http://www.internationalcompetitionnetwork.org/2003_practices.pdf).

ICN (2003b), 'Project on merger guidelines', Merida (http://www.international competitionnetwork.org/analysisofmerger.html).

ICN (2003c), 'Compendium of investigative tools', Merida (http://www.international competitionnetwork.org/ReportIT.pdf).

ICPAC (2000), 'International Competition Policy Advisory Committee: Final Report', Department of Justice, Antitrust Division, Washington, DC.

Jacquemin, Alexis (1995), 'Towards an internationalisation of competition policy', *The World Economy*, **18**(6), S.781–9.

Jansen, Stephan A. and Günter Müller-Stewens (2001), ‚Pre- und Post Merger-Integration bei grenzüberschreitenden Zusammenschlüssen: Trends, Tools, Thesen und empirische Tests von Old und New Economy Deals', in Stephan A. Jansen, Gerhard Picot and Dirk Schiereck (eds), *Internationales Fusionsmanagement – Erfolgsfaktoren grenzüberschreitender Unternehmenskäufe*, Stuttgart: Schäffer-Poeschel, pp. 3–33.

Jenny, Frederic (2003), 'International cooperation on competition: myth, reality and perspective', *The Antitrust Bulletin*, **48**(4), 973–1003.

Karpoff, Jonathan M. and David Wessels (2002), 'Large mergers during the 1990s', in Benton E. Gup (ed.), *Megamergers in a Global Economy – Causes and Consequences*, Westport, CT, Quorum Books, pp. 45–63.

Kaserman, David L. and John W. Mayo (1995), *Government and Business – The Economics of Antitrust and Regulation*, Fort Worth, TX: The Dryden Press.

Kasper, Wolfgang and Manfred E. Streit (1999), *Institutional Economics – Social Order and Public Policy*, reprint, Cheltenham, UK and Northampton, MA, USA: Edward Elgar.

Kerber, Wolfgang (2003), 'International multi-level system of competition laws: federalism in antitrust', in Josef Drexl (ed.), *The Future of Transnational Antitrust – From Comparative to Common Competition Law*, Berne: Staempfli Publishers, pp. 269–300.

Kerber, Wolfgang and Oliver Budzinski (2004), 'Competition of competition laws: mission impossible?', in Richard A. Epstein and Michael S. Greve (eds), *Competition Laws in Conflict – Antitrust Jurisdiction in the Global Economy*, Washington, DC: AEI Press, pp. 31–65.

Kleinert, Jörn and Henning Klodt (2002), 'Causes and consequences of merger waves', Kiel working paper no. 1092, Kiel Institute of World Economics.

Klodt, Henning (2001), 'Conflict and conflict resolution in international antitrust: do we need international competition rules?, *The World Economy*, **24**(7), 877–88.

Kovacic, William E. (1992), 'The influence of economics on antitrust law', *Economic Inquiry*, **30**(2), 294–306.

Kovacic, William E. (1996), 'Downsizing antitrust: is it time to end dual federal enforcement?', *The Antitrust Bulletin*, **41**(3), 505–40.

Ladeur, Karl-Heinz (1997), 'Towards a legal theory of supranationality – the viability of the network concept', *European Law Journal*, **3**(1), 33–54.

Langlois, Richard N. (1986), 'The New Institutional Economics', in Richard N. Langlois (ed.), *Economics as a Process*, Cambridge: Cambridge University Press, pp. 1–25.

Maher, Imelda (2002), 'Competition law in the international domain: networks as a new form of governance', *Journal of Law and Society*, **29**(1), 111–36.

Marin, Bernd and Renate Mayntz (eds) (1991), *Policy Networks – Empirical Evidence and Theoretical Considerations*, Frankfurt a. M: Campus.

North, Douglass C. (1990), *Institutions, Institutional Change and Economic Performance*, Cambridge: Cambridge University Press.

O'Connor, Kevin J. (2002), 'Federalist lessons for international antitrust convergence', *Antitrust Law Journal*, **70**(2), 413–41.

Posner, Richard (2004), 'Federalism and the enforcement of antitrust laws by state attorneys general', in Richard A. Epstein and Michael S. Greve (eds), *Competition Laws in Conflict – Antitrust Jurisdiction in the Global Economy*, Washington, DC: AEI Press, pp. 252–66.

Prahalad, Carl K. and Gary Hamel (1990), 'The core competence of the corporation', *Harvard Business Review*, **68**(3), 79–91.

Pryor, Frederic L. (2001), 'Dimensions of the worldwide merger boom', *Journal of Economic Issues*, **35**(4), 825–40.

Régent, Sabrina (2002), 'The open method of co-ordination: a supranational form of governance?', DP/137/2002, International Institute for Labour Studies, Geneva.

Schaub, Alexander (2002), 'Continued focus on reform: recent developments in EC commission policy', in Barry E. Hawk (ed.), *International Antitrust and Policy: 28th Annual Proceedings of the Fordham Corporate Law Institute*, New York: Juris Publishing, pp. 31–51.

Sullivan, Lawrence A. and Warren S. Grimes (2000), *The Law of Antitrust: An Integrated Handbook*, St. Paul, MN: West Group.

Tarullo, Daniel K. (2000), 'Norms and institutions in global competition policy', *The American Journal of International Law*, **94**(3), 478–504.

Todino, Mario (2003), 'International competition network – the state of play after Naples', *World Competition*, **26**(2), 283–302.

Trebilcock, Michael J. (1996), 'Competition policy and trade policy – mediating the interface', *Journal of World Trade*, **30**(4), 71–106.

Ullrich, Hanns (1998), 'International harmonisation of competition law: making diversity a workable concept', in Hanns Ullrich (ed.), *Comparative Competition Law – Approaching an International System of Antitrust Law*, Baden-Baden: Nomos, pp. 43–74.

Van den Bergh, Roger (1996), 'Economic criteria for applying the subsidiarity principle in the European Community: the case of competition policy', *International Review of Law and Economics*, **16**(3), 363–83.

Van den Bergh, Roger (2000), 'Towards an institutional framework for regulatory competition in Europe', *Kyklos*, **53**(4), 435–66.

Van den Bergh, Roger and Peter D. Camesasca (2001), *European Competition Law and Economics – A Comparative Perspective*, Antwerp: Intersentia.

Vanberg, Viktor and Wolfgang Kerber (1994), 'Institutional competition among jurisdictions – an evolutionary approach', *Constitutional Political Economy*, **5**(2), 193–219.

von Finckenstein, K. (2003), 'Recent developments in the international competition network', address to the 2003 Forum on 'Hands on in Antitrust Heaven: Current Global Issues and Dilemmas', New York (http://www.internationalcompetition network.org/speech_aba.html).

Williamson, Oliver E. (2000), 'The new institutional economics – taking stock, looking ahead', *Journal of Economic Literature*, **38**(3), 595–613.

Young, Oran R. (1999), *Governance in World Affairs*, Ithaca, NY: Cornell University Press.

5. Do multinational enterprises pay less tax? Empirical evidence for Italy

Francesca Gastaldi and Maria Grazia Pazienza

INTRODUCTION

In recent years, multinational enterprises (henceforth ME) have increased their role in more integrated economic systems. As a consequence, international taxation issues have attracted the attention of both economists and policy makers. This focus initially originated in the United States, Canada and the United Kingdom, where both the external attitude of firms and the amount of direct investment flows have been substantial. Recently, following the process of creation of the European Union (EU), these issues have become more important also in Europe and in Italy. In the EU, direct investment (DI) outflows tripled, from 1.5 per cent of GDP in 1993 to 4.6 per cent of GDP in 1998. Inflows more than doubled, from 1.2 per cent of GDP to 2.8 per cent of GDP. In the same period, in the United States, outflows increased from 1 to 1.5 per cent of GDP, while inflows increased from 0.6 to 2.1 per cent of GDP.

This sharp change has raised the question whether the corporate taxation originally introduced in a more regulated financial environment with limited international capital mobility may still be appropriate. Various factors may affect the answer: (a) how taxes affect savings and capital formation in different countries; (b) how they affect the choice between debt and equity; (c) how more integrated systems have increased the opportunity for tax avoidance and/or tax evasion; and (d) the role of the tax systems in leading international competitivity. Theoretical models have been developed on these different topics, yet the answer needs some empirical evidence. International institutions are added to this picture, institutions which, without actually trying to regulate the situation, attempt to establish a basis upon which countries may carry out collaborative efforts amongst themselves.

Empirical studies on corporate taxation have mainly dealt with the effects of tax policy in different countries and with the way tax incentives may affect the international allocation of capital. Results are often uncertain, not least because of lack of data and unclear theoretically grounded tax indicators.

Some recent literature following the methodology used by King and Fullerton (1984), has calculated 'effective tax rates' to analyse the effects of tax incentives on international investments. Other methods, mainly based on tax law prescriptions, describe tax avoidance opportunities left to ME.

According to the 'eclectic' approach *à la* Dunning (1971), the relation between ME economic decisions and tax variables can be represented by a three-stage tree.[1] In the first stage, external-oriented firms decide whether to export or implement a new plant abroad. This kind of choice can be performed as a cost–benefit analysis 'OLI' (ownership, localisation, internationalisation), where the tax variable can be easily included. The abundance of empirical studies on this topic have led to ambiguous results mainly due to the weak role of tax variables in explaining the decision of how to cope with firm internationalisation.

In a second stage, when the decision to implement abroad has been taken, the firm decides where to locate. Also in these cases, many authors have argued that productive process characteristics are more important in explaining location: that is, the probability of either horizontal (market shares) or vertical expansion (raw material provisions) is more important than corporate tax variables. If anything, it is the whole set of institutional variables (tax systems, infrastructure endowment, tax compliance, specific country risk and so on) that might affect location.[2]

In a third stage, when ME enterprises are already located, tax variables may possibly affect ME economic decisions. There is some evidence that this influence is not negligible, especially on investment decisions and the financial structure of the firm, including the dividend policy.

This chapter deals with the third stage, looking for tax minimisation by ME. This issue is important from the point of view of a 'within-border' unfair competition among domestic and ME firms located in the same country. ME can make use of different types of tax planning strategies than those available to domestic firms because of tax differentials between countries. Focusing on textile and clothing companies in Italy, the aim of this chapter is to determine whether there are significant differences in the tax burden of multinational companies (corporations located in Italy but controlled by foreign corporations and Italian corporations controlling foreign corporations) and domestic companies. Some preliminary evidence of profit shifting behaviour is discussed, suggesting a more systematic and thorough approach.

The chapter is organised as follows. The first section describes, in general terms, the problem of unfair tax competition between countries used to attract multinational company tax bases. The second section stresses the role of international institutions. The third section overviews some aspects of ME taxation that are more likely to affect the profit shifting process. Then the fourth section discusses the most relevant features of empirical literature that have sought out evidence of profit shifting. The fifth section provides some evidence that ME actually pay less taxes than domestic firms located in the same country, using information derived from accounting and tax data at firm level and following a micro backward-looking methodology to derive implicit tax rates.

MULTINATIONAL ENTERPRISES AND THE PROBLEM OF HARMFUL TAX COMPETITION

The globalisation process of the economy has caused more linkages between different tax systems. The difference in tax structures make for a different tax burden, depending upon the country in which the tax base is located. Countries having a more advantageous tax regime may attract investors to locate their business activity. In this case, however, their choice is still conditioned by the specifics of the input involved as well as by the fact that there is no perfect way to substitute investments in different countries, owing to the different level of public services offered (a balance between taxation and public expenditure).

This problem takes on even more relevance in regard to ME who, regardless of the location of their productive activity, can more easily place the various balance sheet items that make up their tax base in more fiscally convenient countries. By doing so, they are able to avail themselves of the differences existing (although dealing in a single market) in tax rates and criteria for establishing tax bases and tax incentives. In other words, globalisation is having, above all in reference to ME, a 'positive' effect, guaranteeing ME the chance to lessen the global tax burden by locating business in countries having a higher level of services and directing positive components of the tax base to countries with lower taxation.

As far as the reaction of individual countries is concerned, the more recent European tax reforms, aimed at the lowering of tax rates and broadening of tax bases, were actually influenced by globalisation itself and the subsequent need to lessen the impact of distortions caused by fiscal variables. The process of international integration urged individual countries to 'reconsider' both their national tax systems and their level of public expenditure. This was done for the purposes of identifying the best fiscal 'setting' for investments. At the same time, both nationally and internationally, a heated theoretical debate was ignited regarding the alternatives of tax harmonization (or, more realistically speaking, coordination) of tax bases and rates, and tax competition. For these two hypotheses, characteristics of efficiency, equity and transparency of corporate tax systems are weighed.[3]

Some authors (see Musgrave, 1972) argue that tax competition generates negative effects on wealth as well as causing some distortion in the choices of the public administration, thus resulting in excessive costs for efficiency and equity. Tax competition produces beggar-my-neighbour politics, which results in a level of tax rates on income from capital that are lower than what would be advantageous, with this leading to significant consequences.[4] In particular, the capacity for public funding is reduced, and this may lead to a 'downsizing' or worsening of collective services. Also the displacing of the tax burden to the least mobile tax bases lowers the fairness of overall levying of taxes, thus creating ties to the sustainability (both political and financial) of redistributive policy. And, lastly, adverse effects on employment are cited by critics of tax competition, deriving from the long period of tightening of taxation on labour. On the other hand, tax competition is viewed positively within economic theory on tax federalism. From this perspective, we postulate an analogy between the effects of efficiency of the mechanism of competition within a 'product' market and within an 'institutions' market: 'competition between governments should produce, within the public sector, the same type of benefits that are generally associated with competition between private companies' (McLure, 1986). Countries compete to attract resources and tax bases through offering institutions; this should lead to an optimum arrangement in both levying taxes and in the offer of public services.[5]

Another defence of tax competition (Buchanan and Tullock, 1962; Brennan and Buchanan, 1980) is grounded in the economic theory of political behaviour. Tax competition, in this context, takes on a beneficent role of external ties to the 'leviathan' behaviour of governments, or rather posing limits to potential 'failure of government'. Indeed the tendency to increase taxes in an inefficient manner is punished by a loss of tax base and income, limiting the size of the public sector and the flawed behaviour of governments.[6]

Currently, different countries operate under a regime of tax competition. The OECD Committee has acknowledged that there are no specific reasons why two countries should have the same level and structure of taxation. Levels and structures of taxation, in spite of the implications that these hold for other countries, are basically political decisions taken at a local level by national governments.

Since the inception of the EU, the subject matter of taxation has always been the exclusive prerogative of the member states. It is considered an integral part of national choices and preferences regarding economic and social politics that lie outside the scope of the Convention and EU policies. An exception is established, however, by the rules of the internal market: generally, fiscal measures that create obstacles to the free circulation of goods, services and/or capital, or measures which might distort the rules of competition, are not permissible.

The important question remains how to ensure that competition between different regimes responds to needs for efficiency. Policies of taxation that are mainly or exclusively motivated to attract financing or other mobile tax bases, as well as avoidance behaviour carried out by enterprises, could cause undesirable distortions to international trade and investments and, at the same time, lower global wealth.[7] These considerations have led to the development of the concept of harmful tax competition as a specific issue dealt with in cooperative agreements stipulated to do away with specific distorting effects and behaviour of both taxpayers and of governments attempting to distinguish between fair and unfair tax competition.

On the one hand, the definition of unfair or harmful competition seems to be concerned with the protection of the reasons of the states, and emphasis is placed on the erosion of the national tax bases that the said procedures produce. On the other hand, from the point of view of the company, the problem of harmful tax competition mostly limits itself to the distortions that the policies could cause to the free competition of companies, bringing about, for instance, changes in prices involved in international trade and thus, guaranteeing through the lowering of the tax burden, funding linked to the operativity of enterprises. From this perspective, it is undeniable that national companies have different interests than ME might have in seeking out solutions to the problem of harmful tax competition. Indeed it is clear that any eventual poor functioning of the market tends to harm more the enterprises that, although being open to the international market, carry out their own activity in a national sphere. In contrast ME may avail themselves, to their own advantage, of tax competition, also harmful competition, among the different national systems. This reduces their tax burden and increases their competitivity in the market. Enterprises that mainly operate in a domestic market may be subject (considering equal benefiting from public services) to a greater tax levy than the amount of tax levied on non-resident enterprises. This is due both to fiscal provisions such as 'ringfencing' and, implicitly, to the wider selection of tax avoidance procedures available to ME.

Distinguishing between fair and unfair, or harmful, tax competition is a whole other issue. If an investor who is a resident avails himself of the benefits of a public service in their own country and, at the same time, manages to avoid all taxes by domiciling for fiscal purposes all profit in a 'tax haven', it is not hard to arrive at the conclusion that we are dealing with an example of unfair tax competition. Both the investor and the host country act as a 'free rider', thanks to finance operations that are specifically designed to avoid taxes in the first country.

The case of ME is not as obvious. ME work in several countries, with different tax rates for direct and indirect taxation. They try to achieve the best conditions also for (along with the other aspects of their business) aspects regarding tax burdens: this, in itself, as tax planning, cannot be considered unfair or harmful.

ACTIONS FROM INTERNATIONAL INSTITUTIONS

Under the current regime of different tax systems, actions taken by individual countries are not always helpful. In many countries, tax authorities may effect adjustments to earnings of a resident company, attributing to the transactions contested for tax purposes a transfer price that is in line with the market values. Moreover, often, intra-group transactions are not comparable because of their differences from normal market transactions. Thus this principle is difficult to apply. Competitive adjustment procedures (that are not coordinated) affected by individual countries may also result in cases of double taxation.

In order to adopt fiscal measures and decisions there must be a unanimous decision of the European Union Council (cf. articles 93–5 of the EC Treaty).[8] Article 94 provides for the possibility of directives for coordination and approximation of national tax provisions 'that have a direct effect on the internal market'. The directives for coordination leave the national legislation intact, but set rules for areas of contact and interfacing between national systems for cross border activity. The two main examples in this area are directive 90/435, aimed at eliminating double taxation on dividends, and directive 90/434, which regulates mergers, contributions, splits and other transactions aimed at altering company structure, allowing for the effecting of these transactions under a tax neutral regime.

One example of a cooperative reaction in this area is the convention regarding transfer pricing. This convention has established an arbitration procedure whose objective is to inhibit cases of double taxation that are not covered by the network of existing bilateral conventions. The convention, adopted by the European Council in 1990, entered into force on 1 January 1995 and, after being ratified by the member states, provided that an enterprise could take recourse against the tax authorities in charge of levying taxes on the company profits, by filing a procedure, initially dealing in information and conciliation, and later in arbitration, which must conclude with the elimination of the double taxation involved.

In the EU, coordinated activities on a large scale have, as of today, only been encountered in theoretical studies which have brought about proposals that are yet actually to be applied to a real case study. This, however, is if one excludes the reaction of industrial countries to the strategies of unfair tax competition practised by tax havens, or rather, what is called the CFC (Controlled Foreign Corporations) legislation. The CFC legislation is one example of a non-cooperative solution to the problem of different tax systems interfering with each other. The legislation establishes that the resident holding company be taxed on profit 'produced' (even if said profit has not yet been distributed) by controlled companies located in countries having privileged tax systems (tax havens). This kind of intervention does, however, cause conflict that is difficult to eradicate between the taxation authority of the country that adopts the norm and the authority of the (presumed) tax haven and the other countries having competitive CFC regulations. This occurs above all when there are existing international agreements between these countries aimed at avoiding double taxation.[9]

Almost ten years after the presentation of the Ruding Report, in October 2001 the European Commission published a new report (*Toward an internal market without tax obstacles*) indicating what the EU action should be in regard to fiscal issues for enterprises. The proposals therein are a product of the difficulties encountered in creating a European tax legislation (given the fact that there must be a unanimous vote of the committee and adherence to the principle of subsidiarity) as well as the limited success in applying the provisions suggested in the Ruding Report.

The opinion of the Commission is that the existence of 15 different tax regimes makes for a substantial obstacle in achieving a single market. The Commission deals with this issue by proposing, on one hand, actions that are 'aimed' (in the short term) at eliminating obstacles and, on the other hand, 'global actions' (in the medium to long term) meant to eliminate the factors that result in hindrances to cross-border business activity. Some of the 'aimed' actions are (a) extending of the directive regarding mergers; (b) adjustment of the directive regarding parent–subsidiary companies to eliminate the with-holding tax and to levy tax on profits only on the company producing said profits and not on the company receiving it: a substantial change, mainly in extending the access to this directive also to shareholdings with quotes that are lower than the current 25 per cent limit; (c) the proposal of a new directive on the cross-border offsetting of losses; (d) a directive (the draft has already been drawn up) regarding royalties and interest and the taxation of these only in the country of the beneficiary receiving them, thus eliminating the application of a withholding tax in the country from which they are distributed; (e) a permanent joint forum on transfer pricing, including mem-ber states and enterprises; (f) the submitting of a petition regarding the need to adapt the conventions against double taxation to a standard model that would render them adherent to common principles and thus avoid a mix of individual tax systems.

With a medium to long-term objective, the Commission initiates a debate on whether to adopt a consolidated tax base at a European level. This would allow for the calculation of taxable income of multinational groups by refer-ring to only one set of legislation. Basically this would be an attempt to deal with the problem (currently one issue that ME must deal with) of tax compli-ance formalities required by the different fiscal systems in the countries in which business activities are located. The Commission, however, permits each individual country to decide on its own tax rate to apply to the relevant taxable income, thus granting countries some degree of flexibility for tax competition. In order to reach this objective an efficient and politically feasible route must be found. In particular, member states must reach an agreement on two matters: how to determine the tax base for enterprises operating in different countries, and what mechanism to adopt for the division and attribution of taxable profits to countries. The solution of the first issue is a main priority and is still in the drafting phase.

The Commission have identified four systems. The first of these is a European company income tax (EUCIT). This system provides for the creation of a tax to be levied at a European level. A part, or the whole, of the said tax could go directly to the EU. Originally conceived as an obligatory regime for large ME, at the start it may be seen as an optional system. The idea that all member states may waive all, or even part, of their decision-making power on the levying of corporate income tax does, however, seem to be quite unlikely.

The second system is home state taxation (HST): this provides for a tax base to be calculated according to the tax regulations in the country in which the main headquarters of the company are located. It is conceived as a non-obligatory regime that a company operating in a different country may choose to adopt. This method does not require that member states establish common rules, in that, in order to implement the system, one only needs to have the mutual recognition of the taxation systems involved (although each country would have to recognize 15 systems and, with the prospect of extending the EU, even 25 systems). This has been defined as a route that would be politically feasible and one which should not present any particular obstacles, given that it would not be an obligatory regime for companies. From another point of view, however, the possibility should not be underestimated that more fierce (and likely harmful) competition may result, in contrast to current competition in determining tax bases in several countries having a negative outflow on the income of those companies belonging to enterprises that are part of multinational groups (the risk is that of ending up with very low tax bases or even bases reaching zero). ME tax bases could tend towards a homogeneity, yet at a lower than advantageous level, and thus the problem of arriving at a more substantial agreement setting a limit, even partial, to the decision-making power of each county would only be postponed up to the moment in which this competition is perceived as harmful. Lastly, this method would not solve the potential problem of companies that, although they may be operating in the same country and in the same sector, could be subject to very different tax regimes such as to alter fair competition among companies.

The common base taxation (CBT) system proposes the creation of harmonised rules at an EU level for the purpose of determining a single European tax base. This regime would also be optional. From a technical point of view, CBT offers two advantages over HST: (i) in each member state one would only need to be aware of the EU regulations and not the regulations of the other 14 member states; (ii) a starting point would be created for the establishing of European tax norms. The most relevant obstacle that CBT poses is undeniably the difficulty of defining a common tax base, and obtaining the agreement of all member states. This difficulty is exacerbated by the fact that, currently, each country has a series of more or less extensive 'tax expenditures' or rather, advantages connected to the country they belong to (such as accelerated amortisations). In establishing a common tax base it would be difficult to 'sum up' each individual tax advantage. The system would end up generating a more extensive tax base than the actual tax base existing in each member country. In this case, enterprises would have no interest in choosing a less favourable regime, unless the different countries were to lower their tax rates. This would, however, create repercussions (not considered in the EU plans) also in the tax levy on domestic companies. The problem remains, as is the case with HST, of a coexistence of determining different tax bases, in the same country, for ME who have opted for the EU regime and the domestic companies.

Finally there is the harmonized single tax base in the EU: this system provides for the progressive harmonisation of national directives for determining the corporate tax base. This proposal would be enacted over time: the 15 systems of determining the tax base would be gradually harmonised, but this harmonisation would involve all companies and not only those companies dealing in cross-border activity. It is likely that this method would come up against negotiating difficulties similar to those of the CBT. However, it would bring about a more direct and less costly transition: (a) in solving the problem of taxation of ME in Europe; (b) in lessening, as compared to the other methods, the added costs and requirements deriving from operating in more than one country, thus improving the conditions of international competitivity, (c) in rendering tax competition more transparent among countries in that it would be exclusively confined to setting of tax rates, and (d) in improving competition between companies on a national level as well as internationally. Furthermore this seems to be the method that is most in line with the short-term 'aimed' provisions mentioned above. This is because the said provisions tend (albeit in reference to certain institutions) to harmonise the legislation of different countries.

THE INFLUENCE OF TAXATION ON ECONOMIC–FINANCIAL DECISIONS TAKEN BY MULTINATIONAL ENTERPRISES

In an international context, income produced by companies may be subject to different tax systems, and companies located in certain countries may be eligible for certain tax benefits for which other companies located elsewhere are not eligible. Differences in taxes charged arise, not only during the setting of parameters for taxation (statutory rates, setting of tax bases and tax advantages), but also in determining the accounting profit. The flow of inter-company income is also subject to different and separate tax systems and, under the tax system of one country, there may be differential tax treatments established for income coming from foreign sources rather than internal sources. Given that each jurisdiction has the right to apply its own tax system, the tax burden of companies operating in more than one market is the result of a combination of the different companies which, at times, may be regulated by conventions between different countries.

In an open economy, ME may avail themselves of differences in international taxation through operations of tax arbitration. There could be a specific interest in setting up a multinational company only for gaining from these opportunities. Here we recall the two main channels for lessening tax burdens: the choice of financial policy and the possibility of profit shifting within the different companies belonging to the same group, using transfer pricing.

The financial policies of ME are different from the policies of companies operating in a single market. The former have the possibility of benefiting from a wider choice of financing channels. The convenience of achieving financing through subsidiaries depends on the level of the tax rate, but also on the credit conditions in the different markets (the interest rates and other types of conditions) as well as on the method used by the parent company for financing. Considering the different combinations of these factors, the possibilities for tax arbitration are manifold.

When dealing in ordinary transactions between group companies (purchase of tangible and intangible goods and services, financial activity and allocation of common expenses such as research) ME may apply 'transfer prices' which allow for the lessening of tax burdens and the increasing of overall profit. In conditions in which there are no obligations imposed by the tax authorities, transfer prices between companies belonging to the ME are based on the tax differentials in the different countries in which they are located as well as on the different methods adopted to avoid the problem of double taxation.

A REVIEW OF THE EMPIRICAL LITERATURE

Empirical studies on ME economic decisions may be first distinguished according to the type of economic decision carried out by the ME (whether to produce abroad, where to localise, what to do when located: see Figure 5.1) and to the type of data used (aggregate data on direct investments or micro data). There is in fact a third category, represented by the kind of fiscal indicator used in the analysis (see Table 5.1).[10]

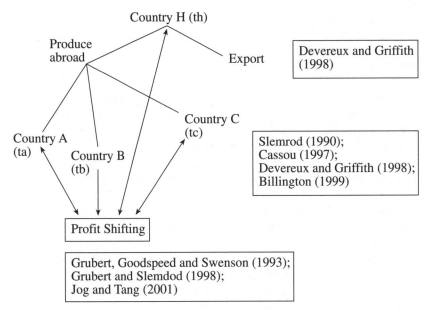

Note:
th = tax note in home country.
ta = tax note in Country A.
th = tax note in Country B.
tc = tax note in Country C.

Figure 5.1   A firm's decision tree: empirical literature

However, whether and how tax variables may affect ME investment choices is quite difficult to establish. Despite improved statistical methodologies and the development of new tax indicators, elasticity coefficients are often dispersed and not significant. In de Mooji and Ederveen (2001), reviewing the most important empirical studies on this topic, it is noted that 53 per cent of estimated elasticities are simply not statistically significant, while more than 4 per cent have a positive sign.[11]

Table 5.1   *Classification of main empirical contributions according to type of data and fiscal indicator*

Type of data	STR	EMTR	EATR	ITR
Macro: FDI time series	Billington (1999)	Slemrod (1990); Devereux and Freeman (1995)		Cassou (1997)
Micro: balance sheet or tax authority	Jog and Tang (2001)		Devereux and Griffith (1998)	Grubert, Goodspeed and Swenson (1993)

Notes: STR = Statutory tax rate, EMTR = effective marginal tax rate, EATR = effective average tax rate, ITR = implicit tax rate.

Using the three-stage tree in Figure 5.1, it is possible to note that the empirical evidence shows tax variables do not affect clearly the first two stages (whether to implement and where), while a relatively stronger impact may be exerted on the choices of already located ME.

With empirical evidence concentrating on the influence of taxation on decisions taken by companies already set up, the focus of analysis is not the level of investment, but rather on financing procedures, distribution of profit or, more generally, the activity of profit shifting which might result in a foreign-owned company being subject to a lower tax burden than a domestic company.

Grubert and Mutti (1991), with a pioneering paper on the topic, find a negative relation between tax levels of the host country (measured by both statutory and effective tax rate) and profitability using a cross-sectional data set (1982) of US subsidiaries for 33 countries.

Grubert *et al.* (1993), having noted that the ratio between gross profits and the total asset was 0.58 for foreign-owned firms and 2.14 for domestically owned firms in 1987, attribute the low profitability of foreign subsidiaries in the USA to many factors: manipulated transfer pricing, tax avoidance, start-up costs, mergers and acquisitions, differences in the cost of capital (lower for foreign firms) and so on. All these factors lead the authors to conclude that there are clear indications of profit shifting in foreign-controlled firms, even though a relevant share of profit differences is attributable to asset values and exchange rate movements.[12] Furthermore there is evidence that profitability does not depend on the home country, nor is it true that the home country adopts either higher or lower levels of taxation as well as either tax credits or tax exemptions.

Grubert (1997) supports the differential level of tax rates between foreign-controlled and domestic firms, while at the same time giving less weight to profit shifting of foreign controlled firms in the USA, finding no differences between tax rates of single-owner and multiple-owner foreign-controlled firms. Harris *et al.* (1993) also support the idea that US ME economic and financial behaviour may be affected by the tax levels of the host country. It is of particular interest that countries are classified as high- or low-tax using the statutory tax rate rather than the effective tax rate.

Grubert (1998) provides a detailed analysis of ME tax reduction policies led by financial choices and dividend distributions. The empirical analysis is conducted on micro data (tax returns) on the main industrial holdings and on about 3500 foreign-controlled firms through inter-company flows. The tax price of financial flows is calculated to verify whether choices are linked to tax parameters, with a positive outcome. Nevertheless changing the tax price of financial flows does not modify the amount of either retained or distributed profits, but only the way in which these flows are repatriated in the home country.

Even though the models on ME economic decisions distinguish between location decisions and decisions on investments and minimisation of the tax burden, there are cases contradicting the previous conclusion. Grubert and Slemrod (1998, p. 365), analysing ways and reasons for US investments in Puerto Rico, argue that 'the results suggest that income shifting advantages are the predominant reason for U.S. investment in Puerto Rico'.

More recently Jog and Tang (2001) have studied profit shifting in Canada as a consequence of the US tax reforms of the 1980s. It is argued that US subsidiaries in Canada have reacted by increasing leverage and consequently reducing taxes paid in Canada. Empirical analysis has shown that domestic companies make generous use of debt tax shields, the relation between the Canadian rates and the US rates affects the choice of debt for companies having connections abroad, the more lucrative enterprises have greater leverage (given the smaller risk implied) and leverage seems to be positively linked to size measured by the total of all activities.

It can be concluded that the empirical analysis conducted on profit shifting, in all but a few cases, shows that foreign-controlled companies behave irregularly, with various entities connected with conduct of tax avoidance. One unresolved issue remains the problem of identifying with certainty which channels are used in order to carry out such behaviour. An economic analysis based on traditional balance sheet data is not able to provide an answer to this question.

AN EMPIRICAL ANALYSIS OF THE TEXTILE SECTOR

Objective of the Analysis

The objective of the analysis is to verify whether ME incur an implicit tax burden that is lower than the tax burden of companies not having foreign associates, through eventual procedures of international allocation of group profit. Therefore this study only considers the tax burden relative to taxes levied by the host country: thus, a first level of taxation is involved[13] which does not take into consideration any interaction between the different tax systems and the aggregate tax debt on invested capital in any given country. In this phase, our objective is not to assess the choice of the location of the company based on differentials of tax rates on an international level, but rather to verify, indirectly, the effects of the practice of profit shifting carried out by already established companies in light of the differentials of taxation with the countries of the associated foreign companies. Indeed we consider that this is a relevant aspect both from a perspective of internal competition in the same market – and in particular between domestic and multinational companies operating in a certain country – and from a perspective of adherence to the benefit principle, connected to the right of the host country to levy a corporation tax on the foreign owned company.

The empirical analysis carried out on the textile sector for Italy is meant to provide a contribution to the verification of eventual tax planning conducted by ME having consequences on competitivity of companies operating exclusively on the domestic market (with potential effects of unfair and harmful tax competition). In fact, we consider that, from this perspective, the effect of tax factors may arise, not so much because of factors of location of investments but owing to factors of location of the tax bases. The analysis was limited to the textile sector, but should be extended to other sectors to further observe differential economic behaviour, attributable to fiscal factors, within the sphere of the same ME.

Tax Indicators

The choice of tax indicators is crucial to conceptualising and verifying empirically the relation between ME and tax systems. Tax burdens may indeed be calculated with different tools and for different aims.

The first rather obvious measure to consider is the statutory tax rate (STR), which gives a general idea of national tax policies. STR is widely used in international comparison; however, it does not give a reliable measure of the actual tax burden, especially in international and intersectoral contexts, as the actual tax burden closely depends on the definition of the tax base, which is far from being harmonised among countries.

For this reason, STR is often replaced by effective tax rates (ETR), that is tax indicators that take into account how the tax base is determined and whether tax laws allow tax incentives. Within ETR it is then possible to distinguish between ex post ETR (backward-looking) and ex ante ETR (forward-looking). The first group, henceforth ex post implicit tax rates (EPITR), includes all those indicators calculated as the ratio between taxes actually paid and a reference economic aggregate (profits, capital, value added and so on).[14] Using taxes actually paid allows the analyst to incorporate the specific rules underlying the determination of a tax base. Average tax rates obtained in this manner measure the size of the potential retained profit that is subtracted from the firm. In this perspective, they are useful when the aim of the analysis is to analyse the income effects of taxation and compare taxation levels of different groups of firms.

The second group, ex ante marginal tax rates (EAMTR), is of a forward-looking nature. It measures a theoretical impact starting from tax laws applicable to a specific investment project at the margin, that is not producing extra profits.[15] This kind of gauge is useful to understand how tax systems affect firms' decisions as well as to spot non-neutralities of tax systems among different alternative investments. For this reason, the indicator is usually expressed as a ratio with the difference between gross and net return as the numerator and the gross return as the denominator. EAMTR are calculated for different types of investment (for example, machinery and intangible assets) and different financing sources (self-financing, debt issues and so on).

Devereux and Griffith (1998) have developed this approach by building a methodology to calculate theoretical tax rates for inframarginal investments which is referred to as the 'average effective marginal tax rates' (EAVMTR).[16] Conceptual differences in indicators imply differences in results. The implicit tax rate (calculated by using a proxy for gross profits as the denominator) is indeed usually lower but not very far from the statutory rate, yet the quality of the indicator strongly depends on the quality of the denominator. Marginal tax rates, instead, may be very far from statutory and average tax rates, since it is possible for them to be negative.

Things may become more complicated when those same measures are applied in an international context. Calculation of tax burden needs not only to look at statutory rates in the domestic country but possibly to consider also withholding taxes applied by the host country, or compensation mechanisms applied by the home country for taxes paid abroad. To provide an example, the STR in Italy has been one of the highest in developed countries since the early 1990s and remains so, even after various reforms. Looking at the marginal tax rates, however, the Italian situation is one of the most appealing in Europe. A recent contribution by the European Commission (2001) identifies Italy as one of the countries in which the cost of capital for a foreign subsidiary is lower (standing at about 5 per cent instead of an average of 6 per cent).

In this chapter the ex post implicit tax rate indicator has been chosen, given the specific interest in pinpointing behaviour aimed at minimising tax burdens and at the difference in the fiscal burden borne by only domestic companies as opposed to those having foreign associates.

Data Source

The AIDA data set[17] (containing 170 000 non-financial corporations' balance sheets with total revenue above one million Euros) is the main database for this study. The data set is not a representative sample, but it gives a good coverage of macroeconomic aggregates for medium and large firms. It covers a period from 1994 to 2000. Our specific subset of data is drawn from 1998, gathering balance sheets and additional external information concerning nationality of majority shareholders and subsidiaries. Corporations included in this subset satisfactorily approximate some figures as calculated in the National Accounts (NA) as well as tax revenue from (non-financial) corporations. Value added from non-financial firms is, in the subset, equal to about 50.3 per cent from NA, while a similar coverage is observed for the labour cost (61 per cent). Even more satisfactory is the comparison with data from the tax authority (TA) reported in Table 5.2.

Firms represent only 20 per cent of the total number of non-financial corporations, whereas about 30 per cent of business comes from the agriculture and manufacturing sectors, as registered by the tax authority.[18] Both earnings before taxes and taxes (corporation tax, IRPEG and regional tax on

Table 5.2   Accounting variables (AIDA data set) as percentage of tax authority data (1998)

		Assets	Turnover	Cost of employees	Value added	Income before taxes	Income taxes
Non-financial	Number	20.4	20.4	20.4	20.4	20.4	20.4
corporations	Amount	67.7	83.9	84.8	78.6	74.4	75.6
Agriculture and	Number	28.6	28.6	28.6	28.6	28.6	28.6
manufacturing	Amount	81.1	85.1	82.2	79.5	85.2	86.1

Source: Authors's calculations on AIDA and tax authority data.

production activity, IRAP) in AIDA amount to 75 per cent and 85 per cent of the figures drawn from income tax returns for non-financial corporations and agriculture and manufacturing, respectively. This supports the idea that corporation tax (liabilities) payments are highly concentrated in Italy.[19] The AMADEUS data set is also used to compare Italian data with data from other countries.[20]

Building the Data Set

In this chapter, we use a micro data set of firms, in order to exploit all the information available in firms' budgets, while at the same time introducing heterogeneity and differentiation between foreign-owned firms and domestic firms located in the same country. This scheme is relatively new among empirical works that try to investigate the relation between ME economic choices and the tax policy of various countries, as existing works are usually more concentrated on the locational choice of companies. The year 1998 is the base of the analysis. For some firms it has also been possible to merge specific elaborations from tax authority data. Data collected from analysing shareholders have allowed us to separate domestic companies (DC) from companies located in Italy but controlled by foreign corporations (FCC), representing inward direct investments. With regards to domestic firms, Italian corporations controlling foreign corporations (ICC) have been separated as well. We analyse only one sector, textile and clothing.[21] This choice is due to the strategic position of this sector in the Italian economy and its high propensity to internationalise.[22] Moreover we have been able to avoid differences in tax burdens due both to differences in the production function and to sector-specific tax rules (for example, tax incentives).[23]

The database has also allowed us to identify firms with at least one foreign shareholder and/or a direct investment in a firm located abroad with a share equal to one-third of the capital. This criterion corresponds to the identification of direct shareholders (or first beneficiary) and not to the identification of the overall structure of the group (that would adhere to the criterion of the last beneficiary).[24] Nevertheless it has been useful to classify as 'multinational' also those firms that, even though lacking a direct link with foreign firms, are at least 50 per cent owned by either an FCC or an ICC. To classify multinational enterprises (FCCs and ICCs), the ownership threshold has been set at 25 per cent, lower than the majority percentage of 50 per cent used in other studies,[25] but well above the limit used to identify direct investment (10 per cent). For our purposes it has been necessary to set a participation threshold that would imply an interest in coordinating tax planning among firms, taking into account the cost of repatriating profits. Finally we apply the same percentage set by the parent–subsidiary directive. For example, multinational groups may be organised in a simple way, with one holding located in Italy that owns a subsidiary located, for instance, in Germany, or in a more complex way, with various residence countries. In the first case, there will be an incentive for tax minimisation stemming from the comparison of only two tax systems. In the second case, any potential shareholder in any country will try to minimise its own tax burden according to tax laws regulating cross-border investment flows.

AN OVERVIEW OF THE TEXTILE AND CLOTHING SECTOR

The textile and clothing sector covered 7891 firms in 1998[26] and 159 of them have consolidated balance sheets. However these latter have not been considered in order to preserve information that would have been lost by using the consolidated accounting variables (for example, the choice of financing sources).[27] At the same time, it is worth noting that the consolidated tax return has no tax relevance in Italy;[28] this is why the analysis has been restricted to non-consolidated balance sheets. A further 1844 firms have been excluded owing to incomplete balance sheets or lack of consistency between budget items. The number of firms considered in the analysis is therefore 6047, out of which 5799 are domestic firms. Of the 248 multinationals, 80 are FCCs and 168 are ICCs. Table 5.3 summarises the main characteristics of the sample.

As information on shareholdings from the AIDA data set is incomplete, it has been necessary to integrate data with other databases: R&S, Business International and Mediocredito Centrale. However the identification of countries of residence of both controlling and controlled firms has not been possible for all firms (Table 5.4).

Table 5.3   Data set for textile and clothing (1998)

Total number of corporations	7 891
Consolidated budget	159
Not included	1 844
Included	6 047
National (DC)	5 799
Multinational enterprises	248
foreign controlled (FCC)	80
Italian controlled (ICC)	168

Source: Author's calculations.

Table 5.4   Localisation of multinational companies

ICC (Subsidiaries)			FCC (Parent company)		
Romania	52	31.0%	USA	14	17.5%
France	19	11.3%	Germany	10	12.5%
Germany	10	6.0%	UK	9	11.3%
UK	6	3.6%	France	8	10.0%
Hungary	2	1.2%	Japan	4	5.0%
Total	168	100.0%	Total	80	100.0%

Source: Author's calculations.

It is worth noting that, even though the investigation is carried out on a data set including only medium and large firms, their distribution is comparable with that of other studies. Statistics in the Cominotti *et al.* report (1999), for example, show 236 companies located abroad with Italian participation, out of which 166 are holders, and 63 located in Italy with foreign participation, out of which 49 are holders in the textile and clothing sector.

Among the 6047 firms of the sample, more than 40 per cent have a total revenue (turnover) below 2.5 million Euros (mainly domestic firms), while about 80 per cent of ICCs and FCCs have a total revenue above 5 million Euros. This fact *supports the common belief that international firms have higher total revenues.* Table 5.5 illustrates the distribution of firms by revenue classes.

With regard to employment, on average, domestic firms have a significantly lower number of employees (38 units) compared with ME (239 and 148 units for ICC and FCC, respectively).[29] Table 5.6 also reveals a different level of productivity between domestic firms and ME. In particular, the share of the value added per employee of the former is equal to about 70 per cent of those observed for ME. Accordingly we can also observe higher average wages and salaries in ME (in particular for FCC) due to the influence of foreign standards.

PROFITABILITY AND TAX BURDEN

The empirical literature shows that multinational corporations usually have lower profit rates and tax payment in comparison with domestic companies. In Italy, our data support this finding – profit indicators (typically ROE and ROI) are lower than for domestic firms, as illustrated by the sample values of

Table 5.5   Number of companies, by turnover class (percentage)

| | Total revenue classes (millions of Euros) | | | | | |
	0–1.5	1.5–2.5	2.5–5	5–25	25 and over	Total
DC						
% row	27.8	19.1	23.1	26.5	3.6	100.0
% column	99.4	99.4	98.0	93.2	68.9	95.9
ICC						
% row	3.0	2.4	10.7	44.6	39.3	100.0
% column	0.3	0.4	1.3	4.6	22.1	2.8
FCC						
% row	6.1	3.7	12.2	45.1	32.9	100.0
% column	0.3	0.3	0.7	2.2	9.0	1.4
Total						
% row	26.8	18.4	22.6	27.2	4.9	100.0
% column	100.0	100.0	100.0	100.0	100.0	100.0

Source: Author's calculations.

Table 5.6   Productivity index and average cost per employee (Euros, 000s)

	Value added per employee	Average cost per employee
DC	41 934	25 107
ICC	47 395	25 983
FCC	63 954	32 686

Note: Average cost per employee = total labour cost/number of employees; value added per employee = value added/number of employees.

Source: Author's calculations.

ROE and ROI of Table 5.7. It can also be observed that ROI (the first column), even though higher for domestic firms, is relatively more homogeneous than returns on equity, still higher for domestic firms.

The dispersion of these two indices is lower than what is observed for other countries, yet it might be interpreted as a signal of profit-shifting behaviour of multinational firms, showing a lower return due to tax burden minimisation. This difference is in fact maintained throughout the period 1994–2000 (Table 5.8)[30] and it does not seem to depend on the age of the

Table 5.7   Profitability indices: ROI and ROE (1998)

	Return on investment	Return on equity
DC	5.06	2.77
ICC	4.84	1.84
FCC	4.56	2.08
Total	5.04	2.73

Note: ROE = profit or loss after taxation/net equity *100; ROI = operating profit (or loss)/total assets *100.

Source: AIDA data.

*Table 5.8   Return on equity (1994–2000)**

	1994	1995	1996	1997	1998	1999	2000
DC	12.2	12.0	6.8	5.2	2.8	3.7	3.5
ICC	9.2	12.9	5.5	4.7	1.8	0.5	3.5
FCC	–3.8	8.5	5.9	1.4	1.8	3.0	–1.0
Total	11.9	12.0	6.7	5.1	2.7	3.6	3.5

Note: * ROE is calculated on panel data for the period 1994–2000.

Source: AIDA data.

multinational firm (still 'not mature') or on a substantial merger or acquisition activity, at least in the period observed in the analysis.[31]

Lower profitability has a consequence in terms of tax liability. This latter is quantified by the implicit tax rate (following the micro backward-looking methodology) defined as the ratio of taxes to total assets. Both taxes and total assets are those relevant for financial reporting and not for tax purposes. On average, taxes paid by domestic firms are higher than those paid by ICCs and FCCs (Table 5.9). This result is marked with respect to the choice of alternative denominators; using sales, conclusions are reinforced further owing to the fact that capital per sales unit is lower in both FCCs and ICCs.[32]

Again in Table 5.9, some interesting observations can be made by looking at the percentage of companies with positive or negative income (profit or loss).[33] It is worth noting that, in our sample, the higher share of firms operating at a loss belongs to FCC (29 per cent), yet the difference when taking the share of domestic firms (22 per cent) does not seem to be a

Table 5.9   Income taxes* as a percentage of total assets and sales

	Taxes/assets	Taxes/sales	Number of companies making a loss	Number of companies in profit
DC	2.83	2.27	22.0	78.0
ICC	2.32	1.96	17.3	82.7
FCC	2.29	1.79	29.6	70.4

Note: * Income taxes are those in the balance sheet and they include the corporation tax (IRPEG) and the regional tax on production activity (IRAP).

Source: Author's calculations.

compelling justification for overall tax rate differences. Finally the ICC is the group with the higher share of firms operating at a profit (83 per cent).

It should also be considered that the tax rate of any firm has been given the same weight in defining the mean average tax rate. Alternatively, as in other studies, we could have calculated the average tax rate as the ratio between the total amount of taxes paid and the total assets (or turnover). In this case, an implicit tax rate is actually computed for each subsample of companies, which is consequently considered as a representative company. This tax indicator smooths extreme values when averages are calculated.[34] Results, not reported here, do not change when using total assets as the denominator, while they weaken when using turnover. In this latter case, there is some evidence illustrating that ICC would pay more than domestic firms, while for FCC a lower tax burden would still emerge.

In spite of the fact that our results are similar to other empirical analyses, we can observe a wide range of implicit tax rates across companies in the same subsample,[35] which is typical in accounting data. To this purpose, we run two statistical tests: the Levene Test on variance homogeneity and the T-test on differences in means (Table 5.10). As a first step, we compare the means of implicit tax rates attached to domestic and multinational companies (adding FCC and ICC). The upper part of the table shows basic statistics on tax notes for DC and the new NF group (FCC plus ICC). In the bottom part the Levene test accepts homogeneity of variances for tax-sales indicators and rejects homogeneity for tax-asset indicators. The difference among average implicit tax rates is statistically significant (see T-test in the lower part of the table) only when total assets is used as the denominator (see significance level). When using turnover, instead, the difference is not significant. A likely interpretation lies in the wider range of extreme values of the corresponding

Table 5.10 Statistical tests on differences in means: T-test and Levene test

		Mean	Standard deviation	Mean Standard error
Taxes/sales	MC=FCC+ICC	1.9050	1.8519	0.1183
	DC	2.2709	303.9931	4.0142
Taxes/assets	MC=FCC+ICC	2.3074	2.6644	0.1692
	DC	2.8272	3.4060	

		Levene test on variance homogeneity		T-test on mean homogeneity					Confidence interval (at 95%)	
		F	Sign.	t	df	Sign (2-code)	Differences in means	Differences in standard error	lower	higher
Taxes/sales	Homogeneous variances	0.2890	0.5910	-0.3080	5978.00	0.7580	-5.9797	19.4230	-44.0558	32.0963
	Variances not homogeneous			-1.4890	5743.87	0.1370	-5.9797	4.0159	-13.8525	1.8930
Taxes/assets	Homogeneous variances	5.5040	0.0190	-2.3730	6045.00	0.0180	-0.5199	0.2191	-0.9494	
	Variances not homogeneous			-2.9710	282.67	0.0030	-0.5199	0.1750	-0.8643	-0.1754

implicit tax rates. The ANOVA test leads to the same conclusion, even though FCCs and ICCs are separately considered.

Higher tax payments for DC are constant over the period 1998–2000, even if evidence from other countries is stronger[36] (Table 5.11.)

Table 5.11   Income taxes as a percentage of total assets (1998–2000)*

	1998	1999	2000
DC	2.8	2.9	2.8
ICC	2.3	2.4	2.3
FCC	2.2	2.2	2.4

Note: * Income taxes are those in the balance sheet and they include the corporation tax (IRPEG) and the regional tax on production activity (IRAP); ratios are calculated on panel data for the period 1994–2000.

Source: Author's calculations.

The same methodology has been used to extend results on the ME behaviour for some other European countries: France, Germany, Romania and the United Kingdom. DCs and MEs (FCC and ICC) are identified for each country. Implicit tax rates, both on assets and on turnover, are higher for domestic controlled firms in all countries, with the corresponding ICC showing the lower tax rate (Table 5.12). Moreover the level of the implicit rates is comparable to other international empirical studies and supports the positions of both Italy as a high tax country and the United Kingdom as a low tax country.

VALIDATION: THE TAX AUTHORITY DATA SET

As is known, taxes resulting from balance sheets might provide an unclear picture of the yearly tax burden. In order to verify whether estimated tax rate levels are meaningful, a restricted data set on domestic and multinational firms from the Italian tax authority is used.[37] Separate tax rates have been calculated for the two most important direct taxes on firms, IRPEG and IRAP. Both of them show a higher variance, compared with our data set, yet findings are confirmed, in that tax rates for multinationals are higher (Table 5.13). Tax differentials are stronger than in our data set if IRPEG and IRAP are taken together, as occurs in accounting data. Results do not change if IRPEG and IRAP are separated.

Table 5.12 Income taxes as a percentage of total assets and of sales: textile and clothing (1998)*

	France		Germany		United Kingdom		Romania		Italy	
	Taxes/ assets	Taxes/ sales	Taxes/ assets	Taxes/ sales	Taxes/ assets	Taxes/ sales	Taxes/ assets	Taxes/ sales	Taxes/ assets	Taxes/ sales
DC	2.80	2.06	2.54	1.22	1.82	n.a.	3.80	2.42	3.31	2.80
ICC	1.06	1.42	1.45	1.20	1.32	n.a.	2.44	1.65	2.58	2.27
FCC	2.54	1.87	1.08	1.40	1.05	n.a.	2.01	1.06	2.82	2.08

Note: * Income taxes are those in the balance sheet.

Source: Author's calculations on AMADEUS data.

115

Table 5.13   Taxes (IRPEG and IRAP)* as a percentage of total assets and of sales (1998)

	IRPEG/ sales	IRPEG/ assets	IRPEG+IRAP /sales	IRPEG+IRAP /assets	Companies with loss (%)	Companies in profit (%)
DC	1.33	1.99	2.40	3.50	33.9	66.1
ICC	0.75	0.88	1.68	1.83	21.4	78.6
FCC	0.84	1.24	1.81	2.54	25.0	75.0

Note: * Taxes are those in tax record data (UNICO, 99): the corporation tax (IRPEG) and the regional tax on production activity (IRAP).

Source: Tax authority (1998).

As already argued in the case of balance sheet data, the difference between tax rates is not due to a greater percentage of multinationals with losses. Tax authority data for IRPEG (the corporation tax in Italy) show on average 23.2 per cent of MEs with negative income, lower than numbers recorded for domestic firms (33 per cent), whereas, for IRAP purposes, only 5 per cent of firms have a negative tax base (net value added) and almost every multinational has a positive tax base.

IS THERE PROFIT SHIFTING?

As already observed, tax rate differentials between multinationals and domestic firms are not particularly wide, yet they suggest a more specific analysis on those budget items representing, indirectly, indicators of profit shifting. The cost of raw materials and interest expenses are two factors determining firms' tax base and, consequently, tax burden. For a multinational firm, these factors may become useful tools for tax avoidance through transfer pricing and thin capitalisation. Indirectly, to find a partial justification for a lower tax burden for multinational firms, one can therefore investigate both leverage and vertical integration indicators, this latter proxied by the share of the value added in turnover (Table 5.14).

Given the assumed homogeneity of the production function in the sector, possible deviations among firms might be a signal for a significant influence of tax factors on profits.

Domestic firms show a much higher leverage than the leverage of multinationals. The same is true for the ratio between interest expenses and turnover and for the implicit interest rate. All these variables are instead very close for

Table 5.14   Leverage indices and values added on turnover

	Leverage	Interest/sales	Implicit interest rate	Value added/sales
DC	55.9	11.6	6.3	44.1
ICC	44.5	3.5	4.4	22.1
FCC	46.4	2.9	4.0	24.2
Total	55.5	11.3	6.2	43.2

Notes: Leverage = total payables (excl. tax and to suppliers)/total liabilities; implicit interest rate = financial charges/total payables.

Source: Author's calculation.

FCC and ICC. Since Italy is thought of as a country with relatively high legal corporate tax rates, this result would seem to contradict the initial hypothesis, but it may reflect a distortion of the Italian firms (mainly small and medium-sized firms) towards financial policy favouring debt financing to equity, not merely to take advantage of tax saving. It is therefore impossible to conclude whether debt is used as a profit-shifting tool by multinationals.

Because of 'anomalous' behaviour by domestic firms, the figures for this indicator could also hide possible avoidance activities of multinationals. However, the average value of the leverage ratio is highly differentiated across companies in the same subsample and does not show statistical significance. Furthermore, in 1998, there was no evidence of a different tax strategy carried out by such firms, even though, as a result of the last tax reform, they have reduced tax advantages of using debt, as interest expenses are included in the IRAP tax base. The leverage of the firms considered in the analysis is almost constant between 1994 and 2000.

The tax strategy followed by multinationals could therefore be better investigated through the analysis of transfer pricing practices that, since 1998, have given more advantages in terms of both corporation tax and IRAP through higher costs of raw materials. Initial evidence is linked to the degree of vertical integration of the firm as measured by the ratio between value added and turnover (Table 5.14). In this case, a substantial difference emerges, with multinationals much less integrated than domestic firms.

Quite obviously, the vertical integration index compounds tax and industrial strategies. In this sense, it is only a weak indicator of the possibility that raw materials have higher prices for external-oriented firms. As already noted above, evidence on profit shifting has not yet led to a clear identification of this possibility. It might only occur through the precise identification of the price differentials between internal and market transactions.

VALIDATION: THE SIZE EFFECT

As indicated above, DCs' higher implicit tax burden, compared with that of MEs, may be, to some extent, interpreted as a signal of avoidance behaviour. At this stage, it is important to provide evidence that our results are not biased by the size effect. Recent studies, when comparing small and large companies, have shown different tax burdens. For selected EU countries, including Italy, Nicodème[38] applies a similar methodology to ours, calculating higher implicit tax rates for small companies. In our data set, the DC subsample includes relatively smaller companies than the ME subsample does; as a consequence, our analysis needs to exclude the presence of correlation with a size effect. This explains why the ratios are computed by selecting companies with over 5 million Euros. On the one hand, the outcome validates previous results in terms of implicit tax burden. On the other hand, we found a reranking of the leverage index. Excluding the size effect, the debt level of the ME subsample is higher than the debt level of DCs. It seems confirmed that the DC position in the total data set may be affected by the financial policy of small and medium-sized Italian companies that is biased towards debt, rather than towards equity or retained earnings (Table 5.15).

Table 5.15   Leverage and tax ratios (companies with turnover of more than 5 million Euros)

	Leverage	Taxes/assets	Taxes/sales
DC	40.25	3.01	2.28
ICC	42.39	2.38	2.00
FCC	46.55	2.58	1.93
Total	40.61	2.95	2.24

Source: Author's calculations.

Moreover, to determine the statistical significance of these differences, we undertake statistical tests on differences in means (see F-test and significance level columns in the table). The T-test and the variance analysis reject the null hypothesis of no differences, giving support to the results obtained for the implicit tax burden as well as for the leverage ratio (Table 5.16).

The evidence shown in this chapter highlights the different financial behaviour of multinationals, yet we need to investigate more regarding tax minimisation instruments. A preliminary examination of data considering the country where MEs are located gives evidence of a level of debt and of

Table 5.16   *Leverage and tax ratios: analysis of variance (companies with turnover of more than 5 million Euros)*

		Sum of squares	df	Means of squares	F	Sig.
Taxes/assets	Between groups	60.375	2	30.187	3.103	0.045
	Within group	18881.289	1941	9.728		
	Total	18942.289	1943			
Leverage	Between groups	2900.812	2	1450.406	3.725	0.024
	Within group	753347.141	1935	389.327		
	Total	756247.953	1937			

Source: Author's calculations.

implicit interest rates related to the country's nominal tax rate differential, such as postulated by the theory on tax planning behaviour.

CONCLUSIONS

The current debate on international corporate taxation is focusing on cross-border discrimination issues driven by complexity and diversity of tax rules, tax incentives and different levels of tax enforcement. This chapter extends the analysis of possible tax discrimination to a domestic level, between firms operating in a single country and firms operating in more than one country (ME). The multiplicity of tax rules and tax planning practices (profit-shifting behaviour, cross-border payments of dividend and so on) affords companies operating at an international level the possibility of legally decreasing or avoiding taxation. This aspect is of great importance, not only from the point of view of the traditional international tax competition literature, but also from the point of view of 'within-border' unfair competition between domestic and ME firms located in the same country. If ME minimise tax burdens, they contribute less than domestic firms to the total tax revenue. Empirical studies have provided some evidence of lower tax burdens for multinational corporations, suggesting tax-motivated income shifting, as in the case of the USA, Canada and the UK.

Empirical evidence supporting discrimination against domestic firms in a sample of 6047 balance sheets of companies registered in Italy and included in the textile and clothing sector has been reported in this chapter by carefully distinguishing among pure domestic companies (DC), foreign-controlled companies (FCC) and Italian companies controlling foreign corporations (ICC).

Using the microeconomic backward-looking approach, implicit corporate tax rates (taxes as a fraction of either sales or assets) have been computed for each firm on individual accounting data. In a first stage, we have compared profit indices (ROE and ROI), finding that, on average, ME profit rates are lower than those of domestic companies, suggesting behaviour aimed at minimising the tax burden. Next we observed higher tax rates for DC over the period 1998–2000, even when expressed in percentage points. Differences are not marked, but the pattern of choosing alternative denominators is noteworthy. Moreover results are confirmed by a restricted data set covering domestic and multinational firms from the Italian tax authority. Compared with our data set, implicit tax rates show even greater differences between DC and ME.

Finally we focused on some balance sheet items representing indicators of profit shifting: leverage and vertical integration indices. The former does not show significant differences across different groups of companies, but it is not sufficient to exclude some practice of thin capitalisation by ME. The second, that is, the value added on sales ratio, suggests that ME are less integrated than domestic companies, signalling the need for further investigation of transfer pricing practices.

NOTES

1. Devereux and Griffith (1998, 2002).
2. See, for example, De Santis and Vicarelli (2001).
3. In the EU, the debate on tax competition was started by the pressure for competition, which, in its turn, derives (for companies in countries with a high level of public expenditure and taxation) from the process of integration of the internal market and the single currency.
4. Countries are obliged to lower tax rates to create competition and to avoid capital leaving the country, which results in corporate income tax rates tending to disappear.
5. In particular, we refer to the well-known contribution of Tiebout (1956), according to which, when electors 'vote with their feet', an optimum market solution is reached for the offer of local public goods.
6. Another line of reasoning, attributed among others to Kehoe (1989), is based on the idea that tax competition could solve the problem of *time consistency* in the taxation of earnings from capital. According to this interpretation, governments benefit from the application of tax rates that are initially lower, thus attracting capital, and later increase said rates once investments have been effected and have lost their mobility (at least in the short term).
7. OECD, (1998).
8. The possibilty of a complete harmonisation of national norms is provided only for indirect tax (art. 93 of the Treaty) 'in the needed proportions so as to ensure the establishing and the functioning of the internal market'.
9. In many countries the adopting of CFC legislation has been an increasingly contentious issue between tax authorities and taxpayers. In addition, the fact that more and more countries are adopting CFC legislation results in an overlapping of tax obligations on companies located in fiscally privileged countries that is difficult to resolve.

10. See Devereux and Griffith (2002) and de Mooji and Ederveen (2001).
11. An analysis of variance of this meta database reveals how the choice of both data and tax indicators has a strong impact on the estimated elasticities.
12. The authors do not, however, find relevant differences in the financing policy and, therefore, in the leverage levels.
13. For an overview of international taxation of capital, see Giannini (1994).
14. Implicit average tax rate can be calculated either on national accounts data or on microeconomic data on individual firms.
15. These indicators have been built following King and Fullerton (1984). Without going into details, it is worth emphasising that the use of this methodology brings with it quite restrictive assumptions, such as perfect competition and the absence of extra profits, to name two of the most striking. For a more detailed explanation, see Martinez Mongay (2000).
16. The 'average' derives from the fact that these indicators are obtained as the average of taxes due on hypothetical investments with different profitability levels.
17. Aida Bureau Van Dijck.
18. In Italy, the number of companies (over 3.5 million units) is higher than the EU average. In this chapter, we are interested in the corporate sector (about 600 000 units) that includes the bulk of multinational companies.
19. In aggregate, corporation tax liability shows the effect of having a high percentage of companies making a loss: during the 1980–98 period this stood on average at more than 50 per cent in each year.
20. The AMADEUS data set includes the balance sheets of large companies (sales over 15 million euros located in the European countries.
21. Following Ateco91codes, sectors 17 and 18.
22. For the recent trends, see Rossetti and Schiattarella (2003).
23. Empirical evidence of differences in tax provisions by sectors has been shown by Nicodème (2002) for selected EU countries.
24. This restriction could be a limit for the analysis of income shifting into the same group (holding group); however, the aim of the chapter is to verify whether ME bear an implicit tax rate lower than DC, considering that they have access to more instruments to avoid taxation.
25. See, for example, Cominotti *et al.* (1999) and OECD (2001b).
26. There are specific difficulties in choosing 1998 as a base year, due to the fact that in the same year a tax reform was started, introducing a dual taxation system (DIT) and Irap. However, this choice has the advantage of providing a reliable data set and some comparability with tax authority data.
27. An opposite choice was made by Grubert *et al.* (1993).
28. Actually, in the law proposal, consolidation for autonomous taxation is a possibility.
29. About 350 firms do not report the number of employees. Average values are therefore conditional.
30. Except for 1995 and 2000, when ROE for ICC is slightly above that of DC.
31. As argued by Grubert *et al.* (1993), frequent acquisitions and mergers would make the actual value of the fixed assets emerge in the total asset, implying an increase of invested capital that could not be found in domestic firms not involved in extraordinary activity.
32. The choice of an appropriate denominator is not an easy task. On the one hand, we need an indicator to take into account the effects of production costs and financial items (mainly interest expenses); on the other hand, the use of assets and sales implies that rates of returns on assets and the true profit margin, respectively, should be equalised across companies.
33. To this purpose the share of firms operating at a loss is of some relevance as IRAP is a tax with a wider tax base than competition tax.
34. In particular, this average indicator is used when negative value can compensate for positive value.
35. For FCC, the highest tax rates recorded are 13 per cent, with turnover as denominator, and 15 per cent, with total assets as denominator. About 13 per cent of the firms have a zero

rate and more than 29 per cent of these firms have negative earnings before taxes. It is worth noting that tax rates may be positive even with losses because they include IRAP, which is a tax on the net value added. Moreover only one firm (using turnover) and five firms (using total assets) have a tax rate greater than 7 per cent. Without these extreme cases, tax rates decrease from 1.8 to 1.6 per cent (turnover) and from 2.3 to 1.8 per cent (assets). Analogous results are observed for ICC, even though the percentage of firms with zero rate is now lower, partly as a consequence of the smaller number of firms with negative earnings before taxes (17.3 per cent). Here the highest tax rates are not higher than 8 per cent (with turnover) and 11 per cent (with total assets), while a particular concentration is observed around 3 per cent (more than 80 per cent of firms). The situation of domestic firms is more articulated, because a substantial percentage of these show losses (even though fewer than FCC) and, consequently, zero tax rates (about 7 per cent). On the other hand, there is a high number of tax rates within 3 and 50 per cent, regardless of the denominator used (turnover or assets).

36.   Grubert *et al.* (1993) show more than three percentage points of distance between domestic and multinational corporations in the USA.
37.   The tax authority sample includes 350 companies for textile and clothing that are also included in our sample.
38.   Nicodème (2002).

REFERENCES

Billington, N. (1999), 'The location of foreign direct investment: an empirical analysis', *Applied Economics*, **31**, 65–76.

Brennan G. and J.M. Buchanan (1980), *The Power to Tax: Analytical Foundations for a Fiscal Constitution*, Cambridge: Cambridge University Press.

Buchanan, J.M. and G. Tullock (1962), *The Calculus of Consent*, Ann Arbor: University of Michigan Press.

Cassou, S. (1997), 'The link between tax rates and foreign direct investment', *Applied Economics*, **29**, 1295–301.

Cominotti, R., S. Mariotti and M. Mutinelli (1999), 'Italia Multinazionale 1998', Documenti CNEL.

de Mooij, R. and S. Ederveen (2001), 'Taxation and foreign direct investment. A synthesis of empirical research', CESifo Working paper No. 158.

De Santis, R. and C. Vicarelli (2001), 'Determinants of FDI inflows in Europe: the role of the institutional context and Italy's relative position', Isae documento di lavoro, no. 16/01.

Devereux, M. and H. Freeman (1995), 'The impact of tax on foreign direct investment: empirical evidence and the implication for the tax integration scheme', *International Tax and Public Finance*, **2**(1), 85–106.

Devereux M. and R. Griffith (1998), 'Taxes and the location of production: evidence from a panel of US multinationals', *Journal of Public Economics*, **68**, 335–67.

Devereux, M. and R. Griffith (2002), 'The impact of corporate taxation on the location of capital: a review', *Swedish Economic Policy Review*, **9**(1), 79–102.

Dunning J.H. (1971), *The Multinational Enterprise*, London: Allen & Unwin.

European Council (2001), 'Company taxation in the internal market', Brussels.

Giannini, S. (1994), *Imposte e Mercato internazionale die capitali*, Bologna: Il Mulino.

Grubert H. (1997), 'Another look at the low taxable income of foreign-controlled companies in the United States', *OTA*, working paper no. 74.

Grubert, H. (1998), 'Taxes and the division of foreign operating income among royalties, interest, dividends and retained earnings', *Journal of Public Economics*, **68**, 269–90.

Grubert, H. and J. Mutti (1991), 'Taxes, tariffs and transfer pricing in multinational corporate decision making', *Review of Economics and Statistics*, **73**, 285–93.

Grubert, H. and J. Slemrod (1998), 'The effect of taxes on investment and income shifting to Puerto Rico', *The Review of Economics and Statistics*, **80**, 365–73.

Grubert, H., T. Goodspeed and D. Swenson (1993), 'Explaining the low taxable income of foreign controlled-companies', in A. Giovannini, R.G. Hubbard and J. Slemrod (eds), *Studies in International Taxation*, Chicago: University of Chicago Press.

Harris, D., R. Morck, J. Slemrod and B. Yeung (1993), 'Income shifting in United States multinational corporations', in A. Giovannini, R.G. Hubbard and J. Slemrod (eds), *Studies in International Taxation*, Chicago: University of Chicago Press.

Jog, V. and J. Tang (2001), 'Tax reforms, debt shifting and tax revenues: multinational corporations in Canada', *International Tax and Public Finance*, **1**, 5–26.

Kehoe, P. (1989), 'Policy cooperation among benevolent governments may be undesirable', *Review of Economic Studies*, **56**, 289–96.

King, M. and D. Fullerton (1984), *The Taxation of Income from Capital*, Chicago: University of Chicago Press.

Martinez Mongay, C. (2000), 'Ecofin's effective tax rate', *Economic Papers*, no. 146, Brussels.

McLure, C.E. (1986), 'Tax competition: is what's good for the private goose also good for public gander?', *National Tax Journal*, **39**, 341–8.

Musgrave, P. (1972), 'Inter nation equity, reprinted in *Tax Policy in the Global Economy: Selected Essays of Peggy B. Musgrave*, Cheltenham, UK and Northampton, MA, USA: Edward Elgar, 2002.

Nicodème, G. (2002), 'Sector and size effect on effective corporate taxation', *European Economy Economic Paper*, no. 175, Brussels.

OECD (1998), *Harmful Tax Competition: An Emerging Global Issue*, Paris: OECD.

OECD (2001a), *Transfer Pricing Guidelines for Multinational Enterprises and Tax Harmonisation*, Paris OECD.

OECD (2001b), *Measuring Globalisation: The Role of Multinationals in OECD Economies, Volume 1: The Manufacturing Sector*, Paris: OECD.

Rossetti S. and R. Schiattarella (2001), 'Un approccio di sistema all'analisi della delocalizzazione internazionale. Uno studio per il settore "made in Italy"', in N. Acocella and E. Sonnino, *Movimenti di Persone e di capitali in Europa*, IL Mulino Bologna.

Slemrod, J. (1990), 'The impact of the tax reform act of 1986 on the foreign direct investment to and from United States', in J. Slemrod (ed.), *Do taxes matter?*, Cambridge, MA: MIT Press.

Tiebout, C.M. (1956), 'A pure theory of local expenditure', *Journal of Political Economy*, **63**, 103–15.

6. Multinational enterprises, core labour standards and the role of international institutions

Matthias Busse

INTRODUCTION

The enormous growth of foreign direct investment (FDI), or the rise of multinational enterprises' (MNEs) activities across countries, is one of the most important signs of the increasing globalisation of the world economy over the past decade. For instance, whereas world production has grown by an annual average of 1.5 per cent in the period 1990 to 2001, trade has risen by 6 per cent and foreign direct investment by 23 per cent (UNCTAD, 2002). While most international investments take place within the Triad, Japan, the European Union and the United States, which make up three-quarters of global FDI inflows and some 85 per cent of outflows in that period, FDI flows to developing countries are relatively small. In the same period, the 49 least-developed countries[1] attracted less than 1 per cent of FDI inflows. Yet the ratio of FDI inflows to GDP in these countries amounted to 2.2 per cent in this period, while the world average was 1.9 per cent, signifying a higher relevance of FDI to least-developed countries.

While the pertinent literature is quite clear on the economic benefits of FDI inflows to the host country, since FDI, among other factors, is likely to increase the capital stock of the host country and to introduce new technologies and management systems,[2] there are concerns that the global competition to attract FDI could lead to undesirable outcomes. In particular, fears have been stated that there will be pressure to lower labour standards to a more 'investor-friendly' environment: in other words, fear of 'social dumping'. For instance, Amnesty International, a non-governmental organisation, has expressed its concern and reported on the actions of MNEs in poor countries:

> Many transnational corporations operate in countries with repressive administrations where the rule of law is weak, where the independence of the judiciary is

questionable, and where arbitrary arrest, detention, torture and extra-judicial ex-ecutions occur. The government may ban free trade union activity and deny its citizens freedom of association. Factory workers in plants from which companies source their products may be subject to inhuman and degrading working condi-tions. (Amnesty International, 2002)

In view of these concerns, it is surprising that only a few studies have explored the relationship between labour standards and FDI. Up to now, three studies have empirically examined that linkage. The OECD (1996, 2000) found no statistical relationship between the observance of fundamental work-ers' rights and FDI inflows. Rodrik (1996) regressed several indicators for labour standards, such as child labour and forced labour or union rights, on the value of investment by majority-owned US affiliates abroad as a fraction of the stock of such investment. Only the indicator for child labour is statisti-cally significant, and the coefficient implies that countries with more child labour attract less capital than democracies that protect child workers. Simi-lar to Rodrik's approach, Kucera (2002) regressed a number of indicators for fundamental labour standards on FDI inflows, but only the indicators for basic union rights are statistically significant. To sum up, the empirical evi-dence available in the literature has been rather inconclusive.

Against this background, this chapter seeks to shed light on the interaction between labour standards and decisions of MNEs on where to invest abroad. It concentrates on three questions: whether countries could gain a competi-tive advantage from low labour standards, and in that way influence FDI flows; whether MNEs have an influence on labour standards in the country of operation or whether they can improve respect for these standards; and what the implications are for international institutions.

In the following, the next section gives a brief overview of different defini-tions of labour standards and the equivalent ILO conventions, while the third section reports the results of empirical tests concerning the effect of labour standards on FDI flows. Subsequently, the reversed causation of that linkage, that is, the possible impact of MNEs on labour standards, is dealt with in the fourth section, and the fifth section continues with a discussion of some policy implications and the role of international institutions. The chapter ends with a summary of the major results and some concluding remarks.

CONCEPTS AND EXTENT OF LABOUR STANDARDS

There are basically two different sets of standards: 'other' and 'core' labour standards (OECD, 1996). The first relates to safety and health standards in the workplace, minimum wages or annual leave with pay. Since these issues are related to actual working and labour market conditions, sometimes called 'acceptable conditions of work', their worldwide introduction would be highly controversial. Core labour standards, on the other hand, focus on fundamental workers' and human rights and include (1) freedom from forced labour, (2) the abolition of exploitative forms of child labour, (3) equal opportunity in employment, and (4) fundamental union rights such as freedom of association and collective bargaining (ILO, 2002b). Because these basic workers' and human rights receive acceptance in nearly all countries and are less controversial than other labour standards, they will become the main focus of this chapter.

The above-mentioned four labour standards are also covered by the Declaration on Fundamental Principles and Rights at Work of the International Labour Organisation (ILO),[3] which was established in 1919 primarily for the purpose of adopting international standards to deal with fundamental labour conditions, such as 'injustice, hardship and privation' (ILO, 2002a). Though the mandate of the ILO was broadened later on, labour standards have remained one of the most important issues of ILO operations, if not the most important one.

All in all, the ILO has set up eight conventions on labour standards, two each on union rights, forced labour, child labour and discrimination (see Table 6.1). The total number of ratifications by member countries is typically within the range of 140 to 160. As for the convention on the worst forms of child labour (no. 182), this convention was only agreed on as recently as November 1999. ILO members are thus still in the process of ratifying this convention. Surprisingly, as of 1 January 2003, 83 countries have ratified all eight. Sometimes the exact wording or the understanding of these conventions does not comply with national regulations or laws (OECD, 1996).

However, the ratification of an international convention does not automatically result in (national) implementation. In fact, the ILO relies essentially on voluntary compliance, but supervises the carrying out of the ratified conventions. If an ILO member country fails to carry out recommendations of a Commission of Inquiry, the governing body is legitimated to recommend actions to the Conference to make sure that a country complies with it (ILO, 1989).[4] In the case of forced labour exacted by Myanmar's military, the governing body invoked the relevant article for the first time in its history. Since the government of Myanmar had not responded to recommendations of a Commission of Inquiry, the governing body and the International Labour Conference instructed the ILO to take a range of actions against the country. For instance, the ILO has recommended that governments and organisations of employers and workers reconsider their relations with Myanmar. Nevertheless it has not directly imposed sanctions against Myanmar. Rather the ILO has asked its member countries and international organisation to do so (ILO, 2002d).

Table 6.1   Ratification of ILO fundamental labour standards (as of 1 January 2003)

ILO convention	Number of countries having ratified the convention
Union rights	
(1) Freedom of Association and Protection of the Right to Organise Convention, 1948 (no. 87)	141
(2) Right to Organise and Collective Bargaining Convention, 1949 (no. 98)	152
Forced labour	
(3) Forced Labour Convention, 1930 (no. 29)	161
(4) Abolition of Forced Labour Convention, 1957 (no. 105)	158
Child labour	
(5) Minimum Age Convention, 1973 (no. 138)	120
(6) Worst Forms of Child Labour Convention, 1999 (no. 182)	132
Discrimination	
(7) Equal Remuneration Convention, 1951 (no. 100)	160
(8) Discrimination (Employment and Occupation) Convention, 1958 (no. 111)	158

Source: ILO (2002b).

EMPIRICAL RESULTS

To analyse the empirical effects of labour standards on FDI flows, a standard starting point would be to develop a basic theoretical model, incorporate these standards and then investigate any change in the level of them. Yet we do not have such a model. Researchers who have looked at the characteristics and behaviour of MNEs have come up with particular management skills, economies of scale and innovative product technologies as important determinants of both FDI and trade.[5] Moreover other studies have identified the market structure, for instance, the dynamics of oligopoly, as a further important factor for explaining FDI or have come up with political and economic stability, market size and growth, infrastructure, exchange rate risks, labour costs and so on as additional determinants.

Regarding the following empirical analysis, we have to rely on the most important variables that determine FDI flows. According to a survey by Chakrabarti (2001), these are the size of the market and growth rates. Hence, for the benchmark OLS regression of the FDI model, only market size (the variable is called GDP), quantified as average GDP per capita in current US dollars, and market growth (GROWTH), measured by average GDP per capita growth, are included. For the dependent variable FDI flows, the data used are net FDI inflows per capita in the reporting economy (FDI). Because FDI flows for a single country can fluctuate noticeably from year to year, a period of seven years, from 1995 to 2001, has been chosen.[6] As with most studies on the determinants of FDI, a semilog model has been used.

For the level of labour standards, five indicators are used. First, the gender-related development index (GDI) as an indicator for the degree of discrimination against women is employed. This is the UNDP (2002) index of discrimination against women in education and working life. The GDI measures gender variations in literacy rates, life expectancy, the combined gross primary, secondary and tertiary enrolment ratio and income levels. The index varies from 0 (very high discrimination) to 1 (no discrimination). Note that, by using the GDI, the definition of ILO 'discrimination with respect to employment and occupation' has been restricted to gender inequalities. Discrimination against minorities is thus not covered, owing to a lack of data. Yet the GDI covers a large extent of the 'spirit' of the two conventions on discrimination.

The next variable is CHILD, representing the occurrence of child labour, which can be defined as the percentage of children ages 10–14 who are active in the labour force. This indicator represents the ILO estimates of child labour. To ensure that a higher number in any of the five indicators implies a higher labour standard and, thus, to guarantee a straightforward interpretation of the following regression results, CHILD has been defined in opposite terms; that is, it measures the percentage of children in that age group who are *not* working: in other words, the non-prevalence of child labour.

The third variable, the indicator for forced labour, has been developed for the purposes of this study. Since the formation of an accurate measure of the extent of forced labour suffers heavily from the lack of precise quantitative data, qualitative measures have to be employed instead. The forced labour indicator used in the following is composed from the number of different kinds of forced labour that occur in a specific country to approximate the extent of forced labour in the country concerned. For each of the most important forms of forced labour, namely slavery and abduction, bonded labour and prison-linked forced labour, a dummy variable is introduced that can take a value of either 0 (form does not occur) or 1 (form occurs). Before adding up, the bonded labour dummy has been multiplied by two, indicating the specific importance and extensive prevalence of bonded labour. Having assessed each country, the respective dummy variables are added up to obtain the indicator value for a specific country. As a result, FORCED can take values between zero (forced labour does not exist) and four (forced labour is used in all three forms).[7]

The fourth variable, UNION, stands for basic union rights, such as freedom of association and collective bargaining rights. UNION is the indicator developed by the OECD (1996, 2000) based on extensive ILO studies as well as reports from international trade union organisations, for example the International Confederation of Free Trade Unions. In compiling their index, the OECD assessed 76 countries on a scale from 1 (union rights almost nonexistent) to 4 (union rights guaranteed in law and practice). And finally, the fifth indicator, CONVEN, represents the total number of ratified ILO conventions on labour standards (0–8).

Turning to the empirical results, column 1 of Table 6.2 reports the results for the benchmark regression. Incorporated were all 130 countries reporting FDI (foreign direct investment), GDP (gross domestic product) and GDP growth rate data for the considered period. Both dependent variables have the expected signs and are statistically significant at the 1 or 5 per cent level. In the remaining columns, 2 to 6, the coefficients for the five labour standards indicators are reported. Given that multicollinearity can be a problem with a set of similar variables, each indicator is included singly in the benchmark regression. Interestingly all four indicators that quantify de facto compliance with the ratification of the ILO conventions have positive signs and are statistically significant at the 1, 5 or 10 per cent level.

These results indicate that a higher level of discrimination against females, more child and forced labour, and poorer union rights are associated with lower FDI inflows; that is, countries with lower labour standards received a smaller amount of FDI per capita in the period 1995–2001 than would have been forecast on the basis of the other country characteristics. Conversely the number of ratified conventions (CONVEN) does not significantly affect FDI flows. CONVEN is slightly below zero, but not statistically significant. Besides, the number of ratifications as an indicator for de jure ratification is a poor measure of de facto compliance. This becomes quite clear if ratification and compliance for each of the four labour standards are compared. For this purpose, the number of ratifications for each of the four labour standards has been calculated. The variables are as follows:

CONDISC for the conventions on discrimination (no. 100 and no. 111),
CONCHILD for child labour conventions (no. 138 and no. 182),
CONFORCE for forced labour conventions (No. 29 and No. 105), and
CONUNION for union rights conventions (no. 87 and no. 98).

Table 6.2 Labour standards and foreign direct investment, OLS regression results for all countries

Independent variables	Dependent variable: FDI					
	(1)	(2)	(3)	(4)	(5)	(6)
Constant	−2.780***	−0.740	−1.397**	−2.189***	−3.240***	−3.082***
GDP	1.059***	0.859***	0.906***	0.994***	1.042***	1.044***
GROWTH	0.083**	0.063**	0.081**	0.088***	0.025	0.084**
GDI		1.198**				
CHILD			1.694**			
FORCED				0.679***		
UNION					0.663*	
CONVEN						−0.066
Adj. R²	0.74	0.77	0.75	0.76	0.79	0.74
N	130	118	126	130	67	130

Notes: See Appendix A for data sources; multicollinearity has been tested by the creation of variance inflation factors (VIF); all regressions pass the test at conventional levels; to save space, the standard errors have not been reported, instead ***, ** and * denote statistical significance at the 1%, 5% and 10% levels, respectively.

Table 6.3   Ratifications of ILO conventions and level of labour standards

Variables	Partial correlation
GDI/CONDISC	−0.01
CHILD/CONCHILD	0.07
FORCED/CONFORCE	−0.15
UNION/CONUNION	0.22

Note: See Appendix A for data sources.

Next, the partial correlations between these four variables and the equivalent indicators for compliance with labour standards have been computed (Table 6.3). The results show that the there is little accord between ratification and observance. The highest number is 0.22, which implies only a weak positive correlation. Even worse, the correlations for forced labour and the discrimination against females are negative, implying that those countries that ratify the corresponding conventions do not put a lot of effort into the monitoring of their observance.

On the whole, these findings clearly indicate that labour standards are positively associated with FDI inflows. Obviously the results are affected by the dominance of FDI flows between industrialised countries and regions like Japan, the European Union and the United States to a large extent (see page 124). To check whether the inclusion of high income has an important role, high and upper middle-income countries have been left out in a second set of regressions. The intention is to include only low-income or lower middle-income countries which, according to the World Bank (2002) are developing countries with a maximum GDP per capita in 1999 of US $2995. In this way, 85 developing countries have been identified and tested regarding the labour standard variables.

As can be seen from Table 6.4, the results are very similar to those of the first set of regressions. Though the overall fit of the regressions worsens, all signs and also the statistical significance of the labour standard variables are very similar. UNION is the exception, which might be explained by the relatively low number of countries for which data on union rights are available. Nevertheless the results do not depend on income levels, since labour standards are positively associated with FDI in low-income countries, too.[8]

Table 6.4 *Labour standards and foreign direct investment, OLS regression results for developing countries*

Independent variables			Dependent variable: FDI			
	(1)	(2)	(3)	(4)	(5)	(6)
Constant	-3.206***	0.135	-0.825	-2.405***	-5.061***	-3.653***
GDP	1.126***	0.729***	0.817***	1.021***	1.291***	1.125***
GROWTH	0.077*	0.049	0.082*	0.094**	0.024	0.092**
GDI		1.295*				
CHILD			1.857**			
FORCED				0.655***		
UNION					0.801	
CONVEN						-0.067
Adj. R²	0.45	0.46	0.46	0.50	0.48	0.45
N	85	76	82	85	31	85

Note: Developing countries can be classified as low- and lower middle-income countries with a GDP per capita in 1999 of US $2995 or less (World Bank, 2002); see Table 6.2 for further notes.

IMPACT OF MULTINATIONAL ENTERPRISES ON LABOUR STANDARDS

Considering the empirical evidence and the methodology used, one might argue that labour standards are not set exogenously as assumed in the analysis. In fact, MNEs may have an influence on labour regulations in the country of operation in that they improve respect for labour standards.[9] As a result, there might be a 'race to the top' rather than a 'race to the bottom' on these standards. In most cases, FDI brings technology, additional capital and new management techniques to the host countries. However, the question remains whether the role model of MNEs with respect to technology and management skills can also be applied to labour standards (OECD, 1996).

The answer to this question depends on two categories of potential influence: the direct and indirect impact of MNEs and FDI on such standards. The direct impact could be related to work relations between MNEs and their local workers, who could be the direct beneficiaries of MNEs' activities in their country. If the (home-country) corporate employment policies of foreign-owned enterprises are put into operation, workers benefit from (usually) higher standards in comparison to legal minimum requirements or actual working practices in the host countries.

An indirect impact may come up as MNEs require that their local suppliers use the same standards as in their own production. Then the workers of the local suppliers will benefit as well. Likewise, if MNEs have good relations with their workers, domestic companies may follow their example. An indirect impact could arise also if FDI raises GDP growth rates of the domestic economy by augmenting the capital stock, improving efficiency and so on. Higher incomes are probably the most important determinant for the level of labour standards. If countries become richer, they are more likely to have higher labour standards. For example, parents could afford to send their children to school instead of relying on their contribution to the overall family income.

Despite these positive effects, links between MNEs' activities and changes in the legal obligations for labour standards cannot be ruled out. Frequently MNEs are accused by non-governmental organisations of trying to lobby governments to lower standards, that is, to change labour legislation to meet their 'wishes'. Apart from anecdotal evidence from sometimes questionable sources, frequently in the form of the presentation of single cases rather than a comprehensive analysis, no published study has been undertaken to support this view (Kucera, 2002).

The empirical evidence available shows that MNEs do not employ child or forced labour (OECD, 2000). Likewise they usually do not discriminate against females or minorities in the host country of their operations. In contrast, there have been a few published accounts that MNE subcontractors violate labour standards, in particular regarding child labour (ILO, 2002c). With respect to the effects of MNE activities on basic union rights, there is contradictory evidence. In OECD countries, union density rates, that is, the percentage of workers that are members of a trade union, are higher in foreign-owned firms than in domestically controlled enterprises. This evidence conflicts with the claim that MNEs prefer union-free locations (Graham, 2000). In developing countries, the data available on union rights are much weaker, yet the much lower level of unionisation in export processing zones in comparison to the domestic economy as a whole tends to underline that MNEs do not improve basic union rights.

Table 6.5   Comparison of MNEs and average domestic manufacturing wages, 1994[1]

	All countries	High-income	Middle-income	Low-income
Average wage paid by MNEs, $000s[2]	15.1	32.4	9.5	3.4
Average domestic manufacturing wage, $000s	9.9	22.6	5.4	1.7
Ratio	1.5	1.4	1.8	2.0

Notes:
[1] Data apply to foreign affiliates of US firms and selected countries for which wage data are available.
[2] Total compensation paid by foreign affiliates of US firms (less wages paid to the firms' expatriate employees), divided by the number of non-US citizens employed by these affiliates.

Source: Graham (2000).

There is, however, strong evidence that MNEs do pay a wage premium, reflecting efforts to recruit relatively skilled workers (see Table 6.5). Wages paid by US foreign affiliates to poor-country workers are about double the domestic manufacturing wage level. In middle-income countries they are about 1.8 times the local wage. Moreover Graham (2000) also shows that wages in Mexico are highest near the border with the United States, a region where American-controlled firms are concentrated. Other studies confirm these results.[10] If MNEs do pay a wage premium to attract higher-skilled employees, it seems rather unlikely that, on average, labour standards are lower than in domestic enterprises, as the wage level and respect for fundamental workers' rights are usually closely linked (OECD, 2000).

POLICY IMPLICATIONS AND THE ROLE OF INTERNATIONAL INSTITUTIONS

In view of the empirical evidence on labour standards and FDI presented in the third section and the discussion of the reversed effects on pages 133–4, recent considerations[11] on whether labour standards should be included in the legal structure of international institutions, for instance, the World Trade Organisation (WTO), to implement multilateral investment rules appear to be inappropriate. But some industrialised countries are still calling for internationally binding rules on investment (and trade) regarding basic workers' and human rights. For instance, during the GATT[12] Uruguay Round, the United States and France tried unsuccessfully to include labour standards in trade talks. Subsequent attempts, at the WTO conferences in Singapore in 1996 and in Seattle in 1999, again failed. Unlike the Clinton administration, the current US President George Bush does not show any interest in international labour standards. Therefore the United States, until that time one of the leading supporters of labour standards within the framework of the WTO, is not pushing the matter forward as before.

The European Union, in contrast, is still strongly in favour of linking investment (and trade) and fundamental workers' rights and brought the issue to the negotiating table at the WTO conference in Doha in November 2001. This attempt was rejected by developing countries, which fear that industrialised nations might justify protectionist measures against foreign competition by claiming that their rivals violate basic workers' rights. It has been agreed that the issue of labour standards remains in the sphere of influence of the ILO. The WTO has been asked to 'take note of work under way in the ILO on the social dimension of globalisation' (WTO, 2001) and will organise talks at expert level about labour standards.

Despite the fact that the empirical results are unambiguous, it is clear that basic workers' rights may influence decisions on where to invest in some cases. To exemplify this, abuses of labour standards have been reported in particular in export-processing zones in Asian and Central American countries, where investors from South Korea and Chinese Taipei have been identified as responsible for violations of freedom-of-association rights (OECD, 1996, 2000). Lower standards in these export-processing zones might appeal to a few MNEs. In a similar fashion, the governments of Bangladesh and Pakistan have exempted export-processing zones from industrial relations and national labour legislation in order to increase their attractiveness as a location for FDI (ICFTU, 2002).

Apart from these reported individual cases, there is simply no justification on humanitarian grounds for extremely poor working conditions to exist in any country. The most important question is, thus, how to improve labour standards in these cases. On the whole, two approaches seem to be feasible: multilateral rules or trying to eliminate individual abuses of labour standards. At the multilateral level, efforts were made with the Multilateral Agreement on Investment (MAI). This agreement was negotiated by OECD countries from 1995 to 1998 (Hoang Mai, 2002).

Before the MAI negotiations started, OECD governments acknowledged two things: first, global rules on how to regulate foreign investment did not exist, and, second, these rules could have some beneficial effects, such as improving the benefits of MNEs' activities, while reducing their (supposedly) negative effects. Whereas the main focus of the MAI talks concentrated on rules for investment protection and dispute settlement, the OECD negotiators also talked about standards related to working practices regarding MNE activities in OECD countries (Graham, 2000). In fact, a provision had been included that intended to prevent the lowering of safety and health standards, as well as labour standards. In principle, the provision required those governments who should have signed the agreement not to lower labour standards as a way to attract FDI inflows. In case of a dispute, conflicting parties were to be able to bring their concern (or accusation) forward to the agreement's dispute settlement procedures. In that sense, the intended labour standard clause would have been enforceable.

At the end of 1998, the MAI talks broke down, partly because the investment talks were held by the OECD, not the WTO (Graham, 2000). The OECD has only 30 members, mainly countries that are relatively open to FDI, but countries like India and Indonesia, where strict regulations on FDI do exist, were excluded. In addition, the main task of the OECD consists of economic research; it had not held complicated negotiations like the MAI before. Finally the OECD does not have a legal apparatus or a dispute settlement procedure to deal with nations or firms that do not follow the agreed rules, while the WTO does. Any lack of practical enforcement power thus further undermined the credibility of the MAI and the talks failed after almost four years of negotiations. Though the MAI negotiations were unsuccessful and the provision on labour standards never came into force, it seems doubtful whether imposing sanctions on countries where poor labour standards prevail by means of multilateral agreements within the WTO, OECD or ILO is the most suitable way forward. To begin with, consider the case that only a single firm abuses labour standards. If sanctions were imposed on the whole country as a response, that would imply that innocent firms would be punished along with the guilty. That is hardly ever a sound economic policy. Furthermore the chance to impose sanctions may be exploited by industrialised countries to protect their markets against suspected 'unfair' competition from developing countries with poorer standards (Graham, 1997). Both effects could then lead to negative economic consequences, since sanctions are likely to be harmful to GDP growth rates (and, thus, FDI inflows) in low-income countries.

A more effective way to punish individual firms for allowing appalling labour conditions to exist on their production sites is product labelling. Freeman (1994) and Rodrik (1996) suggested this method, which has a number of advantages. Some economists favour the approach because the market mechanism can be employed. Product labelling requires that (imported) commodities be correctly distinguished by labels that state that the product has been produced without child labour, forced labour or other such undesired means. Consumers in industrialised countries might be ready to pay a higher price for improved standards. This approach could also lessen concerns about low standards by trade unions (in high-income countries) and non-governmental organisations and could provide an incentive for firms in the exporting nations to upgrade their standards without binding rules. In particular the voluntary participation of all parties involved is the most appealing argument for labelling, as it allows the willingness-to-pay rule to decide the level of harmonisation in labour standards and avoids internationally binding trade restrictions (Rodrik, 1996).

Despite these obvious advantages, there is also an important problem involved with labelling: owing to the likely premium on commodities with higher standards, labelling might create incentives for private firms to overstate the standards by which they abide. Consumers in importing countries cannot easily check the statements made on the labels, since information about the production process regarding working practices cannot be obtained free (Freeman, 1994). A remedy for this problem would be close governmental monitoring, but this involves bureaucratic interference and the problem of protectionism of lobbying groups anew.

A role for international institutions, particularly the ILO, arises in this context. The ILO does have extensive information on violations of labour standards and is (to some extent) able to find out which firms and/or countries do not follow the provisions in their recommendations and conventions. In addition, the ILO would be able to employ corps of inspectors that work within its organisation with the mission to visit production facilities in any (ILO member) country. These inspectors would be able to decide whether standards are being met or not (Varley, 1998). Finally governments of countries which are willing but not able to enforce labour standards should be able to get more financial and technical assistance from the ILO. This is likely to result in much higher effects on the improvement of basic human and workers' rights than binding international regulations within the WTO framework.

CONCLUDING REMARKS

The main focus of this chapter has been the linkage between labour standards and FDI, or the activities of MNEs. The results can be summarised in three points. First, in contrast to the conventional wisdom that MNEs prefer to invest in low-standard countries, improved workers' rights are, in fact, positively associated with FDI. As a consequence, the main argument of non-governmental organisations that, owing to the increasing globalisation of the world economy, countries will take on an intense competition for FDI, with 'social dumping' on these standards as the likely consequence, does not appear to be accurate. The empirical results show clearly that low standards are not a major attraction for MNEs. This outcome of the regression analysis has been soundly demonstrated for all four labour standards, namely abolition of child labour, elimination of forced labour, non-discrimination in employment and basic union rights. Running further regressions with a special focus on low-income and lower middle-income countries indicates that the empirical results are independent of income levels.

Second, considering the reversed causation, there has been little evidence that MNEs are likely to have a major impact on the level of labour standards in the host country of their operation. It can be expected that they actually increase respect for labour standards on account of their production facilities, which might lead to a 'race to the top' rather than a 'race to the bottom' on these standards. Yet the empirical evidence on this issue (in comparison to the first question) is much weaker owing to data deficiencies.

Finally the chapter discussed the arguments in favour of and against internationally binding rules regarding labour standards, showed other ways of improving these standards and argued about the role of international institutions. Clearly there are violations of basic workers' rights in a number of cases/countries. To deal with humanitarian concerns about the sometimes obvious abuse of workers' rights in individual cases, two recommendations have been proposed: sanctions should not be introduced as a means of countering breaches of binding rules within international institutions such as the WTO, as they are likely to be unfair towards guiltless workers and firms and more wasteful with respect to economic welfare and efficiency; product labelling, on the other hand, promises to be a more effective approach, since it allows for voluntary commitments to labour standards. Yet, even with product labelling, there could be an important role for international institutions, in particular for the ILO, in terms of closely monitoring the observance of labour standards, making financial and technical assistance available to poor countries which lack resources and staff, and providing more transparency about the outcome, that is, the observed violations of fundamental workers' rights.

NOTES

1. At present, there are 49 least-developed countries (UNCTAD, 2002) which have in common a GDP per capita of less than US $900.
2. See Klein *et al.* (2001) for a survey of studies on the economic effects of FDI in developing and emerging market countries.
3. For simplicity, the term 'labour standards' will be used for core labour standards in the following, except where stated otherwise.
4. According to Article 32 of the ILO constitution, the implementation of a recommendation can only be challenged before the International Court of Justice.
5. See Chakrabarti (2001) for a recent survey of the literature.
6. More specifically, the annual average for these seven years has been calculated. Accordingly, GDP and GROWTH are also annual averages for the same period. Data sources of all variables are reported in Appendix A.
7. See Appendix B for the assigned numbers for each country.
8. Further sets of regressions have been run to test the influence of income levels, yet neither statistical significance nor signs change considerably if other income groups are included in the regressions. To save space, the results have not been reported.
9. Unfortunately econometric tests on the question of whether labour standards are in fact endogenously determined could not be carried out, as the income level (GDP per capita) is the most important determinant of both FDI flows and labour standards.
10. See, for example, the studies by Aitken, Harrison and Lipsey (1996), Bora and Wooden (1998) and Rosen (1999).
11. For instance, see not only calls for binding labour standards by non-governmental organisations like Amnesty International (2002), but also Morris (2001) for an economic analysis and an overview of the literature.
12. General Agreement on Tariffs and Trade, which is the predecessor of the WTO.

REFERENCES

Aitken, Brian, Ann Harrison and Robert Lipsey (1996), 'Wages and foreign ownership: a comparative study of Mexico, Venezuela and the United States', *Journal of International Economics*, **40**, 345–71.

Amnesty International (2002), 'Business and human rights: a geography of risk' (Internet Posting: http://www.amnesty.org.uk).

Anti-Slavery International and ICFTU (2001), *Forced Labour in the 21st Century*, Brussels and London: Anti-Slavery International.

Avery, Christopher (2002), 'Business and human rights: a resource website (Internet Posting: http://www.business-humanrights.org/).

Bora, Bijit and Mark Wooden (1998), 'Human capital, foreign ownership and wages', working paper series no. 149, National Institute of Labour Studies, Adelaide.

Chakrabarti, Avik (2001), 'The determinants of foreign direct investment: sensitivity analyses of cross-country regressions', *Kyklos*, **54** (1), 89–113.

Freeman, Richard (1994), 'A hard-headed look at labour standards', in Werner Sengenberger and Duncan Campbell (eds), *International Labour Standards and Economic Interdependence*, Geneva: ILO, pp. 117–57.

Graham, Edward (1997), 'Should there be multilateral rules on foreign direct investment?' in John Dunning (ed.), *Governments, Globalization and International Business*, New York: Oxford University Press, pp. 481–505.

Graham, Edward (2000), 'Fighting the wrong enemy: antiglobal activists and multilateral enterprises', Institute for International Economics, Washington, DC.

Hoang Mai, Pham (2002), 'Regional economic development and foreign direct investment', *Journal of the Asia Pacific Economy*, **7**(2), 182–202.

ICFTU (2002), 'Annual survey of violations of trade union rights (various issues), International Confederation of Free Trade Unions' (Internet Posting: http:/www.ifctu.org).

ILO (1989), 'Constitution of the International Labour Organisation and Standing Orders of the International Labour Conference', ILO, Geneva.

ILO (2001), 'Stopping forced labour', International Labour Conference 89th Session 2001, Report I (B), International Labour Organisation, Geneva.

ILO (2002a), 'About the International Labour Organisation' (Internet Posting: http://www.ilo.org).

ILO (2002b), 'Ratifications of the ILO Fundamental Conventions' (Internet Posting: http://webfusion.ilo.org/public/db/standards/normes/appl/appl-ratif8conv.cfm?Lang=EN).

ILO (2002c), 'A future without child labour', International Labour Conference 90th Session 2002, Report I (B), International Labour Organisation, Geneva.

ILO (2002d), 'ILO governing body opens the way for unprecedented action against forced labour in Myanmar', ILO Communication (Internet Posting: http://www.ilo.org/public/english/bureau/inf/pr/2000/44.htm).

Klein, Michael, Carl Aaron and Bita Hadjimichael (2001), 'Foreign direct investment and poverty reduction', World Bank Policy Research Working Paper no. 2613, World Bank, Washington, DC.

Kucera, David (2002), 'Core labour standards and foreign direct investment', *International Labour Review*, **141**(1/2), 31–69.

Morris, David (2001), 'Free trade: the great destroyer', in Jerry Mander and Edward Goldsmith (eds), *The Case Against the Global Economy*, London: Earthscan, pp. 115–124.

OECD (1996), *Trade, Employment and Labour Standards: A Study of Core Workers' Rights and International Trade,* Paris: OECD.

OECD (2000), *International Trade and Core Labour Standards*, Paris: OECD.

Rodrik, Dani (1996), 'Labor standards in international trade: do they matter and what do we do about them?', in Robert Z. Lawrence, Dani Rodrik and John Whalley (eds), *Emerging Agenda for Global Trade: High Stakes for Developing Countries,* Washington Overseas Development Council Essay no. 20, Baltimore: Johns Hopkins University Press, pp. 35–79.

Rosen, Daniel (1999), 'Behind the open door: foreign enterprises in the Chinese marketplace', Institute for International Economics, Washington, DC.

UNCTAD (2002), *World Investment Report 2002*, New York and Geneva: United Nations.

UNDP (2002), *Human Development Report 2002*, Geneva: UNDP.

US Department of State (2002), *Victims of Trafficking and Violence Protection Act of 2000: Trafficking in Persons Report*, Washington, DC: US Government Printing Office.

Varley, Pamela (1998), 'The sweatshop quandary: corporate responsibility on the global frontier', Investor Responsibility Research Center, Washington, DC.

World Bank (2002), 'World development indicators', Data on CD-ROM.

WTO (2001), WTO Ministerial Declaration, Doha, Qatar, 14 November 2001 (Internet Posting: http://www-svca.wto-ministerial.org).

APPENDIX A: DEFINITION OF VARIABLES AND DATA SOURCES

Variable	Definition	Source
FDI	Foreign direct investment, net inflows in current US dollars, annual average for the period 1995–2001	World Bank (2002)
GDP	GDP per capita in current US dollars, annual average for the period 1995–2001	World Bank (2002)
GROWTH	Growth of GDP per capita in per cent, annual average for the period 1995–2001	World Bank (2002)
GDI	Gender-related development index, index 0–1, annual average for the period 1995–2000	UNDP (2002)
CHILD	Percentage of children ages 10–14 who are not working, annual average for the period 1995–2000	World Bank (2002)
FORCED	Indicator for core forms of forced labour (bonded labour, slavery and abduction, prison labour), scale 0–4, 1999	Anti-Slavery International and ICFTU (2001), Avery (2002), ILO (2001), US Depart. of State (2002)
UNION	Freedom of association and collective bargaining rights of unions, scale 1–4, 1999	OECD (1996, 2000)
CONVEN	Number of ratifications of the eight fundamental ILO conventions, 1999	ILO (2002b)
CONDISC	Number of ratifications of the two ILO conventions on discrimination (no. 100 and no. 111), 1999	ILO (2002b)
CONCHILD	Number of ratifications of the two ILO conventions on child labour (no. 138 and no. 182), 1999	ILO (2002b)
CONFORCE	Number of ratifications of the two ILO conventions on forced labour (no. 29 and no. 105), 1999	ILO (2002b)
CONUNION	Number of ratifications of the two ILO conventions on basic union rights (no. 87 and no. 98), 1999	ILO (2002b)

APPENDIX B: INDICATOR FOR FORCED LABOUR

Indicator = 2
Bangladesh, India, Nepal, Pakistan, Sri Lanka

Indicator = 1
Benin, China, Congo (Democratic Republic), Côte d'Ivoire, Indonesia,
Madagascar, Mauritania, Sierra Leone, Sudan

Indicator = 0
Albania, Algeria, Angola, Argentina, Armenia, Australia, Austria,
Azerbaijan, Bahamas, Barbados, Belarus, Belgium, Belize, Bolivia,
Botswana, Brazil, Bulgaria, Burkina Faso, Burundi, Cambodia, Cameroon,
Canada, Cape Verde, Central African Republic, Chad, Chile, Colombia,
Congo (Republic), Costa Rica, Croatia, Cyprus, Czech Republic, Denmark,
Djibouti, Dominican Republic, Ecuador, Egypt, El Salvador, Estonia,
Ethiopia, Fiji, Finland, France, Gabon, Gambia, Germany, Ghana, Greece,
Guatemala, Guinea, Guyana, Haiti, Honduras, Hungary, Iceland, Iran,
Ireland, Israel, Italy, Jamaica, Jordan, Kazakhstan, Kenya, Kyrgyzstan,
Latvia, Lebanon, Lesotho, Lithuania, Luxembourg, Macedonia, Malawi,
Malaysia, Maldives, Mali, Malta, Mauritius, Mexico, Moldavia, Mongolia,
Morocco, Mozambique, Netherlands, New Zealand, Nicaragua, Niger,
Nigeria, Norway, Panama, Papua New Guinea, Paraguay, Peru, Philippines,
Poland, Portugal, Romania, Russia, Samoa, Senegal, Seychelles, Singapore,
Slovakia, Slovenia, South Africa, South Korea, Spain, Swaziland, Sweden,
Switzerland, Syria, Tanzania, Thailand, Togo, Trinidad and Tobago, Tunisia,
Turkey, Uganda, Ukraine, United Kingdom, United States, Uruguay,
Uzbekistan, Venezuela, Vietnam, Zambia, Zimbabwe

Sources and definition: See text and Appendix A.

7. Foreign direct investment and wages

V.N. Balasubramanyam and David Sapsford

INTRODUCTION

Perhaps much more has been written on foreign direct investment (FDI) in the development process than on any other aspect of development economics. This should be of little surprise; the characteristics of FDI, its rapid growth and pivotal role in the process of globalisation in recent years, its intimate relationship with trade and its historical antecedents pose a variety of important and relevant researchable issues. These include the determinants of FDI, its impact on growth, trade, technical change and income distribution in the host countries. Wages, as the return to labour, influence these and other aspects of FDI in a number of ways. This brief chapter analyses the interrelationship between wages and FDI.

STYLISED FACTS

The propositions listed below may be stylised but not necessarily facts, in the sense that they are supported by robust empirical evidence. Nonetheless they provide an informative framework for discussing the relationship between wages and FDI.

1. FDI is attracted to low wage locations.
2. Foreign firms pay relatively high wages; they create a labour aristocracy and increase income inequalities in host countries.
3. Foreign firms pay high wages to skilled labour because of the skill-intensive nature of their technologies and thereby promote income inequalities between skilled and unskilled labour in host countries.
4. FDI reduces the wage gap between skilled and unskilled labour because foreign firms pay relatively high wages to unskilled labour.
5. Foreign firms tend to disperse production across a number of countries, fragment the labour they employ into different labour regimes and thereby weaken the bargaining power of labour unions for better pay and allowances.

Let us consider each of these in turn.

FDI is Attracted to Low Wage Locations

As the wage bill typically accounts for a substantial proportion of total costs, most studies argue that relatively low wage rates are a significant determinant of FDI, especially so in the case of production of labour-intensive goods and services (Dunning, 1993). Also, with globalisation, labour-intensive segments of the production process are hived off and located in low wage locations. As Dunning argues, much of the observed division of labour within multinational firms is accounted for by their desire to seek efficiency by locating capital and information-intensive activities in the developed countries and labour-intensive activities in developing countries. There are a number of empirical studies, mostly cross-section studies across countries and regions within a country, which incorporate a wage variable in regression equations to test the impact of wages on FDI. Although there are studies which appear to detect a positive relationship between wages and FDI, several do find a negative relationship (Pain, 1993; Kumar, 1994; Wei and Liu, 2001; Balasubramanyam and Salisu, 1991).

Several caveats are to be attached, however, to these findings. The first relates to the measurement of wages. Data on wage rates are not easily accessible and what is typically available is the wage bill and the number of employees. Wage rates arrived at by utilising the wage bill and number of employees may differ across countries, not because of differences in basic wage rates, but because of differences in allowances and other non-wage emoluments paid to labour. Also wage rates in these countries are not always adjusted for differences in price levels; that is, they are not based on PPP (purchasing power parity) exchange rates when national wage rates are converted into a common currency. The most significant caveat, though, is that it is not low nominal wage rates but low efficiency wage rates that are sought by profit-maximising firms. Estimating efficiency wage rates is fraught with problems.

Estimating the ratio of the wage rate to productivity of labour yields wage per unit of output. This may be high or low depending on labour productivity for a given nominal wage, but labour productivity may be influenced by the nature of the production function and choice of techniques adopted. Most empirical studies acknowledge the fact that it is efficiency wages and not nominal wages which influence investment decisions, but because of the problems associated with estimating efficiency wages they settle for nominal wage rates. The mixed bag of evidence they report may be due to the statistical problems associated with inaccurately measuring efficiency wages. Those studies which report a positive coefficient on the (nominal) wage variable in regression equations argue that relatively high wages signify relatively high labour skills and it is skills that foreign firms seek. Ideally most firms would seek relatively low wage locations with productivity levels comparable to those in their home countries. Investments in service industries in developing countries, such as those in India's software industry, are attracted by low efficiency wages. Productivity of local labour in software is on a par with that in the home countries, but nominal wages tend to be relatively low because of both substantial supplies of software engineers and the relatively high purchasing power of incomes in India. Then again foreign firms in processing industries located in export processing zones in developing countries are known to be footloose: they move from one locale to another as wage rates increase in the initial location. Wage rates, for instance in the Export Processing Zone (EPZ) in Mauritius may have increased over time, because of both increasing shortages of labour and growth in productivity over time. Firms in the zone may tend to relocate their investments in Madagascar, a low wage location. Here the firms are not seeking low efficiency wages but low nominal wages; if wage rates are sufficiently low in Madagascar they may maintain their profit shares by employing a larger volume of relatively less efficient labour at low wages. In sum the proposition that FDI is attracted to low wage locations is subject to a number of caveats, with the consequence that generalisations can be misleading.

Foreign Firms Pay Relatively High Wages and Create a Labour Aristocracy

The essence of the proposition here is that foreign firms pay relatively high wages compared with those paid in locally owned firms because of reasons unrelated to the productivity of labour. They do so to demonstrate they are good citizens (perhaps they wish to placate local labour unions), they do so to prevent entry of new firms, and they do so because of labour market imperfections in host countries. A further possibility is that they pay higher wages in the belief that this will exert a positive effect on labour productivity. The basic notion here is a development of the longstanding arguments relating to the so-called 'economy of high wages' (for example, Leibenstein, 1957). Somewhat confusing, in the context of the current discussion, is the fact that such models, which see labour productivity as being positively related to wage rates, are nowadays referred to as efficiency wage models (for example, Akerlof and Yellen, 1986).

It may be argued that in China foreign firms pay higher wages compared with those in state-owned enterprises because they have to compete for labour in the so-called 'privileged sector'. The privileged sector consists of educated labour with access to employment in state-owned enterprises which provide a variety of non-wage benefits, such as housing and health benefits. Foreign firms have to pay higher wages to entice these workers away from the state-owned enterprises even though the technology and skills they bring into the country are no different from those in the state-owned enterprises (Zhao, 2001). Unskilled labour, however, is left behind as it does not share the privileges enjoyed by skilled labour in locally owned enterprises. Such relatively high wage rates paid by foreign firms exacerbate income inequalities between skilled and unskilled labour. Zhao produces empirical evidence to show that returns to educated labour in foreign firms in China are substantially higher than those in state owned enterprises.

The proposition raises several issues. First, is it likely that the relatively high wages foreign firms pay merely compensate labour for the loss of social benefits provided by state owned enterprises? In the event that the wage rates are higher than those required to compensate labour for its loss of social benefits there would be a distortion. Second, the wage policies of both foreign-owned and state-owned firms may prove to be a major obstacle for locally owned private firms in China. Also unskilled labour may enjoy none of the privileges and work for low wages in foreign firms. In these cases FDI may prove to be less than favourable for growth of skills and the development of locally owned firms in China. Zhao (2001), though, argues that the wage policies of foreign firms in China may promote education (all training and learning) and schooling (within schools only), as labour would invest in education to gain profitable employment in foreign-owned firms. This may though be a second best policy. The first best policy would be to remove the distortions introduced by state owned firms in the form of housing and medical benefits which results in labour immobility. The case of China, however, endorses the proposition that institutional factors may be important in explaining observed wage differences between groups of labour and these factors may limit the benefits FDI can confer on the economy as a whole.

Foreign Firms Pay Relatively High Wages to Skilled Labour

This is a familiar proposition which merely states that foreign firms bring in skill-intensive technologies and pay relatively high wages to the skilled labour required to operate them. Here there are no distortions from inflows of FDI and it may serve to augment stocks of human capital in the country. Also locally owned firms may be forced to compete for skilled labour with foreign firms, and such competition may promote the diffusion of skills from foreign-owned to locally owned firms. This may be so if locally owned firms not only invest in labour training but also entice labour away from foreign firms with all the training and experience it may have acquired.

Admittedly, increased wages to skilled labour paid by foreign firms would increase income inequalities between skilled and unskilled labour. Technological change and orientation of demand for products towards skill-intensive products are bound to put unskilled labour at a disadvantage. The policy option in this case is labour training and investments in education.

Foreign Firms Pay Relatively High Wages to Unskilled Labour and Reduce the Wage Gap

The relatively high wages paid to unskilled labour here refers to wage rates over and above the opportunity cost of labour in developing countries. Here again it is China which provides an apt case, with FDI in labour-intensive activities, mostly located in export processing zones, absorbing a high proportion of unskilled labour. In these cases the employment creation effect of FDI is much more important than the relatively high wages foreign firms pay unskilled labour. If much of the unskilled labour is either unemployed or engaged in activities with a low marginal product, the wage rates paid by foreign firms may not be 'high'. It is the absorption of surplus resources by foreign firms and the subsequent exports which such investments generate that are the benefits to the host countries. It is likely that there is very little transfer of technology and skills from such investments. Nonetheless foreign firms provide an outlet for surplus resources and generate exports of labour-intensive components and products. These investments would be of the type recognised by Myint as *vent for surplus* benefits of trade and foreign investment. These benefits are, however, subject to mobility of labour between sectors and regions within the host country. The downside of such unskilled labour absorbing FDI may be that it promotes regional inequalities of incomes and employment opportunities, as in the case of China's coastal versus interior regions. The policy option in these cases may be to encourage movement of capital to labour in the regions rather than move labour to capital in the coastal areas where much of China's FDI is concentrated.

FDI and the Fragmentation of Labour

The argument here is that, by dispersing production facilities across a number of countries, multinationals are able to delimit the power of labour unions (Ietto-Gillies, 2002). Dispersion of production facilities fragments labour across countries into differing labour regimes and thereby prevents labour organisations from successfully bargaining for improved pay and conditions. The companies are able to play off one set of labour unions against the others and may move production facilities from organised labour locations to those which have lax labour regimes. However, there is not much evidence in

favour of this proposition. Multinationals do disperse production across countries. Thus they do take advantage of differing locational advantages, including
availability of natural resources and cheap labour. But whether or not they do
so in order to thwart the objectives of labour organisations is arguable. For
the argument to be sustained, evidence has to be provided to show that within
the developing countries labour is organised and it has the resources, expertise and bargaining power. Whilst this may be so in some of the developing
countries, in most countries efficient labour organisations are a rarity. In any
case, in most countries the attitude of labour towards FDI is benign because
of the jobs and relatively high wages it provides. But if multinationals are
able to play one set of labour unions off against the others the policy option,
as argued below, is for the formulation and implementation of an international framework on labour legislation.

MAJOR EMPIRICAL QUESTIONS TO BE ANSWERED

In the cause of symmetry this section raises five major empirical questions
regarding the relationship that exists between FDI and wages. First, which of
the various wage measures that are suggested by theory do MNEs actually
take into account when making decisions regarding whether to invest overseas and, if doing so, precisely where to invest and what sort of investment to
undertake, for example when considering greenfield versus mergers versus
acquisitions?

Second, how important, compared to other factors entering into the FDI
decisions of MNEs, are wages? In terms of the eclectic OLI (ownership,
location and internationalisation) paradigm, how important (for example,
within an ANOVA framework) are wages compared to other 'L [locational]
factors'? Further, as has been made clear in the previous section, the prevailing wisdom is that MNEs take account not of nominal wages but of some
form of efficiency wage (in the language of the trade theorist) or unit labour
cost (in the language of the labour economist). However described and defined, such measures have two components: the nominal wage (presumably
measured in either the currency of the investing country or the US$) as
denominator and some measure of average or marginal productivity as the
numerator. However, nothing is currently known as to the relative strength or
importance in the investment calculus of MNEs of the two separate elements
that are combined to give this ratio.

Third, by their very nature investment decisions involve dynamic considerations (most obviously DCF and IRR-type calculations) into which expected
values must, in practice, be fed. Given that the wage variable that will be fed
into such calculations is a ratio, an important question is whether expecta-

tions of the nominal wage element (the numerator) are more accurately formed than those relating to the productivity term as the denominator). While it might be argued that from the MNE's viewpoint that the latter is inherently more predictable than the former (after all, the MNE may be merely transferring a given production method (with a given, known, capital–labour ratio) from the home to the host country. However, little if anything is known about the actual out-turn of either component relative to expectations and predictions formulated at the time the investment decision was actually made (or not made). Indeed future research that might shed light upon this important question could usefully focus not on FDI, but rather upon foreign direct disinvestment, in order to highlight not only 'what went wrong' but more specifically to investigate in the context of the wage variable whether it was a greater unpredictability of productivity relative to nominal (common currency) wages (or vice versa) that contributed most to the decision to disinvest. Although nothing is currently known regarding potential asymmetries here, there is certainly some anecdotal evidence from recent disinvestment decisions in the context of Taiwanese electronics firms in the UK, and US computer firms in the Republic of Ireland, to suggest that inaccurate predictions of labour productivity, rather than nominal wages, were a major contributing factor.

Fourth, although the currently perceived wisdom is that MNEs pay higher wages than local firms, it is not at all clear that this is actually the case even for a 'properly defined' wage variable when one sees the issue through the eyes of the labour economist who would require that proper account be taken of such considerations as net advantages and non-competing groups, segmented labour markets, not to mention the dynamics of labour quality and prevailing labour market distortions and, most importantly, the potential relationship between high wages and improved labour productivity according to the efficiency wage hypothesis, discussed above.

Finally, given that this volume is produced under the auspices of the University of Innsbruck's Centre for the Study of International Institutions it is appropriate to focus upon the implications of the preceding discussion for the structure of international institutions. In a real sense, what we have here is a situation of fine and mature – but nevertheless old – wine in new bottles. As is abundantly clear from the foregoing discussion, the rapidly growing importance of FDI as a form of international factor mobility takes us towards a situation where certain MNEs are, or will become, monopsonists in certain sectors of the international market for particular sorts of labour (for example, IT specialists of certain sorts). As any intermediate textbook on labour economics reminds us (see, for example, Sapsford and Tzannatos, 1993) the occurrence of monopsony in a labour market not only leads to the possible occurrence of so-called 'monopsonistic discrimination' (as demonstrated long

ago by Pigou, of varying degrees) but also to distortions in resource allocation within the domestic economy. Since by its very nature it seems fanciful
to suppose that the monopsonistic power of MNEs in host country labour
markets can be controlled by legislation, an alternative is to recognise the
result long established in the labour economics literature according to which
it is possible, in principle at least, to return to the Pareto optimal/efficient
allocation of resources by introducing an equal but opposite (or countervailing)
distortion on the other (that is, the seller's) side of the labour market.

The obvious contender here is the formation of an international, or perhaps it
would more appropriately be termed as a multinational, trade union. Bargaining theory suggests that the ultimate outcome of collective wage and
employment bargaining under such a bilateral monopoly depends, amongst
other things, upon relative bargaining powers. It is, however, possible that
one outcome is that of Pareto efficiency in resource allocation of the sort that
exists in the world of microeconomics textbooks, where the usual assumptions of pervasive perfect competition prevail. This idea is not new and was
widely discussed in the labour economics and industrial relations literature
throughout the 1960s and 1970s, especially in respect of the labour markets
for transport workers (including seamen and airline pilots), dock workers and
coal miners. Perhaps the wine has now come to maturity if we substitute the
market for high-level IT analysts for coal miners. However, let us finish on a
note of caution, for Pareto efficiency is only one of a range of possible
outcomes that can emerge from such collective bargaining. Maybe the time
has finally come when we actually need a new international agency to oversee the operation of this sort of international or – more appropriately –
transnational collective bargaining. The objective of this body, perhaps appropriately named the Transnational Labour Court (TLC), might simply be
specified as seeking to ensure that the outcome to emerge from such
transnational collective wage bargaining approaches, as far as is practically
possible, that which corresponds to the Pareto-efficient allocation. This is a
tall order but one which may occupy a prominent position in the future
agenda regarding reform of the international institutions governing world
trading relations.

CONCLUSIONS

In this short chapter we have argued that, although much is known about the
role played by wages in the process of FDI seen as a form of international

capital mobility, there are still a number of important issues (both theoretical and empirical) about which rather too little is known. Therefore we hope that this chapter has provided a first step in the formulation of a research agenda which will ultimately lead to a greater understanding of the wage–FDI nexus. At the institutional level we have recognised some of the major changes that are being made to the structure of world labour markets and suggested the formulation of a new international institution designed to ensure that, at the global level, the gains from FDI as a particular form of trade might be maximised and distributed equitably in the Paretian sense.

REFERENCES

Akerlof, G. and J. Yellen (eds) (1986), *Efficiency Wage Models of Labour Markets*, Cambridge: Cambridge University Press.
Balasubramanyam, V.N. and M. Salisu (1991), 'Export promotion, import substitution and direct foreign investment in less developed countries', in A. Koekkoek and L. Mennes (eds), *International Trade and Global Development*, London: Routledge.
Dunning, J. (1993), *Multinational Enterprises and the Global Economy*, Wokingham, UK: Addison-Wesley.
Ietto-Gillies, G. (2002), *Transnational Corporations: Fragmentation Amidst Integration*, London: Routledge.
Kumar, N. (1994), *Multinational Enterprises and Industrial Organisation: The Case of India*, New Delhi: Sage Publications.
Leibenstein, H. (1957), 'The theory of underemployment in backward economies', *Journal of Political Economy*, **65**(1), 91–103.
Pain, N. (1993), 'An econometric analysis of foreign direct investment in the United Kingdom', *Scottish Journal of Political Economy*, **40**(1), 1–23.
Sapsford, D. and Z. Tzannatos (1993), *Economics of the Labour Market*, London: Macmillan.
Wei, Y. and X. Liu (2001), *Foreign Direct Investment in China: Determinants and Impact*, Cheltenham, UK and Northampton, MA, USA: Edward Elgar.
Zhao, Y. (2001), 'Foreign direct investment and relative wages: the case of China', *China Economic Review*, **12**, 40–57.

8. Coordination failures and the role of foreign direct investment in least developed countries: exploring the dynamics of a virtuous process for industrial upgrading

Brian Portelli

INTRODUCTION

Attitudes towards foreign direct investment (FDI) in least developed counties (LDCs) have changed considerably over the last two decades, in the context of widespread adoption of economic liberalisation doctrine, whether taken up voluntarily or through World Bank-sanctioned structural adjustment programmes. These changing attitudes refer to the so called 'New Economic Model' (Reinhardt and Peres, 2000), characterised by the adoption of outward-looking economic policies, particularly in the emphasis of promoting economic growth through foreign investment and efforts for greater participation in international trade.[1] FDI is seen as having a central, important role to play in national development strategies and is viewed as the engine with which to exploit and sustain the competitiveness of indigenous resources and capabilities (UNCTAD, 1999).[2] The present policy stance vis-à-vis FDI represents in many ways a dramatic turnaround, particularly so in the case of those LDCs which until the 1980s practised the outright barring of FDI activity in domestic markets (Caves, 1982). The marked change in attitudes of LDCs towards FDI also emanates from the recognition of the accelerating pace of technical change and the emergence of integrated production networks of MNEs (Lall, 2000a). Indeed FDI can play an important role in national development strategies, particularly as regards the potential contribution to host country industrial and technological development. It is also becoming increasingly clear that the less developed a country is, the greater usually are the expectations placed on FDI to alleviate resource and skill constraints (Noorbakhsh *et al.*, 2001) through the application of ownership-specific advantages in the form of financial and human resources, technology and knowledge (Dunning, 1993).

In this respect, LDCs explicitly seek to encourage MNE activity as a source of much-needed capital and technology and hope that inward FDI flows will fill the savings, investment and production gaps in these underdeveloped economic contexts. However, whereas some 'gaps' can be filled immediately (investment, production, employment, tax revenue), other 'gaps' inextricably linked to industrial upgrading such as skills, capability and technology development take time to emerge or possibly never take place. Furthermore benefits of inward FDI are more likely to emerge from that kind of FDI which is likely to generate positive spillovers (Lall, 1993; Narula and Dunning, 2000). This 'right' kind of FDI tends to shy away from LDCs. All these factors prompt some uncertainty about the extent of realising this potential contribution of FDI in the host country industrial development.

We think it is important to place this current policy 'fervour' towards FDI in the context of what is actually happening with regard to the development and upgrading of the host country competitiveness and industrial development in general. Although there is a tendency to categorise economies within a dichotomy of either inward-looking, import/substituting policy orientation (IL–IS) or outward-looking, export-oriented policy stance (OL–EO) (Ozawa, 1992; Narula, 1996) this may be an oversimplification, since in reality there tends to be a hybrid policy orientation. Even though LDCs may be adopting outward-looking economic policies, their industrial policies and productive capacities are still mired in development models implicitly based on inward-looking, import substitution policy stances. Therefore, whereas LDCs have registered some success in attracting much-needed FDI flows to their economies (as a result registering some success in their outward-looking economic strategies), it is increasingly evident that the host of socioeconomic systems are still characterised by weak absorptive capacities. The extent of these underdeveloped domestic capacities is to a certain extent reflected in the generic location factors (L_H) that LDCs possess, particularly with regard to the low quality of human capital and the weak absorptive capacity and capabilities of the domestic firms.

This chapter is motivated by the belief that in LDCs a coordination failure exists between the progress registered in outward-looking policies, specifically FDI policies, on the one hand, and the stagnant, underdeveloped domestic capability systems, on the other. At the outset, this coordination failure seems to undermine the potential to leverage FDI for industrial upgrading purposes. Indeed we argue here that this coordination failure is tantamount to the limitations of FDI as a *sine qua non* for industrial development. Notwithstanding that the role of MNEs is seen as a means to actualise the process of technology transfer and FDI does represent the most efficient option to promote a process of industrial development (Narula and Dunning, 2000), there are obvious limitations of FDI as a driver of technology and industrial development. FDI does not automatically lead to positive externalities in the host economy. For example, when MNEs seek to transfer knowledge, they prefer to use technologies that are suited (first and foremost) to their particular needs, and the purposes for which they have made the investment. MNEs tailor their investment decisions to the existing market needs, and the relative quality of location advantages (especially skills and capabilities that the domestic economy has a comparative advantage in; see Lall, 2002a). Hence the extent to which FDI is a driver of industrial upgrading depends on the quality of location advantages and how these advantages are developed over time.

A process of industrial development which has its roots at the micro level essentially must start with the interaction of MNEs with host country economic agents (domestic firms and individuals). Industrial upgrading presupposes that there is a virtuous interaction between ownership-specific advantages of the MNEs and the location-specific advantages of the host country that emerge from the assets and capacities of domestic economic agents. The virtuous process refers to the cumulative causation mechanism between the respective advantages, which potentially leads to industrial upgrading over time (Dunning, 1988). However, whether this virtuous process occurs depends on the nature of location advantages possessed by domestic economic agents. In an optimal scenario, location advantages in LDCs should be transformed from 'generic' to more 'created' asset types (Narula and Dunning, 2000). Central to the upgrading of local assets is the issue of the development of absorptive capacities and capabilities. The point here is that the process of developing location advantages, primarily through improved capabilities of domestic economic agents, determines the application of more sophisticated ownership-specific advantages of the MNE which are tenable to industrial and technological development. Hence it is essentially non-FDI changes in a host country location-specific advantages that determine FDI-induced changes crucial to industrial upgrading, for FDI-led industrial upgrading needs to be domestically enabled through the upgrading of host location factors.

The challenge lies in the process of upgrading location factors, which is essentially a gradual process when taking into account the socioeconomic context of LDCs. We stress the point that a virtuous process is essentially a gradual process spanning various successive phases, since capabilities and asset development follow a certain path dependency. In this chapter we present a simple micro model through which we project the dynamics of a virtuous process between MNEs and host country economic agents over different phases. We operationalise the interaction between location advantages and ownership advantages and the determinant feature of location advantages by referring to MNE linkages and spillovers in the host economy. As linkages provide a channel for spillovers (Lall, 1980), we use a taxonomy of linkages that potentially take place as a result of FDI entry and analyse spillovers that emerge from them. This idea is based on the premise that there is an interdependence between types of MNE domestic linkages and resultant spillover effects and that the nature of linkages/spillovers depends on the interaction between respective ownership and location advantages.

In the first section of the chapter, we take a closer look at what lies at the heart of this coordination failure in LDCs, focusing on why FDI is not a *sine qua non* for industrial development since the upgrading in the host country absorptive capacity is the determinant factor. We operationalise absorptive capacity and capability with reference to the domestic economic agents that potentially interact with MNEs. In the following section, we present the micro model to explain the trajectory and dynamics of a virtuous process leading to FDI-led industrial upgrading. The last section will present the main conclusions.

COORDINATION FAILURES AND THE LIMITATIONS OF FDI AS A DRIVER OF INDUSTRIAL DEVELOPMENT

FDI is nowadays regarded as a primary (and explicit) means by which industrial development can be promoted. This is based on the premise that the availability of foreign capital and technology is an important means of economic catch-up for LDCs. This importance has been further propagated by the idea that FDI is a *sine qua non* for development, an idea implicit in the Washington Consensus approach. This idea is based on the notion that markets for knowledge are efficient, that FDI is the same thing as technology imports (with the addition of capital flows) and that these technological imports will generate positive externalities and spillovers to domestic economic agents and lead to host country industrial development. However, as will be argued, this argument may have a number of flaws.

We maintain that FDI is not a *sine qua non* for development. FDI does not automatically lead to positive externalities in the host economy, nor are MNEs in the business of economic development, ready to serve host government economic development objectives. When and where MNEs seek to transfer technology and knowledge, they prefer to use technologies that are suited (first and foremost) to their own needs, and to the purposes for which they have made the investment decision. The kinds of activity and the level of competence of the subsidiary are also codetermined by the nature of the location advantages of the host country. That is to say, while MNE internal factors such as their internationalisation strategy, the role of the new location in their global portfolio of subsidiaries and the motivation of their investment are pivotal in the structure of their investment, they are dependent on the available location-specific resources which can be used for that purpose. Location-specific factors include all aspects of industrial and investment policy which can determine the kinds of incentives provided by the host country, as well as more 'traditional' location advantages such as market size, agglomeration economies, infrastructure and asset availability.[3]

In LDCs, FDI is largely 'received' in underdeveloped host socioeconomic systems, characterised by weak domestic capacities and capabilities. These systems comprise economic agents (individuals and firms) and institutions,[4] and refer to the wider concept of a host country's socioeconomic framework, which shapes the receptor conditions of the host country. Gray (2000a) argues that 'a policy of open industrialisation which encourages inward FDI requires that the country develops its 'socio-economic infrastructure' in order to be able to attract inward direct investment and to produce goods of quality required by foreign customers' (p. 1).[5] A socioeconomic system receiving FDI becomes a determinant factor for the objective of industrial upgrading objectives. Inherent in the systems concept is the notion of social capability. The concept of social capability, first introduced by Ohkawa and Rosovsky (1973), generates extensive debate and analysis, since it incorporates a wide variety of issues, including the adequacy of political, financial, educational and economic systems, all of which have an impact on development and, our specific concern here, on industrial development. Abramovitz (1990, 1994, 1995) uses social capability and technological congruence to explain what factors can undermine or enable technological and industrial development. Abramovitz uses technological congruence in the sense that technological and industrial development depends on past evolution of knowledge, competencies, economic conditions and technical capabilities. As 'a country's ability to exploit the opportunities afforded by existing best practice is limited by its current capabilities' (Abramovitz, 1994, p. 25), industrial development necessitates that a country's ability to exploit knowledge opportunities be in place. Laggard economic units must possess (inter alia) the social capability and the absorptive capacity to catch up and converge with economic units at the frontier.

Our argument here is that the absence of or weaknesses in absorptive capacity relates to the weak 'sophistication' of a country's socioeconomic infrastructure. Absent or underdeveloped capacity, in institutions, physical and human capital or the private sector undermine the ability to absorb and efficiently utilise knowledge that may potentially be made available to them.[6] Absorptive capacity (or lack of) supports (or undermines) the accumulation of technological knowledge and technological progress supports (or undermines) the further development of absorptive capacity in a cumulative, interactive and virtuous (vicious process) during the process of industrial development.

Even though LDCs attract marginal shares of global inward FDI flows, the absolute value has been increasing over the last two decades. This partly reflects the warming of attitudes towards foreign investment and more out-ward-looking economic policies. From the early 1970s to 2000, inward FDI to LDCs as a group increased from $103.6 million to $4.4 billion (see Table 8.1). The relevance of these flows to aggregate economic activity in LDCs is marked, as emerging from the share of inward FDI stock to GDP and the share of inward FDI flows to gross investment (Table 8.1). These indicators partly reflect the potential contribution of FDI to economic activity and industrial development in least developed hosts. However, the reality of leveraging FDI for industrial upgrading must be analysed in the context of the socioeconomic systems of LDCs. It is evident that FDI flows are attracted in relatively stagnant economic socioeconomic systems. Human capital re-mains low and the technological structure of industrial activity remains extensively resource and low technology-based (Lall, 2000b, 2000c) (see Table 8.2). What is more, LDCs' position in terms of industrial value added and international competitiveness reflects the underdeveloped capacity and capabilities of the local firms (see Table 8.3).

The conditions, especially with regard to the location factors (absorptive capacity of human capital and the domestic private sector), are still untenable for the process of industrial upgrading. A virtuous process of technological accumulation and investment, FDI-led but domestically enabled, necessitates that an adequate minimum level of absorptive capacity be present initially in the host country. The importance of having appropriate receptor conditions in place is highlighted by Borensztein *et al.* (1998) and Xi (2000). Both show that FDI has a positive impact on economic growth only in those developing countries that have attained a certain minimum level of absorptive capacity. Romer (1993) reports evidence of a similar threshold effect for the ability of a country to benefit from spillovers generated by imports of machinery and equipment. LDCs are still in a pre-catching up stage (Criscuolo and Narula, 2002) since their systems still lack a threshold level of absorptive capacity. Henceforth efforts first and foremost need to be directed at reaching that threshold level of absorptive capacity that will determine the movement along the gradual process of industrial upgrading.

The attainment of a threshold level of absorptive capacity reflects the efforts to develop 'generic' location advantages, in the context of the signifi-cance and the necessity of a host country possessing more 'created' location advantages (Narula and Dunning, 2000). The development of absorptive capacity essentially involves the creation of the appropriate quality and quan-tity of human capital and domestic private investment. There is strong empirical evidence showing that the development of capacities and capabilities is cru-cial to more FDI inflows, consolidation of existing MNE activity and enabling

Table 8.1 FDI indicators

	Annual averages of FDI inflows (millions of dollars), 1970–2000						
	1970–74	1975–9	1980–84	1985–9	1990–94	1995–9	2000
World	17 444.9	30 029.4	58 179.6	129 492.2	200 950.7	592 297.9	1 270 764.3
Developed countries	14 038.5	22 143.9	39 449.8	105 984.8	131 338.5	401 502.1	1 005 177.6
Share of total	80.5	73.7	67.8	81.8	65.4	67.8	79.1
Developing countries	3 406.4	7 872.3	18 711.9	23 400.3	65 570.8	172 712.8	240 167.4
Share of total	19.5	26.2	32.2	18.1	32.6	29.2	18.9
LDCs	103.6	344.7	349.4	598.9	1 459.7	3 259.4	4 414.3
Share of total	0.6	1.1	0.6	0.5	0.7	0.6	0.3
Africa	92.3	316.6	306.3	565.2	824.7	2 693.3	3 893.5
of which oil exporting	4.1	0.7	74.8	192.4	218.0	929.8	1 800.0
Latin America and the Caribbean	5.0	8.1	8.3	6.8	3.0	9.3	13.2
Asia and the Pacific	6.3	20.0	34.9	26.9	632.1	556.7	507.5
Share of Africa LDCs in total LDCs	89.1	91.8	87.6	94.4	56.5	82.6	88.2
Share of oil exporting African LDCs in total Africa LDCs	4.4	0.2	24.4	34.0	26.4	34.5	46.2

The relevance of FDI, by economy and region

Inward stock as percentage of GDP	1980–84	1985–9	1990–94	1995–9
World	6.7	8.1	9.3	13.1
Developed countries	5.2	6.6	8.4	11.3
Developing countries and economies	11.9	14.5	14.4	20.1
LDCs	3.8	4.4	7.0	11.4
Africa	4.9	6.2	11.9	20.3
Latin America and the Caribbean	6.0	5.6	6.9	5.1
Asia and the Pacific	1.7	1.5	2.8	4.9

Inward flows as a percentage of GFCF		1989–94	1995–9
World		4.1	9.2
Developed countries		3.7	8.6
Developing countries and economies		5.2	10.6
LDCs		5.7	6.1
Africa		6.6	16.4
Latin America and the Caribbean		–	1.9
Asia and the Pacific		4.2	1.6

Source: World Investment Report, various issues, UNCTAD.

Table 8.2   Human capital and technological structure

	Tertiary total and technical enrolments					
	1987			1995–8		
	Number (thousands)	World shares (per cent)	Number per 1000 population	Number (thousands)	World shares (per cent)	Number per 1000 population
Total tertiary enrolment						
Industrialised economies	26 630	56.5	34.3	33 775	44.9	40.1
Developing economies	20 473	43.5	6.3	35 346	47.0	8.7
High and upper-middle income	5 998	12.7	15.6	8 849	11.8	18.3
Lower-middle income	6 741	14.3	12.8	12 443	16.5	18.4
Low income	7 734	16.4	3.3	14 053	18.7	4.8
Low income (without China and India)	1 198	2.5	2.4	2 644	3.5	3.8
Least developed countries	634	1.3	2.5	785	1.0	2.3
Technical enrolment						
Industrialised economies	4 508	48.4	5.8	5 850	40.0	7.0
Developing economies	4 814	51.6	1.5	6 670	45.7	1.6
High and upper-middle income	1 400	15.0	3.6	2 100	14.4	4.4
Lower-middle income	1 136	12.2	2.2	1 937	13.3	2.9
Low income	2 278	24.4	1.0	2 633	18.0	0.9
Low income (without China and India)	223	2.4	0.4	325	2.2	0.5
Least developed countries	135	1.4	0.5	138	0.9	0.4

Technological structure of industrial activity

	Manufacturing value added 1998			Manufacturing exports 1998		
	Resource-based	Low tech	Medium and high tech	Resource-based	Low tech	Medium and high tech
World	27.1	14.1	58.7	17.4	18.8	63.8
Industrialised economies	25.5	13.3	61.2	16.8	15.5	67.8
Developing economies	33.7	17.6	48.7	18.2	28.0	53.8
High and upper-middle income	30.5	16.1	53.4	15.8	19.3	64.9
Lower-middle income	43.9	20.7	35.4	27.3	30.1	42.7
Low income	31.7	18.4	49.9	13.1	51.9	35.0
Low income (without China and India)	47.6	27.0	25.4	17.8	72.9	9.2
Least developed countries	44.4	31.6	24.0	12.6	84.0	3.4

Source: *UNIDO Industrial Development Report 2002/2003* (Tables A2.3 and A2.5).

industrial upgrading.[7] An improvement in location factors is an imperative path for host countries to follow since the competition for FDI among developing countries is heavily intensifying (Mytelka, 1996; Mudambi, 1998). Noorbakhsh *et al.* (2001) argue that, as a result of the adoption by MNEs of complex global integration strategies, a significant factor in influencing locational decisions is the presence of sophisticated, created assets in host countries. It is therefore crucial, especially in the context of intense competition for FDI, that developing countries formulate policies that improve local skills and build human resource capabilities (World Bank, 2000).

However, whereas much of the literature considers it axiomatic that human capital represents a core aspect of absorptive capacity,[8] its presence per se is not a *sine qua non* for knowledge accumulation. Human capital, represents but one of several aspects related to absorptive capabilities. While both physical and human capital are necessary inputs for catching up, the lack of appropriate incentives for production and investment can undermine the success of technological upgrading (Lall, 1992). The availability of a large stock of suitably qualified workers does not in itself result in efficient absorption of knowledge. This requires the presence of institutions and economic actors within industry which defines the stock of knowledge in a given location, and the efficient use of markets and hierarchies, be they intra-firm, intra-industry or intra-country. This knowledge is not costless, and must be accumulated over time. Important externalities arise which impinge on the ease of diffusion and efficiency of absorption and utilisation of external knowledge. For example, Freeman and Lindauer (1999) show that, in the case of Sub-Saharan Africa, the focus on investing in education and improving skills and capabilities to achieve economic growth is somewhat misplaced, arguing instead that it is more important to improve the institutional and business environment. This argument is backed up by Pack and Paxson (1999) where they emphasise that, without the efforts of a more competitive environment and export growth, continued efforts to develop high levels of industrial skills can be wasteful.[9] Appleton and Teal (1998) convincingly show that low rates of investment in physical capital have implications for the rates of return on human capital, particularly education. Clearly, in an environment where there are no incentives for production and investment, it is futile to focus only on human capital as a necessary and sufficient factor for technological and industrial upgrading. Human capital alone cannot make all the difference.

Similar arguments can be made with regard to the importance of the domestic sector. The impacts of MNEs in host countries can lead to costs and benefits for the indigenous private sector and the domestic entrepreneurial class (see, for example, Lall and Streeten, 1977), but essentially, if FDI is to lead to any benefits, the domestic sector must have the absorptive capability in an appropriate social capability system. It is important to emphasise that

Table 8.3 *Industrial base and competitiveness*

	Manufacturing value added 1998			Manufactured exports 1998		
	Value (billions of dollars)	World shares (per cent)	Per capita (dollars)	Value (billions of dollars)	World shares (per cent)	Per capita (dollars)
World	5 636.1	100.0	1 094.0	4 230.0	100.0	821.0
Industrialised economies	4 240.8	75.2	5 040.0	3 125.5	73.9	3 714.4
Developing economies	1 225.8	21.7	300.0	987.4	23.3	242.2
High and upper-middle income	560.2	9.9	1 161.0	614.5	14.5	1 273.5
Lower-middle income	210.4	3.7	311.0	159.8	3.8	236.2
Low income	455.2	8.1	156.0	213.2	5.0	73.1
Low income (without China and India)	35.8	0.6	51.0	19.7	0.5	28.1
Least developed countries	12.1	0.2	35.0	6.0	4.4	17.5

Source: UNIDO *Industrial Development Report 2002/2003* (Tables A2.1 and A2.2).

industrial development efforts in host LDCs are notoriously hindered by a continued failure to develop indigenous technological capacities in the host economies, predominantly private sector based. An important feature is a lack of fit between the industrialisation models adopted and the environment: of factor, product markets and social structures. The capacity and capability of the domestic sector is crucial in this process. If no domestic sector were to exist there could be no conditions for the FDI to establish linkages. In order to benefit from linkages, domestic capabilities need to be in place to benefit from potential spillovers. The benefits of FDI only occur when there is domestic investment and where the domestic investment has the ability to internalise the externalities from FDI.

The notion that FDI-led industrial upgrading needs first and foremost to be domestically enabled highlights the interrelatedness between MNE ownership advantages and host country location advantages. The following section presents a model examining the dynamics of a virtuous process between MNEs and host economic agents, highlighting the possible scenario of the way in which the process of industrial upgrading takes place.

MODEL OF INDUSTRIAL UPGRADING

This model shows the dynamics of a virtuous process between ownership (O_F) and location (L_H) advantages enabling industrial upgrading. This model draws on previous work by Scott-Kennel and Enderwick (2001), on FDI-led industrial upgrading, and work by Turok (1993) and Barrow and Hall (1995), who analyse the FDI contribution to industrial development as a continuum from enclave to full integration. Reference is also made to the work by Sally (1996) on the degree of embeddedness of FDI in the host country. The relevance of this model is that it introduces different phases of an evolving virtuous process, exemplified by weak, moderate and strong effects. These three distinct phases represent the upgrading process brought about by the interaction of different O_F and L_H as emerging from potential trajectories of non-FDI and FDI-induced changes. We explicitly focus on the virtuous 'side' of the argument since we are interested in the potential role of FDI in industrial upgrading. Figure 8.1 depicts this model.

We also use a taxonomy of linkages and spillovers, within different time scales (UNCTAD, 2001). In the immediate term, labour linkages are the primary apparent form of integration of the MNE in the host economic context. Other linkages at this stage may take place indirectly through agglomeration and demonstration effects. Later on, after FDI entry, a foreign affiliate can also establish direct backward and/or forward linkages, or enter into horizontal linkages or cooperative agreements with domestic economic

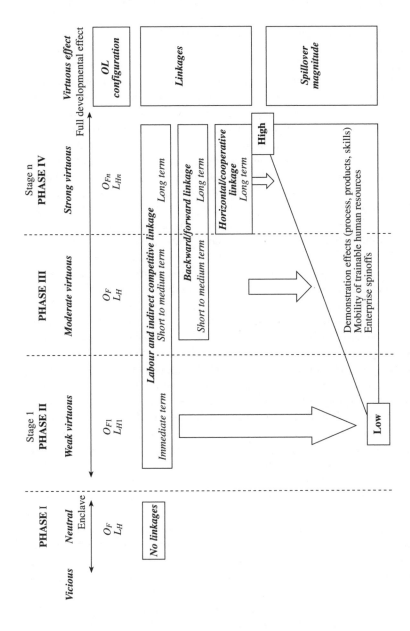

Figure 8.1   Scale of virtuous process, linkages and spillovers

units. We base our model on the premise that different linkages from the MNE potentially result in different kinds of spillovers. Moreover, the cumulative effects of different types of linkages realised, as well as the different time frame of linkage involved, results in different magnitudes of spillovers. By 'cumulative effect' we refer to the scenario where more than one type of linkage is realised simultaneously (for example, labour and backward linkages). By the 'different linkage time frames' we refer to time frames in which the linkage takes place (long-term linkage is stronger than a short-term linkage). The spillover effects varies from low to high, and it is argued that, when spillover effect is high, it will be so since location factors permit it to be so. The spillover effect is the lowest (less tenable for industrial upgrading) in the immediate term when labour and indirect demonstration linkages take place. The spillover effect is the highest in the scenario where long-term labour, indirect linkages, backward and forward and cooperative linkages occur simultaneously.

Central to the realisation of different linkages and subsequent spillover effects is the interaction between O_F and L_H, and how changes in L_H determine changes in O_F. As the magnitude of spillover depends on the extent of the technology and knowledge 'gap' between the foreign affiliate and domestic economic units (the level of absorptive capacity), an upgrading in domestic capacity structure will determine the movement along the successive phases. This process highlights the important fact that FDI needs to be enabled, through domestic upgrading, before it can lead industrial upgrading, since it depends on L_H (absorptive capacity) upgrading over time. Evolving L_H enables the upgrading in the type of O_F assets employed by the foreign affiliate in the host country. Gradual changes in the configuration of O_F and L_H lead to the evolution of a virtuous process, from weak to moderate and strong effects. This classification is based on Scott-Kennel and Enderwick (2001) and is used to categorise the different upgrading impacts of linkages and spillovers: 'weak virtuous process' relates to the most immediate form of MNE linkages and low spillover effects; 'strong virtuous process' refers to the most developed form of MNE linkages and high spillover effects.

A number of caveats are in order. What this model aims to present is an evolving, stage process. It does not mean that this evolving process, once started, will continue uninterrupted, because this process from weak to strong virtuous effect will be determined by the upgrading in the host country's location advantages. Nor does it mean that every FDI project will follow neatly along the different phases. What we attempt to model here is an evolving scenario of development, placing the different types of linkages in different phases along the continuum. This is done according to the sophistication of the location factors and components of L_H. Hence factors constituting L_{Hn} in Phase IV are more sophisticated than L_H in Phase I, II and III. This difference reflects the nature and extent of linkages and spillovers that in turn determine the extent of industrial upgrading. FDI activity can have negative impacts on domestic economic units. We explicitly focus on the virtuous process which assumes that the immediate micro impact between the foreign affiliates and domestic economic units is positive, especially so in an under-developed context such as in an LDC. As development proceeds, other extents of the virtuous process will emerge.

Next we describe the evolving process in detail.

Phase I

The foreign affiliate enters the host economy and brings certain O-specific advantages (O_F). These are unique to the firm and/or are not available to local economic units. In LDCs, the entry of the affiliate will certainly represent a form of breakthrough in alternatively stagnant industrial contexts, most probably characterised by the general absence of the domestic private sector and weak capabilities in economic activity. The O-specific advantages will be determined by the motive for FDI and will correspond to the location factors or advantages possessed by the host country. These advantages are unique to the firm and may potentially become available to domestic firms, economic agents (including individuals) and be spilled over to the host economy in general.

The starting position in phase I is the enclave position, where the foreign affiliate has no linkages with domestic economic units, not even the engage-ment of domestic labour in industrial activity. In such a scenario, FDI is attracted by the generic location factors (primarily natural resources). In this phase, the 'generic' location advantages will be just sufficient to attract FDI but not sufficient to establish linkages and generate subsequent spillovers. An immediate example of this scenario is resource-extracting industries, where the location advantage in the form of natural assets secures the foreign investment. Other examples may be dilapidated formerly state assets put up for privatisation, which are 'generic' in the sense that they are attracting FDI. This phase is most likely to be characterised by investment in and/or rehabili-tation of industrial equipment and facilities. No linkages at this stage means that spillovers are unlikely to emerge. Hence the effect on host country industrial upgrading is at best neutral.

Phase II and Phase III

After FDI entry, non-FDI-induced changes in the form of government policy (specifically industrial and technology policy), incentives and other changes taking place in the establishment of the actual FDI project, the MNE potentially starts to establish linkages with domestic economic agents. The point here is that the conditions in the host economy determine whether an FDI project carries on as projected.

In phase II, the immediate linkage to be established with domestic economic units (primarily in the case of FDI through privatisation) is through the engagement of domestic labour and also through indirect competitive effects in the sector, and the economy in general. These types of linkages will take place in the immediate term, but they may also occur in the short, medium and longer term. No further linkages are expected to occur in this phase because the location factors are not conducive to this. For example, an unfavourable business environment, weak domestic demand conditions or an unsatisfactory socioeconomic framework may all form part of the location factors that preclude backward or forward linkage with domestic economic units. However, spillovers will emerge as a result of this labour linkage and the indirect competitive effect at a sectoral or intersectoral level. However, given that these are the only effects of MNE activity, the spillover effects will be low. In phase II, the virtuous process is *weak*. In the parlance of the OLI framework, full internalisation of O_F advantages is apparent because the FDI project only forms indirect, competitive linkages or establishes direct labour linkages. The initial interaction between O_F and L_H results in spillovers that occur through indirect demonstration effects. The weak virtuous process reflects the low level of linkage and low magnitude of spillover effect, as the technology gap between actors is substantial.

Moving on to phase III, as long as the foreign affiliate will keep employing domestic labour and as long it continues to operate in the host economy, labour and indirect competitive linkages will emerge. But, in addition to these linkages, potential improvements in socioeconomic infrastructure make possible backward and forward linkages with domestic economic units.[10] For example, improved economic conditions, regulatory frameworks or local sector capacity, may all lead to feasibility of backward or forward linkages. In the first instance, backward and forward linkages may represent short to medium-term contractual arrangements for the sourcing and distribution needs of the foreign affiliate. Clearly the L_H in this phase will be different from previous stages, since now backward and forward linkages are taking place as host country conditions will have developed from the previous phase. Also the upgraded L_H will mean that, for instance, the capacity of labour employed in phase III will be different from labour employed in phase II, maybe because of more dexterity on the job or through training. The emergence and incremental process of FDI linkages (labour, indirect, backward and forward linkages) is correlated with the strengthening of the virtuous process between O_F and L_H advantages, in the sense that the emergence of more linkages will reflect an upgrading of location advantages and an improved socioeconomic system. For example, the presence of reliable suppliers or distributors partly reflects the fact that the host country location has become more advantageous for the MNE affiliate. Since our emphasis is on both the quantity and the quality of linkages over time, in phase III the accumulation of labour and indirect competitive linkages with backward and forward linkage will mean that the spillover magnitude from phase III will be greater than in phase II. Hence the virtuous process between the two sets of advantages is now *moderate*; there will be evidence of direct labour, backward and forward linkages, such as in the employment of domestic labour and the use of local agents and suppliers. These linkages emerge as the *L* advantages change as a result of the socioeconomic system upgrades. Hence L_H become more sophisticated and more knowledge-intensive and quasi-internalisation of O_F takes place in the transfer of non-core, codifiable knowledge (Scott Kennel and Enderwick, 2001) to domestic economic units. Hence a moderate contribution to upgrading is registered. The moderate virtuous process therefore reflects the improved magnitude of spillover effects emerging from greater intensity of linkages as the technology gap starts to diminish.

Phase IV

The fourth and final phase in the model will involve all the forms of linkages registered so far and the emergence of a horizontal/cooperative type of linkage in joint projects between the foreign affiliate and domestic economic units. At this stage, ownership augmentation and full embeddedness of FDI will take place, representing the optimal integration of FDI in the host economic structure. In this phase, the most specialised linkage may happen if the foreign-owned entity enters into a horizontal, cooperative linkage with domestic economic units, which may involve joint projects, the establishment of new ventures or any other specialised undertaking. Hence this leads to a virtuous process which we refer to as *strong*. This will involve an accumulation and consolidation of previous linkages plus horizontal cooperation, or partnership between the foreign entity and domestic economic units will take place. A strong virtuous process has the potential of resulting in a two-way transfer of *O* advantages between the foreign entity and domestic economic units and vice versa. Here internalisation of O_{Fn} advantages is at the highest possible level, made possible by the upgrading of L_{Hn} to a level where domestic economic units are at par with the foreign affiliate. Hence the strongest contribution to upgrading is registered. The strong virtuous process reflects the optimal linkage formation and spillover effect as the technology gap is bridged

The point of the model is that the movement along the virtuous cumulative process continuum very much depends on the nature and extent of upgrading in the host country absorptive capacity systems, which will lead to a more created and less generic type of location factor. Hence it is very much non-FDI-induced change (essentially, but not only, government intervention) that triggers and sets the pace for FDI-induced changes in the O_F. The relevance of FDI-induced changes to the industrial development process of the host country is widely acknowledged, so much so that, as argued before, FDI is rather erroneously regarded as a *sine qua non* for development. However, less emphasis is given to the fact that it is non-FDI-induced changes that lead to FDI-induced changes.

A movement to successive stages implies a change in the nature of the competitive advantages of MNEs and host economic agents. In the upgrading of location advantages, government plays several important roles. The work of Lall (see for instance Lall, 1996) points to the need for a holistic approach to selecting and leveraging sectors for dynamic growth, for stable governments, transparent policies and the provision of basic infrastructure and skills. The provision of certain basic location advantages is perhaps most significant to note, especially for pre-catching up and catching-up economies, where firms (foreign and domestic) rely on governments to make available public and quasi-public goods. First, they have a passive role in developing the appropriate public and quasi-public goods that are the background to economic activity. As countries reach a threshold level of technological capabilities and become catching-up economies in earnest, governments need to provide more active support through macroorganisational policies. This implies developing and fostering specific industries and technological trajectories, such that the location advantages they offer are less 'generic', more specific and highly immobile so that they encourage mobile investments to be locked into these assets. In other words, the role of policy making as market facilitator, enabler and provider of complementary created asset-based location-specific advantages increases in importance.

A virtuous process conducive to industrial and technological development is an incremental gradual process. Not only is a forward shift in a country's stage of development associated with the occurrence of a virtuous technology circle, but the ability to maintain this momentum is associated with continuing structural adjustment that may be necessary over time (Narula, 1996). The intensity of this structural adjustment depends on how far an LDC can go in terms of developing its location factors, while simultaneously attracting FDI. LDCs are not expected to progress along the various phases in an orderly, systematic manner, especially given the gradual nature of the industrial upgrading process. However, short of conditions tenable to the strong virtuous process (as visible in phase IV), other virtuous processes can occur, albeit short of the full developmental effect of FDI, but still representing important steps in this process.

OPERATIONALISING THE MODEL

In the previous section we set out to present a model describing the virtuous cumulative process at different stages, by which domestic economic units upgrade their resources and capabilities via linkages and spillovers from foreign affiliates. It has been argued that this upgrading necessitates the upgrading of the location factors. The next step is to operationalise this model at the firm level and test how this virtuous process evolves in practice in relation to our hypothesis that there is a link between linkages and spillovers and that this link is correlated to the socioeconomic system of the host country; as exemplified by the location factors. To this end, we attempt to determine the evolving role of FDI in industrial upgrading.

At the outset the focus should be on describing the type of O_F that the FDI brings and which, alternatively, would not be available in the host country. Different motives for FDI determine different types of O_F (Dunning, 1993). For example, affiliates established through privatisation are likely to have stronger links with domestic suppliers than those established through greenfield investment (UNCTAD, 2000; Scott-Kennel and Enderwick, 2001). It is important to ascertain the role assigned to the affiliates as this may have a strong bearing on the extent of local linkages (Zanfei, 2000). The distinction between the ownership-specific advantages of affiliates of MNEs and other free-standing foreign companies (Jones, 1996) is also important in an LDC, as one expects that the nature and extent of O_F will be different in respective cases. The possible variations in O_F potentially imply that different L_H advantages attracted the foreign investment decision in the first place. Therefore it is important to ascertain the location factors that lead to the FDI project. It is important at this stage to determine also the foreign affiliate characteristics such as the country of origin of foreign investors, age (in terms of the number of years since first establishment in the host country) and size (in terms of the number of employees and value of sales). These firm characteristics are likely to influence the configuration of the O_F and L_H advantages. Many studies have found that local procurement by foreign affiliates increases over their time of establishment in the host country, as a result of investment experience, upgraded location factors and lower costs of local sourcing (Driffield and Mohd Noor, 1999; McAleese and McDonald, 1978; Gorg and Ruane, 1998; Scott-Kennel and Enderwick, 2001). In any case, linkages increase as a result of developments in host country location factors.

Once a set of characteristics at the firm level is determined, we turn to the linkages established in the host economy. The aim here is to ascertain the nature and extent of linkages established between the foreign companies and domestic economic units, according to the different types of linkages identified over time (short-term, medium- and longer-term). The types of linkages established over time will determine the magnitude of spillover.

Labour linkage will be assessed by the share of the local employees in total employment. A distinction needs to be made between the type of employment categories in which domestic labour is engaged and patterns over time starting from the year first established in the host country. Spillovers from labour linkage will be determined according to type of training given to the labour force as well as to labour mobility (Gerschenberg, 1987; Slaughter, 2001; Fosfuri *et al.*, 1999). The indirect competitive linkages are most difficult to ascertain. However, we attempt to proxy this indirect linkage by the number of competitors in the same sector as the foreign affiliate (Scott-Kennel and Enderwick, 2001).

The rest of the linkages (backward, forward and horizontal) are distinguished according to the time scale involved (UNCTAD, 2001). Therefore, with respect to backward linkages relating to the local sourcing and subcontracting from domestic units, and forward linkages relating to the distribution or end custom by domestic economic unit, a distinction will be made between short-term linkage (temporary contract relationship) and longer-term linkage (permanent contract arrangements). As well as determining the presence or absence of linkages, it is important to ascertain the quality of such linkages. In addition it is important to determine their evolution over time in relation to changing host country determinants. The decision to source locally depends on many factors (see, for example, UNCTAD, 2001). However, if and when this happens very much depends on the nature of the location factors, L_H that are most conducive to foreign affiliate linkages.

CONCLUSIONS

Liberalisation acts as a major 'shock' to the socioeconomic systems within LDCs, since it has not just introduced new economic actors (MNEs), but it has also required major restructuring of existing national systems, especially in terms of absorptive capacities and capabilities of domestic economic agents. The coordination failure means that, in the immediate term, MNE activity and flows of inward FDI may well lead to an increase in productivity and exports in the host country, but this does not necessarily result in increased competitiveness of the domestic sector or increased industrial capacity. Domestic capacity and capability is what ultimately determines economic growth. FDI per se does not provide growth opportunities unless domestic economic agents have the necessary technological capacity and capability to lead to and profit from the externalities from MNE activity. An FDI-led industrial upgrading process needs to be domestically enabled. Given this interrelatedness and the gradual nature of the industrial development process, we have argued that there are many facets to the virtuous interactive process between MNEs and host economic agents. Each of these facets of the virtuous process have specific implications for the development and policy making process.

NOTES

1. This economic model draws some of its inspiration from the belief that the success of the Asian NICs can be applied to LDCs. For an overview of the NICs' development success, see World Bank (1994).
2. Substantial efforts are being undertaken to improve investment climates, through FDI-friendly legislation and the setting up of investment promotion agencies.
3. The host country's location advantages play an important role in determining the level of competence of the subsidiary (Benito *et al.*, 2002).
4. Appropriate institutions are needed to determine the interaction between participants of a 'sophisticated' socioeconomic framework. By the term 'institutions' we refer to the 'sets of common habits, routines, established practices, rules or law that regulate the interaction between individuals and groups' (Edquist and Johnson, 1997). Institutions thus create the environment within which upgrading is undertaken and establish the ground rules for interaction between the various economic agents. Institutions shape the development process and influence the dynamics of the industrial upgrading process.
5. Gray elaborates that a country's socioeconomic infrastructure consists of its Northian institutions (North, 1990) and the skills of its population in the use of these institutions.
6. For a discussion on absorptive capacity and technological capability, see Narula (2002).
7. The evolution of created assets is reflected in Porter (1990) and Ernst (2000), amongst others. Pearce (1999) highlights the need for location advantages to develop with a view to consolidating existing FDI.
8. This is an area which has attracted considerable interest and work. See, for example, Noorbakhsh *et al.* (2001), Pfeffermann and Madrassy (1992), Zhang and Markusen (1999), Borensztein *et al.* (1998) and Dunning (1988). Also Verspagen (1991) and Borensztein *et al.* (1998) used human capital measures as proxies for absorptive capacity.
9. In their study, Pack and Paxson (1999), however, stress that skill upgrading is an inevitable process in upgrading.
10. The focus on economic units rather than firms here is not accidental. There are many instances where foreign affiliates link backward to individuals and/or firms, for example in agriculture-based products, such as in tobacco. Hence linkages may not necessarily be only with firms.

REFERENCES

Abramovitz, M. (1990), 'The catch-up factor in postwar economic growth', *Economic Inquiry*, **28**, 1–18.
Abramovitz, M. (1994), 'The origins of the postwar catch-up and convergence boom' in Jan Fagerberg, Bart Varspagen and Nicholas von Tunzelmann (eds), *The Dynamics of Technology, Trade and Growth*, Aldershot, UK and Brookfield, US: Edward Elgar.
Abramovitz, M. (1995), 'The elements of social capability', in D.H. Perkins and B. Koo (eds), *Social Capability and Long-term Growth*, Basingstoke: Macmillan Press.

Appleton, S. and F. Teal (1998), 'Human capital and economic development', background paper for the African Development Report.

Barrow, M. and M. Hall (1995), 'The impact of a large multinational organization on a small economy', *Regional Studies*, **29**(7), 635–53.

Benito, G., B. Grogaard and R. Narula (2002), 'Environmental influences on MNE subsidiary roles: economic integration and the Nordic countries', mimeo, Oslo.

Borensztein, E, J. De Gregorio and J.W. Lee (1998), 'How does foreign direct investment affect economic growth?', *Journal of International Economics*, **45**, 115–35.

Caves, R.E. (1982), *Multinational Enterprise and Economic Analysis*, Cambridge: Cambridge University Press.

Criscuolo, P. and R. Narula (2002), 'A novel approach to national technological accumulation and absorptive capacity: aggregating Cohen and Levinthal', MERIT research memorandum 2002–16.

Driffield, N. and A.H. Mohd Noor (1999), 'Foreign direct investment and local input linkages in Malaysia', *Transnational Corporations*, **8**(3), 1–24.

Dunning, J. (1988), *Multinationals, Technology and Competitiveness*, London: Unwin Hyman.

Dunning, J. (1993), *Multinational Enterprises and the Global Economy*, Reading, MA: Addison-Wesley.

Edquist, C. and B. Johnson (1997), 'Institutions and organisations in systems of innovation', in C. Edquist (ed.), *Systems of Innovation, Technologies, Institutions and Organisations*, London and Washington: Pinter.

Ernst, D. (2000), 'Global production networks and the changing geography of innovation systems: implications for developing countries', East–West Centre working papers, economic series.

Fosfuri, A., M. Motta and T. Roended (1999), 'Foreign direct investment and spillovers through workers' mobility'. CEPR discussion paper no. 2194, Centre for Economic Policy Research, London.

Freeman, R.B. and D.L. Lindauer (1999), 'Why not Africa?', NBER working paper 6942.

Gerschenberg, I. (1987), 'The training and spread of managerial know-how, a comparative analysis of multinational and other firms in Kenya', *World Development*, **15**(7), 931–9.

Gorg, H. and F. Ruane (1998), 'Linkages between multinationals and indigenous firms: evidence for the electronics sector in Ireland', Trinity Economic Paper Series, technical paper no. 98/13.

Gray, Peter H. (2000a), 'Socioeconomic infrastructure, inward direct investment and economic development', mimeo, State University of New Jersey, January.

Gray, Peter H. (2000b), 'Globalization and economic development', *Global Economy Quarterly*, **1**, 71–96.

Jones, G. (1996), *The Evolution of International Business: An Introduction*, London: Routledge.

Lall, S. (1980), 'Vertical inter-firm linkages in LDCs: an empirical study', *Oxford Bulletin of Economics and Statistics*, August, 209–22.

Lall, S. (1992), 'Structural problems of African industry', in F. Stewart, S. Wangwe and S. Lall (eds), *Alternative Development Strategies for Sub-Saharan Africa*, London: Macmillan.

Lall, S. (1993), 'Introduction: transnational corporations and economic development', in S. Lall (ed.), *Transnational Corporations and Economic Development*, vol. 3, United Nations Library on Transnational Corporations, London: Routledge.

Lall, S. (1996), 'The investment development path: some conclusions', in R. Narula and J. Dunning (eds), *Foreign Direct Investment and Governments. Catalysts for Economic Restructuring*, London: Routledge.

Lall, S. (2000a), 'FDI and development: policy and research issues in the emerging context', working paper number 43, QEH Working Paper Series, Queen Elizabeth House, University of Oxford.

Lall, S. (2000b), 'Skills, competitiveness and policy in developing countries', working paper number 46, QEH Working Paper Series, Queen Elizabeth House, University of Oxford.

Lall, S. (2000c), 'The technological structure and performance of developing country manufactured exports, 1985–1998', working paper number 44, QEH Working Paper Series, Queen Elizabeth House, University of Oxford.

Lall. S. and P. Streeten (1977), *Foreign Investment, Transnationals and Developing Countries*, London: Macmillan.

McAleese, D. and D. McDonald (1978), 'Employment growth and the development of linkages in foreign-owned and domestic manufacturing enterprises', *Oxford Bulletin of Economics and Statistics*, **40**(4), 321–9.

Mudambi, R. (1998), 'The role of duration in MNE investment attraction strategies', *Journal of International Business Studies*, **29**(2), 239–62.

Mytelka, L. (1996), 'Locational tournaments, strategic partnerships and the state', mimeo, Carleton University, Ottawa.

Narula, R. (1996), *Multinational Investment and Economic Structure*, London: Routledge.

Narula, R. (2002), 'The implications of growing cross-border interdependence for systems of innovation', MERIT-Infonomics Research Memorandum series, number 17, Maastricht Economic Research Institute on Innovation and Technology.

Narula, R. and J. Dunning (2000), 'Industrial development, globalisation and multinational enterprises: new realities for developing countries', *Oxford Development Studies*, **28**(2).

Noorbakhsh, F., A. Paloni and A. Youssef (2001), 'Human capital and FDI inflows to developing countries: new empirical evidence', *World Development*, **29**(9), 1593–1610.

North, D. (1990), Institutions, Institutional Change and Economic Performance, Cambridge: Cambridge University Press.

Ohkawa, K. and H. Rosovsky (1973), *Japanese Economic Growth*, Stanford: Stanford University Press.

Ozawa, T. (1992), 'Foreign direct investment and economic development', *Transnational Corporations*, **1**, 27–54.

Pack, H. and C. Paxson (1999), 'Is African manufacturing skill-constrained?', Policy Research Working Paper no. 2212, The World Bank Development Research Group, October.

Pearce, R. (1999), 'Multinationals and industrialisation: the bases of "inward investment" policy', *International Journal of Economics and Business*, **8**(1), 51–73.

Pfeffermann, G. and A. Madrassy (1992), 'Trends in private investment in developing countries', IFC Discussion Paper no. 14, World Bank, Washington, DC.

Porter, M.E. (1990), *The Competitive Advantages of Nations*, New York: Free Press.

Reinhardt, N. and W. Peres (2000), 'Latin America's new economic model: micro responses and economic restructuring', *World Development*, **28**(9), 1543–66.

Romer, P. (1993), 'Two strategies for economic development: using ideas and producing ideas', *Proceedings of the World Bank Annual Conference on Development
Economics 1992*, Washington: World Bank, pp. 63–91.

Sally, R. (1996), 'Public policy and the Janus face of the multinational enterprises:
national embeddedness and international production', in P. Gummett (ed.), *Globalization and Public Policy*, Cheltenham, UK and Brookfield, US: Edward Elgar.

Scott-Kennel, J. and P. Enderwick (2001), 'Economic upgrading and foreign direct
investment: exploring the Black Box of the IDP', University of Waikato, New
Zealand.

Slaughter, Matthew. J. (2001), 'Skill upgrading in developing countries: has inward
foreign direct investment played a role?', FDI, Human Capital and Education in
Developing Countries, Technical Meeting, 13–14 December, OECD, Paris.

Turok, I. (1993) 'Inward investment and local linkages: how deeply embedded is
"Silicon Glen"?', *Regional Studies*, **27**(5), 401–417.

UNCTAD (2000), *World Investment Report 2000: Cross-border Mergers and Acquisitions and Development*, New York and Geneva: United Nations.

UNCTAD. (2001), *World Investment Report 2001: Promoting Linkages*, New York
and Geneva: United Nations.

Verspagen, B. (1991), 'A new empirical approach to catching up or falling behind',
Structural Change and Economic Dynamics, **2**(2).

World Bank (1994), *The East Asian Miracle*, Oxford: Oxford University Press.

World Bank (2000), *Entering the 21st Century: World Development Report 1999/
2000*, New York: Oxford University Press.

Xi, B. (2000), 'Multinational enterprises, technological diffusion and host country
productivity growth', *Journal of Development Economics*, **62**, 477–93.

Zanfei, A. (2000), 'Transnational firms and the changing organisation of innovative
activities', *Cambridge Journal of Economics*, **24**, 515–42.

Zhang, K. and J. Markusen (1999), 'Vertical multinationals and host country characteristics', *Journal of Development Economics*, **59**, 233–52.

9. Market entry strategies of multinational firms in local and regional markets and their consequences for regional development: the case of the accommodation and food industry in Western Austria

Klaus Weiermair and Mike Peters

TOURISM: NO LONGER A FRAGMENTED INDUSTRY?

Tourism is certainly not as global as the car or electronics industry but it is more global than food processing, education or retailing. Globalisation in tourism is driven on the demand side by global competition for tourist destinations offering 'global product bundles' thereby producing similar types of fantasy worlds or tourism experiences and facilitated by increasing international flows of capital, technology and labour (Smeral, 1996; Weiermair, 2001b).

What type of changes in Austria's tourism have been brought on by or can be attributed to globalisation phenomena? About 40–55 per cent of the decline in Austrian tourism can be attributed to relative prices in comparison to other destinations. This has been greatly enhanced through the opening of new markets and the greater transparency of market prices (for example, introduction of the Euro and use of the US dollar in new markets). A variety of studies have shown quality deficits in Austria's tourism industries to exist, notably in the areas of animation, cultural attractions, shopping and transport, with an overwhelming proportion of tourists received from neighbouring Germany and some uncertainties as to a continuation of this tourist flow in the future (Freitag, 1996; Fuchs and Weiermair, 1999; Mazanec and Zins, 1996). Immediate strategic questions evolve around the exploration of new products and new markets, and the associated operational questions of improved destination management (Bieger, 2001), better provision of risk capital and exploitation of scale economies in strategic alliances or other forms of inter-firm cooperation in tourism (Smeral et al., 1998).

As with the world of work, individuals experience careers as tourists and an aged population of potential tourists today can be viewed as being at the height of their careers, displaying high levels of tourism experience with attendant high levels of quality expectations and lower levels of perceived risk regarding more distant and exotic tourist destinations. As a consequence the chain of substitution in the eyes of the customer (tourist) has been widened to include hitherto heterogeneous tourism places and/or services such as new Caribbean resorts competing with alpine Austrian tourism resorts during the winter season (Opaschowski, 1993).

The opening up of new tourism resorts worldwide, deregulation in transport and other subbranches of tourism, along with the development of global leisure and tourism products (such as fast food, eclectic global design and architecture, a global choice of tourism products) have challenged local small tourism enterprises with respect to the quality, price and choice of tourism products and services (Weiermair, 1998). In addition tourists have undergone substantial changes in lifestyle and values in terms of individualisation, flexibility and spontaneity in travel decision making as well as a new configuration of available working, learning, household and leisure time (Friedl, 2002).

A third major factor impinging on the competitiveness of tourist destinations stems from the accelerating pace of technological change, particularly in the field of information and communication technologies (Buhalis, 1996). More efficient and qualitatively new forms of information processing have served both as means and as ends in tourism, providing at the same time increased efficiencies and new products (Horillo, 2001). All of these factors have dramatically changed the production and marketing function of the tourism enterprise with respect to economies of scale, economies of scope and the efficient form of corporate governance leading to new minimum optimum size requirements or determinants for enterprises' alliances.

Probably the two most important (and interrelated) factors of a destination's competitiveness are its information-processing capability both towards the client (tourist) and towards all other stakeholders in tourism (particularly tourism firms, suppliers and employees) and the efficiency characteristics associated with different size, scope and agglomeration configurations and attendant levels of capacity utilisation (Flagestad and Hope, 2001).

Tourism has become an 'information business' where those firms will gain competitive advantages that can provide faster, more (emotionally) appealing and cost-effective information to actual and potential tourists in existing and emerging tourist-sending regions. The introduction of new information technologies poses a number of short-term financial and psychological costs and risks to small and medium-sized enterprises. At the same time we have seen the development of the Internet as 'the' tourism information platform of the future (Main, 2001). And although diffusion rates for new computer reservation systems (CRS) vary greatly in Europe with a typical North–South (Scandinavia to Sicily) difference, they have nevertheless become the most important and effective distribution and marketing tools in a globalised world. The potential of Internet technology is enormous, but communication and pricing logic processes remain future challenges for the hotel sector. The need to address incursions from no-frills providers is pushing the leading hotel consortia to further differentiate themselves with upgrades such as Lexington Services' improvements of its SPIRIT© hotel reservation system with detailed web property information, revenue and marketing management services, advanced reporting capabilities and direct interfaces (Wolchuk and Lerner, 2002).

As is true of other branches of economic activity, the globalisation of tourism so far has mainly engulfed developed countries with similar demand and supply conditions. However, many new tourism regions and markets are being added, with globalisation benefits going in the main towards emerging markets in South East Asia and Latin America. Asia, notably China, India and Pakistan, are expected to become leading tourist-sending regions of the world by 2010 (Foot, 2002). Eastern Europe, on the other hand, has seen a rather slow development of its incoming tourism on account of lack of infrastructures, management know-how, capital and technological backwardness (Frauendorfer and Lanschützer, 1992; Reisinger, 1994). The second sphere where liberalisation and globalisation have strongly affected tourism as a hitherto largely fragmented industry is efficiency and effectiveness characteristics of tourism destinations stemming from optimally structured (configured) tourist enterprises with respect to size, scope and governance characteristics (Pechlaner and Weiermair, 1999). Worldwide deregulation of air and other transport industries emanating from the USA and the associated cost, price and airline alliance consequences have led to increased concentration and market power of the remaining few. It has led to new forms of knowledge acquisition and knowledge management in new forms of international alliances (or network) organisations with new forms of corporate governance. Inter-firm cooperation between related firms and industries, a major determinant of competitiveness in Porter's diamond model (Porter, 1990), has been greatly facilitated across borders in a globalised and deregulated world (Weiermair, 2001a, p. 21). Increasing concentration in many of the subbranches of tourism will eventually also allow tourism firms other than airlines to apply such efficiency and effectiveness tools as yield management (Weiermair and Mathies, 2002).

But while tourism is gradually becoming global, yielding new market structures, processes and performances, Europe's tourism has until recently been considered a rather 'fragmented' industry. A fragmented industry typically consists on the supply side of many small or medium-sized enterprises producing and selling very competitive or slightly differentiated products (services) which face on the demand side small regional markets with buyers displaying strong local and locational preferences. Fragmentation has been far stronger and more prevalent in vacation tourism as compared to business tourism and has also played less of a role in underdeveloped or newly developing economies where tourism arrived late and with the helping hand of multinational and transnational enterprises (see, for example, Clegg, 1987). In 1996, over 6.5 million people in the European Union were employed in about 1.4 million enterprises in the tourism industry. This corresponds to 7.7 per cent of all enterprises and 5.8 per cent of the total number of employees in the EU. Although the number of tourism enterprises diminished over the last four years, SMEs are still dominating the hospitality industry.

The historical importance and dominance of the small business sector in tourism can be easily illustrated with a few stylised facts from the hotel sector. In the European Union, 94.4 per cent of the accommodation and food sector is classified as small businesses employing nine employees or fewer. The big companies with more than 250 employees cover 17.2 per cent of all employees. SMEs are still more prevalent in the hospitality industry as compared to other industries: in Europe, SMEs employ 83 per cent of all hospitality workers, while across all industries SMEs provide employment for 66 per cent of the labour force (Hubertus, 2000). For instance, most typical of the situation in central and southern Europe, the average size of hotels was 35.3 beds in 1994, changing only marginally, to 37 beds, by 1998. Figures for Finland, Italy, Spain and France for the same period are shown in Table 9.1.

Mergers, acquisitions and the development of international hotel chains account for the sharp increase in hotel size and bed capacities in Spain. The

Table 9.1   Average number of beds, 1994–8

Country	Average number of beds (1994)	Average number of beds (1998)	Growth (per cent)
European Union	46.0	48.8	6.0
Austria	35.3	37	4.8
Italy	49.9	52.4	5.0
France	70.2	74.2	5.6
Finland	111.5	114.5	1.0
Spain	104.6	130	24.3

Source: Hubertus (2000).

trend towards fewer hotels with higher bed capacities and towards higher levels of concentration is also confirmed in the hospitality industry all over Europe.

Multinational enterprises in tourism are mostly to be found in the hotel and restaurant industries. Forerunners were the fast growing hotel chains: already in 1973 the 100 biggest hotel chains and corporations offered more than 8100 hotels with 1.2 million rooms (Roekarts and Savat, 1989). By 1999 the 100 biggest hotel chains grew to 36 625 hotels with 4.87 million rooms (Marsan and Wolchuck, 2000). These multinational hotel enterprises are able to profit from economies of scale and aim at maximising sales and minimising costs or improving service and hardware quality. Thus scale effects reduce fixed costs and do positively influence the entrepreneurial risk. In the 1980s the study of Klien (1991) could prove that international hotel chains (in the luxury segment) generated competitive advantages whilst the small and medium-sized hotels faced competitive disadvantages.

Multinational hotel enterprises appear to have been very stable in terms of their growth behaviour: advantages of internalisation and ownership are obvious even in the aftermath of 11 September, and in the wake of the economic downturn hotel companies were able (slowly) to enhance their growth (measured in number of rooms) see Figure 9.1. This also demonstrates how much more sophisticated hotel companies have become: stable financial structures, strict discipline at the negotiating table and unexpected levels of operational flexibility left the giants of the industry virtually unassailable (Wolchuk and Lerner, 2002). At the same time the number of hotels of the ten biggest hotel companies increased from 22 024 in 1997 to 28 448 in the year 2001. Thus

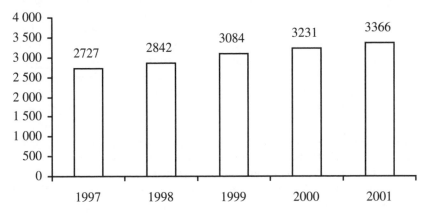

Source: Data provided by Hotels' 325 (see www.hotelsmag.com).

Figure 9.1   Development of rooms (000s) of the ten biggest hotel companies

the average hotel size has remained relatively stable, between 108 and 112 rooms per hotel.

Mark Wells, president and CEO of the no. 1 hotel consortia Utell, sees the future of hotel concentration with two kinds of deals: hotel giants will acquire each other and consolidators will look to fill geographic, product or business niches such as Central and South America, as well as strategic locations in Asia offering ideal growth options for leading hotel companies (Wolchuk and Lerner, 2002). Before attempting to forecast the further continuation of this process of globalisation and concentration in an otherwise local and fragmented business such as tourism, we need to consult existing theories which have provided explanations for the internationalisation of service businesses and the rise of the multinational enterprise.

THE RISE OF THE MULTINATIONAL AND GLOBAL FIRM IN TOURISM

A number of theories have attempted to explain the rise of international, multinational or global firms. Invariably starting with observations of differently staged product life cycles across the globe (Vernon, 1966), both industrial organisation and resource-oriented approaches have supplied at least partial explanations regarding the size and varying nature of foreign investment and foreign ownership. In particular the theory of the MNE[1] has become of great value to the understanding of internationalisation phenomena of service firms. However, certain service industry characteristics need to be taken into account and as a result the theory does require some adaptation (Roberts, 1998).

In his modestly called 'eclectic theory of international production', Dunning (1989) combines elements of the international monopoly theory (Hymer, 1976) and the literature of internalisation theory[2] to provide general explanations for the occurrence and global distribution of foreign direct investments (Dunning, 1988). The approach is particularly interesting as it has already been applied to the services sector (see Table 9.2) (Dunning, 1989). The three theoretical pillars are the development of ownership-specific advantages, internalisation incentives and location-specific advantages (Dunning, 1988) which are furthermore preconditioned by a correspondence of the firm's internationalisation and long-term management strategies (Dunning and McQueen, 1982). The fundamental principles constituting and/or governing these various types of competitive advantages apply not only at the enterprise level but also at the regional, national or branch level and as such may be directly compared to Porter's five forces of internationalisation (Porter, 1990).

*Table 9.2   Some OLI (ownership, location and internationalisation)
            advantages of hotel enterprises*

Ownership advantages (OA)
   Product innovation, licences, patents
   Access, control and efficient use of information
   Quality and branding
   Reputation
   Marketing strengths: market research, information access and so on
   Human capital in the hotel enterprise, career paths, incentive systems,
   standards of employee training
   Financing: sources of financing, networking, risk venture partner and so on
   Cooperation advantages: economies of scope, economies of scale and so on
   Internationalisation advantages: knowhow about foreign markets and
   customer segments, diversification of political and currency risks, growing
   management and internationalisation experience and so on

Internalisation advantages (IA)
   Low negotiation costs in new markets
   Low search costs in new markets
   Quality control and securement
   Control of supplier and customer distribution and communication channels
   Internalising non-existing services in tourism destinations to provide a
   complete product and service bundle
   Avoidance of buyer uncertainty (for example in the area of wellness
   products and services such as spa areas)

Location-specific advantages (LA)
   Governmental support for innovations in the target market
   Low transport and communication costs
   Factor prices and quality, labour productivity, energy and other resources
   and so on
   Physical distance, such as language, culture, management culture and so on
   Unequal distribution of natural and man-made resources and markets

---

Source: Dunning (1988).

Owner or Firm-specific Advantages

These are usually tied up with the firm in question and create competitive
advantages. The following are typical examples: management knowhow,
screening and organisation methods for trained personnel, cooking recipes or
patents and licences; many specific ownership advantages themselves arise

from internationalisation, such as access to efficient resources and/or finances or clients in the receiving country (Macharzina, 1992). Owner-specific advantages typically create entry barriers and hence monopoly rents for specific knowhow and/or technology (Roberts, 1998, p. 51) particularly as they pertain to the family of new information and/or communication technologies, which according to Johnson (1970) should always be easily transferable within the firm and across national boundaries, displaying the characteristics of a public good within the growing firm.

Advantages of Internalisation

Dunning employs here transaction economic arguments as pioneered by Coase (1937) and further refined by Williamson (1975), who demonstrates the usefulness of this approach. If internalisation advantages exist, enterprises will use their own firm or internalisation advantages rather than selling or renting them. Good examples are costs of search and/or negotiation. Ownership-specific advantages do not explain per se why domestic hotels should choose to exploit their monopolistic advantage through foreign production rather than by licensing a provider abroad. It is argued that the market is costly and inefficient for certain types of transactions: when the firm is able to carry out transactions at lower costs within its organisation, transactions will be internalised (Roberts, 1998).

Location-specific Advantages

If the first two types of advantages are fulfilled and there exists no contradictory long-term enterprise strategy, a firm will choose to become internationally active if location promises additional competitive advantages. If that was not the case the enterprise would wish to export rather than to invest in the foreign market. Location-specific advantages are, however, no guarantee of the attainment of long-run competitive advantages as local enterprises could similarly exploit local advantages across the market place (through licensing or outright purchase).[3] The latter suggests the necessity of integrating additional variables such as the size of the market or market growth (Dunning, 1979). In this context it is worthwhile mentioning that countries (regions) with a large home market may also command local specific advantages abroad, particularly if domestic customers are also international customers. For example, the internationalisation of the American hotel industry has been largely facilitated by the presence of US tourists and their associated demand for hotel space and typical American home services of a certain quality abroad (Porter, 1990).

Dunning's eclectic theory of international production can be used successfully to explain the internationalisation of services in general and those of hotels in particular (Dunning and Kundu, 1995). Even where personal contacts between service providers and users are of primordial importance, the above quoted internationalisation motives may still apply and be binding. This approach has been most successfully tested in the banking sector (see, for example, Sagari, 1992; Yannopoulos, 1983). The competitive advantages of multinational hotels are manifold and vary within their place in the tourism value chain of tourist destinations (Weiermair and Peters, 1998).

Already in 1989 Dunning had investigated different economic branches of activity according to the prevalence of OLI advantages in them. In the survey carried out the hotel industry provided information concerning owner-specific advantages such as experiences of multinational enterprises in their home market regarding services distribution, training of key personnel, quality control and referral systems, as well as better access to inputs and economies of geographical distribution. Hotel enterprises, on the other hand, were location-bound when selling a foreign service and the export development was induced by tourists and business people visiting the home country.

Observed internalisation advantages were that hotels are capital-intensive, quality control can generally be ensured through contractual relationships (such as a purchase or management contract) and governments usually prefer non-equity arrangements; referral systems can be centrally coordinated without equity control. The organisational form of the hotels varied, but minority ventures and contractual relations dominated the sample (Dunning, 1989, p. 20).

In 1995, Dunning and Kundu analysed OLI advantages in 34 multinational hotel enterprises in 13 countries. The most significant factors perceived by the hotel executives were the following.

Ownership specific advantages:
1. the knowledge of tastes and requirements of the home country clients,
2. trademark and brand image of the parent company,
2. investment in training of key personnel.

Location specific advantages:
1. size and growth rate of the host country,
2. the opportunities for tourism,
3. the availability and quality of hotel related infrastructure (location-related assets complementary to the ownership-specific advantages of foreign hotels),
4. political, social and economic stability.

Internalisation advantages:
1. quality control,
2. coordinating capabilities of the parent firm,

3. host country's inward investment policy,
4. political and economic stability.

What was interesting in these empirical results was the observations that MNEs seem to have developed skills and knowledge which normally can be expected to be skills and competitive advantages of local hotel entrepreneurs and owners: the knowledge of customers' tastes and requirements as well as knowledge about the regional or local infrastructure were identified as owner-ship and location advantages of multinational hotels. However, the question remains as to the extent to which size disadvantages may be compensated by local advantages of domestic Austrian enterprises and which competitive industry structure evolves in small and medium sized structured industry in Austria.

EVOLVING COMPETITIVE RIVALRY BETWEEN INDIGENOUS AND SMALL VERSUS INTERNATIONAL AND LARGE TOURISM COMPANIES

Even though Austrian tourism still appears to have some symptoms of chronic sickness, in that there exist asymmetries between entry and exit conditions (Weiermair, 2000), it appears that novel conditions and barriers of market entry exist in the 'new tourism' of today (Weiermair, 2001b).

The latter indicates the necessity to change and/or transform enterprises towards man-made competitive advantages where previously, in a seller's market, nature, natural attractions and the natural charm of people (including the manager owners of tourism enterprises) have been the dominant (local) competitive advantages. The 'new tourism' requires new qualifications in the form of further training or post-secondary education of owner management instead of only occupational preparation and training. Similarly it requires the firm's ability to differentiate itself better in the market place through new core services (rather than merely adding related services) and through con-tinuous product planning and development. This, however, raises the question of whether these entrepreneurial tasks can be better performed or more effi-ciently and effectively carried out by large foreign MNEs than by small family tourism enterprises and/or whether small local family enterprises can grow into more efficient large domestic MNEs in Austria. Below an attempt is made to address the general theoretical and tourism-specific empirical question regarding the industrial organisation dimension of innovation, com-petitive rivalry and the enterprises' ability to differentiate.

Innovation

Early industrial organisation research in the 1930s had postulated U-shaped long-run cost curves and an associated minimum optimum plant size (Kaldor, 1934; Viner, 1932). Thus, at least from a static perspective, some small firms may be considered as inefficient. It was only 40 years later that industrial economists took a more dynamic view of optimum firm size and attempted to explain the coexistence of size and survival of different plant sizes (Lucas, 1978).

The latter include for the first time the qualification and role of the entrepreneur as a key element for optimal size configuration. This leads to questions of interdependence and interrelationships between innovation and the plant size, on the one hand (Acs and Audretsch, 1989, 1990; Audretsch, 1993) and innovation behaviour and new (established) versus existing firms, on the other hand. Of particular interest are innovation behaviour and plant size for new market entrants, where suboptimal plant or firm size may produce a disproportionate amount of innovations (Audretsch, 1993). As long as asymmetries between entry and exit behaviour exist, we should expect that low innovation and rent-seeking (inefficient) tourism enterprises will attempt to prevent the entry of new and dynamic small firms.

Intensity of Competition (Rivalry)

The Austrian tourism market (industry) can be characterised by a large number of small enterprises competing strongly with each other. As a corollary, cut-throat competition has led in the past to low rates of profitability, thereby lowering and preventing normal or superior rates of enterprise growth (Peters and Weiermair, 2001b; Weiermair, 2001b). The structural weaknesses of the industry have in the past also been reinforced by an entrepreneurial class of 'lifestyle entrepreneurs' or 'valley lords' (local tourism monopolies), who in contrast to the Schumpeterian entrepreneur have shied away from major restructuring, change exercises and/or innovation (Ateljevic and Doorne, 2000; Peters and Weiermair, 2001a).

This market situation in turn has created new challenges and opportunities. Strong local rivalry has made it very difficult to create new and more 'economical' business organisations and/or novel forms of corporate governance such as strategic alliances, destination holding companies or other forms of cooperation and integrated networks. Individualistic and protective behaviour of 'valley lords' in tourism has prevented the entry of new and more competitive tourism enterprises.

The only market niches left particularly for small and/or micro enterprises are those for individualised personal services provided by the entrepreneur him(her) self, termed *'Gastfreundschaft'* (or guest hospitality) (Peters and Raich, 2002).

Enterprises' Ability to Differentiate

As was shown above, entrepreneurs and enterprises generally lack the ability to develop realistic strategic business plans and implement them both conceptually and practically. The ability to innovate new products/service niches includes above all the ability to conceptualise customer-driven problem solution, create customer benefits and standardise products/services along similar customer benefit segments (Heskett, 1988). The latter, however, requires a different mix of production factors such as technology, risk capital and, above all, qualified and professional human resources, all of which at present can be considered constraining rather than creative factors of expansion (Weiermair, 2001a, p. 18). This brings us back full circle into arguing for innovation as the most important and new factor of production and source of competitive advantage in tourism (Peters and Weiermair, 2002).

Viewed from a different vintage point, Austria's mass tourism is somewhere around the middle, displaying medium prices and medium quality which translates into a weak positioning strategy particularly when compared to international hotel companies and chains, which pursue clearly formed competitive market strategies.

WHERE IS THE RIVALRY BETWEEN SMES AND MNES IN TOURISM LEADING?

Using either Dunning's eclectic theory of international production (Dunning, 1979), Porter's analyses of the competitive advantage of nations (1990), Bartlett and Goshal's concept of the transnational firm (Bartlett and Goshal, 1991), or Yip's globalisation drivers (Yip, 1989), all seem to yield similar predictions regarding future competitive (dis)advantages of small versus large and integrated tourism enterprises.

First of all, as far as local advantages are concerned, MNEs will, using their global market knowhow, tap growth markets in Asia and the Americas and exploit Austria's locational advantages for inbound tourism in Austria. Their superior knowledge of customer preferences will make their products and services more attractive.

Austria's tourism firms will similarly be disadvantaged with respect to managerial knowhow and other qualifications of its personnel, which are largely based on the traditional dual-type apprenticeship programmes as the final preparation for entrepreneurship and management in tourism. The problem is aggravated by the phenomenon of 'brain drain' of the most capable and skilled workers, facilitated by a borderless world. Family businesses, where the emphasis is on the family and its proper succession and which are run like families, will increasingly become endangered by the risk of being tied to the fate of the individual owner. This sharply contrasts with the large MNE where change, innovation and learning have become routinised through proper knowledge management practices (White and Poynter, 1990, p. 103) making large tourism enterprises very flexible and fast changing compared with small and medium-sized family-owned businesses (Prahalad and Doz, 1987, p. 159).

Already a number of new forms of integration and concentration of tourism enterprises can be observed, as can be seen in the rising number of average bed capacity per establishment (Hubertus, 2000), and efforts to regionalise and centralise otherwise local business functions, notably with respect to market research and marketing, outsourcing product development and destination management.

Furthermore concentration and integration tendencies are enhanced by the necessity to form tourism clusters in such fields as culture, sports and/or health and tourism requiring diagonal integration (Poon, 1993). Tourism clusters offer at the same time, through their local authentic nature, entry barriers against foreign competitors, and here exist the greatest opportunities for local tourism enterprises to develop sustainable competitive advantages through innovation and differentiation, with the possibility of further growth and internationalisation.

Dunning's OLI theoretical framework provides, contrary to other attempts to explain industrial organisation phenomena in tourism (Johanson and Wiedersheim-Paul, 1975; Sharma and Johanson, 1987; Teece et al. 1997), the first useful answers and insights regarding the questions why MNEs are competitive, where they invest and in which form (governance) such investments take place in tourism (Dunning and Kundu, 1995). By playing down somewhat the monopolistic preconditions for internationalisation (Itaki, 1991; Meffert, 2000, p. 58; Weiermair, 1996) Dunning, however, provides little guidance regarding potential and possibly necessary policy interventions. Indeed, if the development of competitive disadvantages among SME tourism enterprises were the pure result of myopic behaviour only government-sponsored education and training systems for entrepreneurs and staff of tourism enterprises could be suggested on account of the well known arguments about market failure in education markets and/or training systems (Tschurtschenthaler, 1998; Weiermair, 1996). If it can be shown that monopolisation and monopolistic practices (such as limit pricing to ward off local competition or cross-subsidisation of markets to achieve long-term monopoly rents) were preconditions and/or essential long-term motives, the policy situation would have to be evaluated very differently, in that appropriate international rules for competition or competition policies would have to be worked out. In the absence of such international competition policies, a second-best policy would be to create market conditions at home which boost growth through innovation and new forms of organisations in tourism within a framework of promoting at the same time more quality competition among SMEs.

Although there is only scant and/or causal empirical evidence available regarding the declared market entry strategies of tourism MNEs into the Austrian market, it is worth noting that many MNEs in the USA suffer from high levels of rivalry and low profits, making small markets such as Austria more and more attractive.

NOTES

1. For example, the Hymer–Kindleberger approach (Hymer, 1976; Kindleberger, 1969), the ownership theory, the internalisation theory and the locational theory.
2. See Coase (1937) or Buckley and Casson (1976).
3. Services underlie several restrictions in terms of internationalisation (Vandermerwe and Chadwick, 1989).

REFERENCES

Acs, Z.J. and D.B. Audretsch (1989), 'Innovation, market structure and firm size. An empirical analysis', *American Economic Review*, **78**(4), 678–90.
Acs, Z.J. and D.B. Audretsch (1990), *Innovation in Small Firms*, Cambridge, MA: MIT Press.
Ateljevic, I. and S. Doorne (2000), 'Staying with the fence: lifestyle entrepreneurship in tourism', *Journal of Sustainable Tourism*, **8**(5), 378–92.
Audretsch, D.B. (1993), *Kleinunternehmen in der Industrieökonomik. Ein neuer Ansatz*, Berlin: Wissenschaftszentrum für Sozialforschung.
Bartlett, C.A. and S. Goshal (1991), *Managing across borders*, Boston, MA: Harvard University Press.
Bieger, T. (2001), *Management von Destinationen*, Munich: Oldenbourg.
Buckley, P.J. and M.C. Casson (1976), *The Future of the Multinational Enterprise*, London: Macmillan.
Buhalis, D. (1996), 'Information technology as a strategic tool for tourism', *The Tourist Review*, **2**, 34–7.
Clegg, J. (1987), *Multinational Enterprises and World Competition*, London: Macmillan.
Coase, R.H. (1937), 'The nature of the firm', *Economica*, **4**, 386–405.
Dunning, J.H. (1979), *Explaining International Production*, London: Unwin.
Dunning, J.H. (1988), *Explaining International Production*, London: Unwin.
Dunning, J.H. (1989), *Transnational Corporations and the Growth of Services: Some Conceptual and Theoretical Issues*, New York: UNCTC.

Dunning, J.H. and S.K. Kundu (1995), 'The internalization of the hotel industry – some new findings from a field study', *Management International Review*, **35**(2), 101–33.

Dunning, J.H. and J. McQueen (1982), 'The eclectic theory of the multinational enterprise and the international hotel industry', in A.M. Rugmann (ed.), *New Theories of the Multinational Enterprise*, London: Routledge, pp. 79–106.

Flagestad, A. and A.C. Hope (2001), 'Strategic success in wintersports destinations: a sustainable value creation perspective', *Tourism Management*, **22**(1), 445–61.

Foot, D. (2002), 'Leisure futures: a change in demography', paper presented at the Leisure Futures Conference, Innsbruck, Austria.

Frauendorfer, P. and F. Lanschützer (1992), *Erfolgreich im Neuen Osten*, Vienna: Signum.

Freitag, R.D. (1996), 'International mountain holidays – a pan European overview based on results of the European travel monitor', in K. Weiermair, M. Peters and M. Schipflinger (eds), *Alpine Tourism – Sustainability: Reconsidered and Redesigned*, Innsbruck: ITD University of Innsbruck, pp. 12–41.

Friedl, K. (2002), 'New work-Auswirkungen von Arbeitszeit und Arbeitsort, Flexibilisierung auf den Arbeitsplatz der Zukunft', paper presented at the 1st Leisure Futures Conference, Innsbruck, Austria.

Fuchs, M. and K. Weiermair (1999), 'Measuring tourist judgment on service quality', *Annals of Tourism Research*, **26**(4), 1004–21.

Heskett, J.L. (1988), *Dienstleistungsunternehmen*, Wiesbaden: Gabler.

Horillo, M.A.R. (2001), 'Resources and capabilities of tourist firms in the knowledge economy: towards a framework', in P.J. Sheldon, K. Wöber and D. Fesenmair (eds), *Information and Communication Technologies in Tourism 2001*, Vienna and New York: Springer, pp. 33–41.

Hubertus, J. (2000), *KMU-Statistik: Hotels, Restaurants und Gaststätten*, Luxemburg: Eurostat.

Hymer, S.H. (1976), *The International Operations of National Firms: A Study of Direct Foreign Direct Investment*, Cambridge: MIT Press.

Itaki, M. (1991), 'A critical assessment of the eclectic theory of the multinational enterprise', *Journal of International Business Studies*, third quarter, 445–61.

Jenster, P.V. and J.C. Jarillo (1994). *Internationalizing the Medium-sized Firm*, Stockholm: Handelshojskolens Forlag.

Johanson, J. and F. Wiedersheim-Paul (1975), 'The internationalization of the firm: four Swedish case studies', *Journal of International Business Studies*, **8**(Spring–Summer), 23–32.

Johnson, H.J. (1970), 'The efficiency and welfare implications of the international corporation', in C.P. Kindleberger (ed.), *The International Corporation*, Cambridge MA: MIT Press.

Kaldor, N. (1934), 'The equilibrium of the firm', *Economic Journal*, **44**(March), 60–76.

Kindleberger, C.P. (1969), *American Business Abroad*, New Haven: Yale University Press.

Klien, I. (1991), *Wettbewerbsvorteile von Groß- und Kettenhotels und deren Kompensierbarkeit durch Hotelkooperationen*, Vienna: Service Fachverlag.

Lucas, R.E. (1978), 'On the size distribution of business firms', *Bell Journal of Economics*, **9**(Autumn), 508–23.

Macharzina, K. (1992), 'Internationalisierung und Organisation', *Zeitschrift für Organisation und Führung*, 4ff.

Main, H.C. (2001), 'The use of the Internet by hotels in Wales. A longitudinal study from 1994 to 2000 of small and medium enterprises in a peripheral location with a focus on net technology', in P.J. Sheldon, K. Wöber and D. Fesenmair (eds), *Information and Communication Technologies in Tourism 2001*, Vienna and New York: Springer, pp. 215–23.

Marsan, J. and S. Wolchuck (2000), 'Hotels & Restaurant International, Special Report: Hotels 325', *Hotels*, **34**(7), 50–86.

Mazanec, J. and A. Zins (1996), 'Alpine winter tourists and guest satisfaction – an exploration of the typological relationships', in K. Weiermair, M. Peters and M. Schipflinger (eds), *Alpine Tourism Sustainability: Reconsidered and Redesigned*, Innsbruck: ITD University of Innsbruck, pp. 262–89.

Meffert, H. (2000), 'Internationalisierungskonzepte im Dienstleistungsbereich-Bestandsaufnahme und Perspektiven', in C. Belz and T. Bieger (eds), *Dienstleistungskompetenz und innovative Geschäftsmodelle*, St. Gallen: Forschungsinstitut für Absatz und Handel, Universität St. Gallen, pp. 504–19.

Opaschowski, H.W. (1993), *Freizeitökonomie. Marketing von Erlebniswelten*, Opladen: Leske & Budrig.

Pechlaner, H. and K. Weiermair (1999), 'Neue Qualifikationsanforderungen in Destinationsorganisationen', in H. Pechlaner and K. Weiermair (eds), *Destinationsmanagement: Führung und Vermarktung von touristischen Zielgebieten*, Vienna: Linde, pp. 79–90.

Peters, M. and M. Raich (2002), 'Die Rolle der persönlichen Interaktion im Dienstleistungser-stellungsprozess am Beispiel der Tourismusbranche', in H.H. Hinterhuber and H.K. Stahl (eds), *Erfolg durch 'Dienen'? Zur wertsteigernden Führung von Dienstleistungsunternehmen*, vol. 4, Renningen: Expert, pp. 337–55.

Peters, M. and K. Weiermair (2001a), 'The Schumpeterian entrepreneur and the entrepreneurial culture: half a century later', in V. Orati and S.B. Dahiya (eds), *Economic Theory in the Light of Schumpeter*, Rotak: Spellbound, pp. 301–314.

Peters, M. and K. Weiermair (2001b), 'Theoretical contructs and empirical evidence of entrepreneurial growth modes in the hospitality industry', paper presented at the 'Entrepreneurship in Tourism and the Contexts of Experience Economy' Conference, Rovaniemi, Lapland, April.

Peters, M. and K. Weiermair (2002), 'Innovationen und Innovationsverhalten im Tourismus', in T. Bieger and C. Laesser (eds), *Schweizer Jahrbuch für Tourismus 2001/2002*, St. Gallen: pp. 157–78.

Poon, A. (1993), *Tourism, Technology and Competitive Strategies*, Wallingford: CAB International.

Porter, M.E. (1990), 'The competitive advantage of nations', *Harvard Business Review*, **68**(2), 73–93.

Prahalad, C.K. and Y.L. Doz (1987), *The Multinational Mission*, New York: The Free Press.

Reisinger, H. (1994), *Marktoffensive in Osteuropa-Übernahme oder Neugründung von Unternehmen*, Vienna: Signum.

Roberts, J. (1998), *Multinational Business Service Firms*, Aldershot: Ashgate.

Roekarts, W.T. and K. Savat (1989), 'Mass tourism in South and Southeast Asia. A challenge to Christians and the churches', in T.V. Sing and F.M. Go (eds), *Towards Appropriate Tourism: The Case of Developing Countries*, Frankfurt a. M.: Peter Lang, pp. 35–70.

Sagari, S.B. (1992), 'United States foreign direct investment in the banking industry', *Transnational Corporations*, **1**(3), 93–23.

Sharma, D.D., and J. Johanson (1987), 'Technical consultancy in internationalization', *International Marketing Review*, **4**, 20–29.

Smeral, E. (1996), 'Globalization and changes in the competitiveness of tourism destinations', in P. Keller (ed.), *Globalisation in Tourism*, vol. 46, St. Gallen: AIEST.

Smeral, E., A. Weber, W. Auer, M. Fuchs and M. Peters (1998), *The Future of International Tourism*, Vienna: WIFO.

Teece, D.J., G. Pisano and A. Shuen (1997), 'Dynamic capabilities and strategic management', *Strategic Management Journal*, **18**(7), 509–34.

Tschurtschenthaler, P. (1998), 'Humankapitalentwicklung als tourismuspolitisches Instrument zur Bewältigung der Tourismuskrise', in K. Weiermair and M. Fuchs (eds), *Zukunftsentwicklung für eine optimale Humankapitalentwicklung/-verwertung in der Tourismuswirtschaft*, vol. 4, Innsbruck: Institut für Tourismus und Dienstleistungswirtschaft, Universität Innsbruck, pp. 16–39.

Vandermerwe, S. and M. Chadwick (1989), 'The internationalisation of services', *The Service Industries Journal*, **1**, 79–93.

Vernon, R. (1966), 'International investment and international trade in the product cycle', *Quarterly Journal of Economics*, **80**(2), 190–207.

Viner, J. (1932), 'Cost curves and supply curves', *Zeitschrift für Nationalökonomie*, **3**, 23–46.

Weiermair, K. (1996), 'Globalisation in Tourism: impact and implications for tourism manpower, employment and systems of training/schooling', in P. Keller (ed.), *Globalisation and Tourism*, vol. 38, St. Gallen: AIEST, pp. 245–57.

Weiermair, K. (1998), 'Globalisierung: Chancen und Risiken für die österreichische Tourismuswirtschaft', in H. Handler (ed.), *Wirtschaftsstandort Österreich*, Vienna: Bundesministerium für wirtschaftliche Angelegenheiten, pp. 111–20.

Weiermair, K. (2000), 'Know-how and qualification gaps in the tourism industry: the case of alpine tourism in Austria', *The Tourist Review*, **2**, 45–53.

Weiermair, K. (2001a), 'The growth of tourism enterprises', *Tourism Review*, **56**(3/4), 17–25.

Weiermair, K. (2001b), 'Neue Organisations-, Koordinations- und Führungsprinzipien im alpinen Tourismus', in K. Weiermair, M. Peters and E. Reiger (eds), *Vom alten zum neuen Tourismus*, Innsbruck: Studia, pp. 108–17.

Weiermair, K. and C. Mathies (2002), 'Use and misuse of yield management practices in tourism: a lesson from the airline industry?', in P. Keller and T. Bieger (eds), *Air Transport and Tourism*, vol. 44, St. Gallen: AIEST, pp. 143–63.

Weiermair, K. and M. Peters (1998), 'The internationalization behaviour of service enterprises', *Asia Pacific Journal of Tourism Research*, **2**(2), 1–14.

White, R.E. and T.A. Poynter (1990), 'Organizing for world-wide advantage', in C.A. Bartlett, Y. Doz and G. Hedlund (eds), *Managing the Global Firm*, London: Routledge, pp. 95–113.

Williamson, O.E. (1975), *Markets and Hierarchies Analysis and Antitrust Implications*, New York: The Free Press.

Wolchuk, S. and M.S. Lerner (2002), 'Special Report: Hotels' 325', retrieved from the World Wide Web (www.hotelsmag.com).

Yannopoulos, G.N. (1983), 'The growth of transnational banking', in M.C. Casson (ed.), *The Growth of International Business*, London: Unwin, pp. 236–72.

Yip, G. (1989), 'Global strategy in a world of nations?', *Sloan Management Review*, **31**(2), 29–41.

10. Institutional and policy variety, the role of IFIs and economic development*

Daniel Daianu

INTRODUCTION[1]

Variety, or let us call it diversity, is the essence of economic life in the sense of underlying choice; economic calculation gives numerical substance to the way people make choices in their daily endeavours, either as consumers or as entrepreneurs.[2] As Kevin Lancaster pointed out years ago, variety has value in itself,[3] for we enjoy a wider range of choices instead of a smaller one. How does variety/diversity take shape in the realm of institutions and policy making? Is the range of choices open-ended?

The last couple of decades have revealed an overwhelming offensive of the neoliberal paradigm in terms of defining 'best practices' and spreading the gospel of its policies throughout the world; this offensive was carried out by IFIs (international financial institutions) as well. Even language was shaped accordingly, with market reforms being seen in a single theoretical and policy framework. Are we heading towards increasing uniformity (according to the logic of this paradigm) with regard to institutional and policy set-ups, world-wide? A sceptical answer would highlight the economic challenges which confront societies, whether rich and poor, and the international community in general. One could mention also the partial counter-offensive represented by the so-called 'Third Way' paradigm,[4] the new vigour found by neo-Keynesian ideas and last, but not least, the powerful insights of the 'New Theories', as Robert Gilpin calls them.

This chapter argues that there is substantial scope for institutional and policy variety to operate as a means to foster economic development and that there might be paradigmatic cyclicity in the dynamic of economic policies. The demise of the 'New Economy', the metaphysical notion of the 1990s, the late spate of corporate scandals across the Atlantic and recurrent financial and currency crises throughout the world (which evince major flaws in the international financial system) and the controversies surrounding the role of IFIs, should compel 'ideologues', of all sorts, to be more humble in their prescriptions.

A HIGH AGE OF POLICY VARIETY

Institutional and policy variety was quite obvious in the aftermath of the Second World War. I am not referring to the philosphical and practical underpinnings of command (communist systems). What I have in mind is the wide spectrum of views with regard to economic development, the macromanagement of capitalist economy, trade policy arrangements, foreign exchange regimes for dealing with capital movements and so on. One can argue that a national economy-centred view dominated policy making, as against the modern conception of a 'borderless world' (Kenichi Ohmae, 1995).

That was a period in which Keynesianism fought monetarism in the realm of macroeconomic policy and got the upper hand, structuralism gained a high profile in relation to key problems afflicting developing countries and the theory of the developmental state was embodied by Asian accomplishments. Trade policy, too, was used by various countries to acquire new competitive advantages.

There was much confidence in the regulatory power of the state and in its ability to make the economy (markets) function better, a vison which may have been reinforced by the tasks of postwar economic reconstruction and post-colonialism. But these policies were frequently abused during that period and wishful thinking influenced policy making not infrequently. Arguably this policy thrust did undermine the vigour of market forces. Nonetheless the record showed positive results: these included economic reconstruction in Western Europe, a string of economic miracles in Asia and Brazil's economic growth (however fractured and skewed that was).

THE NEOLIBERAL ZEITGEIST OF RECENT DECADES

I would submit that globalisation is driven by both technological and institutional (policy) factors. Therefore it can be seen as a facet, too, of the neoliberal offensive which started a couple of decades ago.[5] But one should make a distinction between technological change (progress), which has economic and institutional consequences and which is, historically, of inscrutable vintage, and the range of policies initiated in the framework of wide-ranging financial and trade liberalisation, as well as of massive privatisation.

During this period one meets the retreat of Keynesianism (against the background of rising inflation in several advanced economies and the setbacks of profligate welfarism) together with a belief in the preponderance of government failures in macro and micro-managing economies; market coordination failures are largely dismissed. Likewise the poor record of economic progress in large areas of the world speeded up the decline of development economics. As a matter of fact, mainstream (neoclassical) economics was seen as providing a valid toolbox for any circumstances. Thence emerged a policy framework, supported by the IFIs (the so-called 'Washington Consensus'), which supplanted the much wider conceptual policy approach of the 1950s and 1960s.

In the 1980s there was much talk about a clash of models: the Anglo-American model versus a so-called 'continental model', and an Asian model. Nonetheless trade liberalisation, market deregulation and privatisation contained ideological fervour and were pushed by the IFIs unrelentingly. The collapse of communism gave a further impetus to this vision and policy orientation.

The complete independence of central banks, fiscal conservatism and neutrality, rejection of macromanagament of the economy, 'downsizing' of the public sector and market deregulation were seen as epitomes of sound economics and policy, to be generalised worldwide. And globalisation supplied the world arena for thinking that there is 'one way, and only one way' in order to achieve economic progress and, eventually, catching up. The natural inference would be that policy variety in policy making is senseless in a world which appears to have discovered the ultimate *best practices*, either at the macro or at the micro level.

THE DISAPPOINTING RECORD

There are numerous facts which invalidate the rosy picture portrayed above and invite soul searching and honest debate. First, the Washington Consensus[6] has performed much below expectations and there is an increasing number of top-level economists who question some of its working hypotheses; theoretical premises are severely questioned[7] and the work of the International Monetary Fund (IMF) and the World Bank (WB) has come under fire.[8]

Policies aimed at fostering growth in developing countries seem to have fared quite poorly, in many respects, in the last couple of decades, at a time of apparent firm application of the main tenets of the 'Washington Consensus'. According to a leading development economist, William Easterly (until recently on the World Bank staff), during 1980–98 average per capita income growth in developing countries was practically 0.0 per cent, as compared to 2.5 per cent during 1960–79.[9] I would add that this discrepancy becomes even larger when singling out the economic performance of some Asian countries which, as an increasing number of economists would concede, did pursue export orientation, but also implemented measures which, often, were at odds with the 'orthodox' policies;[10] these countries shaped their own particular strategies. As Easterly also points out, 'the increase in world interest rates, the increased debt burden of developing countries, the growth slowdown in the industrial world, and skill-biased technical change may have contributed' to this stagnation.[11] Easterly also stresses the inability of governments' policies worldwide to make good use of incentives for growth. This state of affairs begs a simple question: why is it so difficult to use incentives in order to foster sustained growth?[12] Easterly goes on, 'We economists who work on poor countries should leave aside some of our past arrogance. The problem of making poor countries rich was much more difficult than we thought.'

Mainstream (neoclassical) theory has still to explain why divergence is so prevalent in the world economy.[13] Moreover endogenous growth models[14] and economic geography models have reinforced misgivings about the unqualified optimism regarding the distribution of benefits of free trade and free capital movements. Hence a natural question arises: is opening (integration) to the outer economy advantageous, irrespective of circumstances?

There has been insufficient attention paid to the reality of asymmetries and informational problems in the functioning of both domestic and international markets, and to the key role of institutions. Partly this is mirrored by the talk regarding 'second-generation reforms', 'good governance' and 'reinvigorating the state's capabilities'. But, as Dani Rodrik remarked, 'The bad news is that the operational implications of this for the design of development strategy are not that clear', and 'There are many different models of a mixed economy. The major challenge facing developing nations is to fashion their own particular brands of mixed economy.'[15] In this respect, he stresses the key role of institutions regarding property rights, conflict management and law and order. This search for country-specific solutions does not clash with the need to use so-called 'best practices', but one should equally acknowledge that 'best practices' are not always clear. In this context, one has to give a fair hearing to Mauro Guillen, who argues that globalisation should not be understood as encouraging 'convergence toward a single organisational pattern' and that 'organisational outcomes in the global economy are contingent on country-specific trajectories'.[16] The implication is that variety does matter and adds value.

The issue of asymmetries acquires particular salience in the international economy, where there is increasing disenchantment with the distribution of trade gains[17] and the functioning of financial markets. In this respect, one has to stress both the distribution aspect of trade (which relates to the rules of the game and to the way in which industrial countries defend their own markets[18]), and the institutional dimension.

Prominent voices argue that the world community needs new arrangements and new institutions, which should be capable of addressing the problems of world governance.[19] For instance, it is disconcerting to see that the efforts initiated in the field of financial markets reform by the Financial Stability Forum, in 1998, subsided. As Larry Summers astutely pointed out, world integration demands financial integration, but, as the 1920s and 1930s prove, recurrent financial crises can lead to world disintegration.[20]

Furthermore post-communist economic transition has had very mixed results and the mantra of quick privatisation and liberalisation has clearly indicated its limits and oversimplicity. Under the term 'the second wave of reforms' there is an attempt to renew transformation economics by acknowledging the role of institutional change (and its consuming nature), the importance of competition and structures of governance (in the public and the private sectors), the need of public goods (which cannot be supplied by the private sector), and so on.

The backlash against globalisation is a stark reminder of the perils of succumbing to a simplistic economic cosmology. Growing economic gaps in the world,[21] increasingly unstable financial markets and recurrent crises, the deterioration of the environment and the challenge of sustainable development in the world, spreading diseases and so on have brought home much bad news. There is now talk of the need to manage (correct) globalisation and reform the international financial system.

The fading away of the myth of the 'New Paradigm' and 'the New Economy' in the USA, the spate of corporate scandals in the USA[22] and the plunging stock markets worldwide, and very rocky recovery in the USA together with poor growth in the EU, are not without policy consequences. In the USA, the Bush Administration has resorted to a heavy dose of Keynesian economics in order to stem recession.

In sum, the discrepancy between preaching and practice, particularly in the case of advanced economies,[23] should give much food for thought, quite apart from its hypocritical undertones.

WHERE DO WE STAND?

One can hardly question basic rules of the economic game, which underlie a sound functioning of economies. Such rules are, for instance, that free prices are essential for resource allocation, hard budget constraints need to operate ubiquitously in order to have financial stability, over the longer term low budget deficits are better than large ones, and money printing is bad for monetary stability. But intellectual bigotry and doctrinal fundamentalism are detrimental to good policy making, for the latter needs to be pragmatic and not skewed towards vested interests.

At the beginning of the new century the jury is still out on many central issues which have divided economists over the decades. This ambiguous reality and theoretical situation should trigger more candid debate in the places where policy is formulated or among those organisations which advise governments. Let me single out some of these central issues.

First, although free trade is deemed desirable by most economists, the existence of considerable asymmetries and dynamic effects provides a rationale for developing countries to seek some protection; in this respect, some distinguish between free and fair trade. As Dani Rodrik put it, free trade is not always conducive to economic growth.[24]

Second, free capital flows have been revealed to be quite threatening for emerging markets, and the IMF no longer recommends the opening of the capital account unless proper regulatory and institutional prerequisites exist.

Third, the role of the government in dealing with market coordination failures is widely debated and there is acknowledgment that there is scope for government intervention; the proliferation of financial and currency crises and gross irregularities in the functioning of other markets (energy trading, for example) are making a compelling case for strengthening regulatory frameworks and law enforcement by the state.[25]

Fourth, the role of government in providing public goods is undeniable and some would argue that fostering industrial and technological development is also part of a government's attributes. As a matter of fact, what else but industrial policy is the EU's Eurika programme?

Finally, fiscal neutralism can be deceptive in a world of huge asymmetries.

Economists nowadays, while underlining the pre-eminence of markets in resource allocation and the rewarding of entrepreneurship, debate fiercely about the economic role of governments. This debate has been fuelled by theoretical insights brought about by 'The New Theories':[26] the theory of multiple equilibria, which posits the possibility of persistent bad equilibria; the theory of endogenous growth, which undermines some basic constructs of neoclassical economics (such as 'the law of diminishing returns'); the thesis of path dependency (the role of history) and the importance of geography; the role of information costs and asymmetries, the importance of clusters for achieving competitive advantages,[27] and so on.

'The New Theories' rely on, or bring back into the limelight, theses of the old development economics. For Albert Hirschman, Paul Rosenstein-Rodan, Ragnar Nurkse, Gunar Myrdal and Harvey Leibenstein all highlighted the role of institutions, structural features of poor countries which keep them hostage to various types of traps and the need for assistance (what Rosenstein-Rodan termed as the 'Big Push' in a famous article written in 1943).[28]

To sum up: the current debate on development economics has rediscovered several of its old issues and, in this context, it re-emphasises the existence of externalities, multiple equilibria, bad path dependencies, vicious circles and 'underdevelopment traps', all of which pose numerous challenges to public policy. For it is increasingly obvious that public policy (at the national and the international level) has a role to play in order to address coordination failures. This is because 'There may be a social equilibrium in which forces are balanced in a way that is Pareto improving relative to one in which the government's hands are completely tied – and certainly better than one in which the private sector's hands are completely tied.'[29] In this context, one needs to underline the importance of good institutions, of proper structures for public and corporate governance, which condition the overall performance of the economy.

It is increasingly clear that the wide variety of economic performance in transition (post-communist) countries has to be related to the different functioning of institutional set-ups and policy variety. It may be that we are on the verge of a new age of development economics against the backdrop of the very disappointing record of economic advance in most of the developing world (if one excludes China and parts of India), transition failures in many post-communist countries, and the backlash against globalisation. Dani Rodrik, Paul Krugman, Joseph Stiglitz, Olivier Blanchard and others form a remarkable platoon of brilliant economists who can inject more realism and creativity into policy making.

WHAT INFLUENCES INSTITUTIONAL AND POLICY VARIETY?

Ideology

As John Maynard Keynes said, economists are intellectual prisoners of famous ideas. But ideas do not operate in a social vacuum. This is why, where democracy exists, it is not hard to detect linkages between the dynamic of political life (which is influenced by ideas or doctrines) and changes in economic policies. This is because the constellation of interests in society, which are articulated politically, drives policy formulation. When circumstances modify the texture of interests and also entail variations in the power (relevance) of ideas (some decay and others are resuscitated), policies change.

Complexity

Complexity does affect the ability of policy to influence economic outcomes. Undoubtedly, growing complexity magnified the costs of command-type planning in the former communist states and speeded up their collapse. Another example is provided by the European Union. Thus the EU encounters mounting difficulties in its quest for institutional reforms (the Common Agricultural

Policy included) owing to its growing size and complexity. And it is clear that enlargement would not make this task easier. Japan achieved an economic miracle during the 20th century, especially after the Second World War; her success was fuelled by an ingenious combination of market-based economic structures and state intervention. Nonetheless the increasing complexity and export orientation of the Japanese economy has entailed changes in its functioning and is forcing policy makers to rethink their policy tools in order to cope with new policy dilemmas[30] (I refer here, in particular, to the decade-long stagnation and not, necessarily, to the consequences of the crisis in the banking system). And the recent corporate scandals in the USA show the proliferation of conflicts of interest and the dangers of excessive market deregulation against the background of increasingly complex financial innovations.[31]

Economic Openness

The more open and smaller is an economy the more severely its national policy is constrained by external stimuli (phenomena). This is why open macroeconomics are quite different from macroeconomics in a relatively closed economy. Size matters considerably in explaining the intensity of transmitted effects, the power of interdependencies.

International Agreements

International agreements operate as a constraining factor unless a country's policy makers obtain derogations, or enter into special arrangements with partners.

Policy Conditionality

In a world of growing interdependencies, the effectiveness (performance) of policy making hinges on local expertise and the bargaining power of local negotiators in dealing with IFIs and other entities (such as the EU). Policy conditionality is to be linked to policy ownership. Lately the IFIs increased their concern for enhanced policy ownership, although, sometimes, this smells more of a rhetorical exercise or an attempt to diffuse the blame for failed programmes.

The Rules Imposed by the Functioning of Economic and Monetary Blocs

For example, the EU accession countries have to comply with the so-called *Acquis Communautaire*. However, there is room for bargaining and the EU itself should be interested in better policy venues in view of its own reform pains and the need to help accession countries to catch up economically.

Special Circumstances

Powerful adverse shocks force policy makers to change their views and entrenched habits. Think, for example, of the rescue package mounted by the Republican Administration in the USA in order to help airline companies (following the tragedy of 11 September) or the credits granted by the central bank of Brazil to firms which were badly affected by credit lines withdrawn by foreign banks (during late 2002).

VALUES, INSTITUTIONS AND ECONOMY

Lately the issues of ethical behaviour and social responsibility of firms and individuals have come prominently to the forefront of public debate. Widespread corruption and unethical behaviour are primarily seen as features of institutional fragility and lack of democratic credentials, which are to be found in the developing world in particular. Nonetheless the late spate of corporate scandals in the USA and similar cases in the rich part of Europe illustrate a more complex reality. One should remember that a similar wave of scandals gripped the USA in the 1980s. Is there a cyclical pattern in advanced economies, linked with unavoidable behavioural excesses during periods of exuberance, which would subside over time following policy and institutional adjustments? Or can one establish institutional circumstances and peculiar policies which enhance unethical behaviour, and which do not trigger adequate/counteracting responses automatically? Can one link social and economic dynamics of capitalism to apparent shifts in some of the values which drive entrepreneurs' behaviour? Is the profit motive similar to greed, or, to use Alan Greenspan's famous words, to 'irrational exuberance'? What is the role of norms (formal and informal) in constraining socially irresponsible behaviour?

Post-communist transition is replete with cases of corruption and unethical behaviour. The handy answer in explaining them would be the very institutional weakness of post-communist societies, a precarious functioning of checks and balances and a corrupted judiciary together with very feeble law enforcement capacity. In an optimistic vein, the same reasoning would highlight the advance of structural and institutional reforms, which would allow these societies gradually to diminish considerably any malign (unethical) behaviour. Joining the European Union can be seen through the lenses of this upbeat logic. A more broadly defined answer would include the issue of governance in both the public and the private spheres and scrutinise lessons worldwide, in both rich and poor countries. A pessimistic answer would talk about a bad 'path dependency' and point at the persistence of widespread corruption, precarious institutions and malfunctioning markets in large parts of the world.

In transition societies the prospect of joining the EU has operated as a catalyst for reforms and a strong support for dealing with the pains and frustrations of social change. But numerous citizens are disappointed by the results of reforms, and the widespread corruption and unethical behaviour incense most of the population; some citizens relate these phenomena to market reforms, and this perception does show up unabashedly in the polls. Once the first wave of accession took place benefits would accrue to many citizens, but disappointments, too, are likely to become more intense. Such likely outcomes beg a candid discussion on the linkage between values, morality and the dynamic of capitalism and what it takes to make it more fulfilling for most of the population. This is why the public debate on effective regulations (law enforcement) and institutions, which should strengthen the ability of markets to deliver to the satisfaction of most citizens (consumers) and avoid massive social exclusion has not lost any relevance. The scope of the state in providing public goods should be judged in the same vein, albeit this role should be judged in conjunction with the need for a streamlined and more efficient public sector, which should not crowd out (undermine) the profficiency of the private sector.

The public debate on ethics and economy acquires new overtones when looking at the world under the impact of globalisation and other forces at work. Besides international terrorism, one can point to the dark side of globalisation: inability to cope with global issues (such as global warming), massive illegal immigration, increasing poverty in many areas of the world, poor functioning of international financial markets and so on. In this context, the issues of governance, in both the public and the private spheres, gain more salience, and governance cannot be dissociated from the values and mindsets of those who make decisions.

The years following the Great Depression brought about new regulations, aimed at restraining excesses and unethical behaviour in markets' functioning. An example was the Glass–Steagall Act in the USA, which separated investment banking from commercial banking. The recent scandals in corporate America and on Wall Street question the wisdom of wide deregulation which occurred in the banking industry in the late 1990s. Institutional adjustments followed the end of the Second World War as well. History seems to indicate a cycle of policies and institutional adjustments following large economic dynamics. It may be that, after the 'deregulation euphoria' which featured so highly on the agenda of governments, especially in the Anglo-

Saxon world, during the last couple of decades, a new phase is about to set in. This phase would underline the need for effective market regulations and a more enlightened working together between the public and private spheres. This logic would also have to apply to the international economy, which needs public goods so badly, which further demands reshaped international institutions capable of ensuring global governance. The latter, clearly, asks for more international cooperation and a common vision on how to tackle the major challenges confronting mankind. These challenges cannot be dealt with unless economic rationality blends with social and moral values, which should preserve the necessary social cement of societies.[32]

MORE ON THE ROLE OF IFIS

Perfection does not exist in life and criticism is part and parcel of what prods progress. This reality applies to the activity of large organisations as well, including the IFIs; the latter are supposed to provide public goods to the world community and, for this reason, their endeavours are constantly examined by governments, NGOs and citizens at large. The activity of IFIs has been surrounded by intense controversies starting in the late 1990s. The recurrent financial and currency crises worldwide, the disppointments of trade liberalisation (particularly in developing countries), the record of economic development in poor countries and the ambiguous effects of globalisation have brought the IMF, the WTO and the World Bank more under the scrutiny of public debate in academic, policy and wider circles. This section tries to sum up some of the ideas which are scattered through this chapter.

There are several areas which stir debate on the role of IFIs in economic development. One is the set of ideas (the paradigm) which has driven their policy recommendations over the last couple of decades. Is the neoliberal framework the more suitable framework for fostering economic development, irrespective of circumstances? In certain respects it is, as is the case of stimulating entrepreneurship and fighting excessive welfarism and central regulation. But, as Dani Rodrik and others argue, this framework is far from sufficient in enabling policy makers to deal with the complexity of development efforts in a world which is replete with asymmetries, market imperfections and precarious equilibria.

Another area of debate concerns the very policy advice of IFIs. The most notorious policy turnaround, probably, is capital account liberalisation (CAL). The latter was strongly recommended by the IMF to developing countries in the 1990s, following the logic of free capital flows and the creation of a 'level playing field' in a (supposedly) increasingly globalised world economy. It is fair to acknowledge that capital account liberalisation has exposed many institutional and policy weaknesses in various countries; but it is also correct, for those who advocated this policy drive, to acknowledge that CAL was a mistake in view of the turbulence it caused in many countries and the contagion effects it entailed. Nowadays the IMF admits, both explicitly and implicitly, this mistake when it links CAL with sound macroeconomic policy, proper institutions (including the banking/financial system) and solid prudential regulations. The financial débâcle in Argentina and the demise of the currency board question are another major tenet of the late 1990s (following the financial crises): the corner solutions[33] as inescapable exchange rate regimes in a world of free capital flows. Life shows again its complexity and the danger of oversimplifications.

Trade policy is also under scrutiny. The World Bank and the World Trade Organisation (WTO) advocate free trade as a means of satisfying consumers and making good use of comparative advantages. But free trade can be highly inequitable when asymmetries are blatant and increasing returns dominate growing industries. One has to stress also here the discrepancy between what some rich countries preach and what they practise. Trade in farm products and textiles is highly relevant in this regard.

Tax policy is an issue for debate as well. Rich countries used a different level and structure of taxes when they were at an inferior level of economic development. How does this fact bear on the suggestion – which some make – of using their current taxation systems as signposts for tax reform in developing/transition countries? Several questions can be raised in this respect:

- Which best practices does one have in mind? Can an economy leapfrog development stages by just trying to imitate (import) institutions?
- Do best practices mean uniform rates?
- Does it make sense to look at the experience of economies, be they very few, which achieved remarkable economic progress during recent decades (the succcessful catching-up stories) too?
- To what extent do globalisation and the rules and regulations of the international economic system (WTO and so on) allow an economy room for using fiscal devices with the aim of fostering growth? (The case of Ireland is conspicuous in Western Europe; and, among transition countries, the Visegrad group, which attracted most of the FDI by using fiscal incentives as well, is pretty well known.)

But one can broaden the discussion and look at Asian economies, too. The developmental challenge may be less relevant for the accession countries (even though they themselves have to close major gaps vis-à-vis the West), but it is certainly becoming of paramount importance for south-east Europe.

The conventional wisdom (and the advice provided by the IFIs) stresses the need for fiscal neutrality. But how can the least distortionary effects of taxes be judged in a world in which there are numerous externalities, asymmetries, adverse external shocks, multiple equilibria and the rest? How can one deal most effectively with the frequency of second-best situations? And what are policy implications, in general, and for taxation, in particular?

Policy conditionality has been mentioned already as a high-profile issue. The IFIs seem to be ambivalent in this respect; on one hand they seem to concede the need to allow governments more room in formulating their own national policies; on the other hand, the IFIs have a hard time devising new procedures to this end and, also, show a sort of organisational/intellectual inertia in absorbing new ideas. This represents a major challenge for the IFIs when they are seen as a repository of knowledge and providers of sound advice. The IFIs would have to engage in a more candid debate on the policy challenges facing the developing world (the World Bank is, apparently, more open in this respect) and explore new policy avenues by assimilating what Robert Gilpin called 'the New Theories'. As a matter of fact, these new insights hook up with some of the main ideas of the classical development economics.

Last, but not least, the IFIs would have to come to grips with the issue of 'global governance'; this involves their own operations as well as some substantive institutional reform, as in the case of the international financial system. But here one meets the vested interests of the main players in the international economic system, which may delay changes unless a major event (such as a major crisis) forces a radical shift in their policy propensity.

THE EUROPEAN UNION (EU) FACTOR

In the above context, an interesting question appears: are the efforts to adopt the *Acquis Communautaire* by EU accession countries the equivalent of an effective strategy for economic catching up? In many domains, they may well be so, to the extent that good institutions are smoothly 'imported' and function effectively, and to the extent that technology transfer and upgrading of production (via FDIs) occur intensively, for the benefit of a majority of the citizens (and social cohesion is not impaired).

The EU, as a phenomenon, is exceptional, in a historical perspective; it is unique both economically and politically in modern history. This is why one can hardly establish an analogy between NAFTA (North American Free Trade Agreement) and the agreements which the accession countries have with the EU. As a matter of fact, the accession countries see in the EU enlargement an historical chance to speed up their economic development and modernisation. Can integration into the EU be viewed as a grand strategy for economic catching up (beta-convergence) and modernisation for the 'Big Push', which most Central and East European countries (CEECs) have been seeking during the 20th century?[34] It is worthwhile recalling what Paul Rosenstein-Rodan had in mind when he wrote his famous article in 1943. In that article, he referred to key interdependencies in an economy which may preclude its development unless there is effective coordination among its constituent parts (industries). Development calls for complementary changes of action and resources, and such simultaneous endeavours may not be possible in the absence of a strong stimulus, of a 'big push'. This is a crucial question to be addressed by policy makers.

Central and Eastern European societies do not look poor in important respects (such as the literacy rate of the population, general educational standards and behavioural patterns), but most of them face a set of challenges which are specific to poor countries: still fragile institutions, worrying growth of inequality[35] (precarious social cohesion), incompetent governments (political elites), endemic corruption, which distorts and taxes business, and so on. Therefore these countries need to formulate policies which should tackle the type of problems confronted by poor countries as well; they need development (catching up) strategies.

Empirical analyses show that the opening up of the economy and integration with the outside world have better chances of fostering economic growth when there is an intense inflow of foreign direct investment, which upgrades the capital stock and human capital of the recipient countries while it does not crowd out domestic investment. It is no surprise, therefore, that the frontrunner accession countries have received a disproportionate share of FDI.

Equally a strategy of economic development (catching up) requires 'policy ownership', which refers both to domestic intellectual capabilities (expertise), and to the capacity to formulate policies. This is the lesson of the most impressive cases of catching up of the last century (whether one thinks of Japan, South Korea, Singapore, or, more recently, Ireland).

It may be that the EU arrangements could partially supplant the need for domestic policy capabilities. But, as the reports of the European Commission consistently document, particularly in the case of the less performing accession countries, public administration reform is critical for development, which is a clear indication of the essential tasks of domestic policy. It is true, however, that, within the constraints of the institutional functioning of the EU, domestic policy formulation acquires a new connotation. But the problem remains, since Brussels cannot be a substitute for makers of key decisions at the national level.

Here is a caveat about the linkage between EU integration and convergence. Some Central and Eastern European countries' premises for catching up may clash with the strict conditionality of the Maastricht Treaty criteria, in the case where the accession countries intend to join the Exchange Rate Mechanism (ERM2) and, later on, the Monetary Union. A related situation is entailed by the implications of the 'Balassa–Samuelson effect',[36] which may make it impossible for accession countries to comply with the requirement of a low inflation rate in order to fit in with the EU (ERM) area.[37] And, should they try to attain a very low inflation rate, this may undermine growth and, therefore, catching up. If this is the case, should some of the accession criteria be made more flexible?[38] How would the EU member countries view such a weakening of criteria? To what extent can the logic of a 'variable geometry' play a role in this context? Would such a variable geometry process of enlargement be manageable?

For the EU candidate countries, the low inflation criteria (and, further, the Maastricht Treaty provisions) and the negotiations with Brussels raise two main sets of questions: one regards trade links and, more specifically, the capacity of accession countries to withstand competitive pressures when trade asymmetries disappear; the other issue regards the possibility for the candidate countries to accommodate the stern exigencies of a very low inflation environment, even if they do not adopt the single currency.

It should also be highlighted that, against the backdrop of vagaries in an increasingly uncertain world environment, the EU can provide a shelter, which should be seen in the context of attempts, worldwide, to form economic and monetary blocks.

CONCLUDING REMARKS

Moving away from theoretical fundamentalism in policy making would enhance the room for institutional and policy variety, which fosters economic development. By this I do not mean governments reneging on the basic rules of sound behaviour in economic policy making. Instead, I have in mind creative policy making, which should shun policy fundamentalism and acknowledge particular circumstances. At the same time, 'bad governance' in poor countries would have to be fought against unswervingly.

The IFIs would have to be more candid about past and present failures in development policy and be faithful to the idea of policy ownership, which, it should be said, does not preclude policy conditionality. Likewise Western governments should practise more what they preach in order to be more credible in their dialogue with the developing world. This would concern policy making at the national level and the production (protection) of public goods for the benefit of mankind (current and future generations).

One should also re-examine the functioning of the international economic system, which should draw on the insights of 'the New Theories' and try to deal with the proliferation of bad equilibria, recurrent financial and currency crises, growing economic gaps, the deterioration of the environment and conflicts in the world. Institutional and policy variety does have a meaning and a future.

NOTES

*   An earlier version of this chapter was published in 2003 as 'Institutional and policy variety: does it matter for development?', in V. Franiceric and H. Kimura (eds), *Globalisation, Democratisation and Development: European and Japanese Views of Change in South East Europe*, Zagreb: Masmedia, pp. 15–36. I hereby thank Masmedia for the permission to use parts of that version.

1.   The comments made by Ivo Bicanic, Vlado Gligorov, Kunibert Raffer, Slavo Radosevic and Tsumeaki Sato are highly appreciated. I bear sole responsibility for the content of the chapter.

2.   As Sherwin Rosen says, 'Diversity is the stuff of economics'(*American Economic Review*, **92**(1), March, 2002, p. 1.

3.   Kevin Lancaster, *Variety, Equity and Efficiency*, Oxford: Blackwell, 1979.

4.   The guru is Anthony Giddens. The 'new social democrats' talk about a worldwide political movement which should embrace their ideas.

5.   George Soros, among others, calls it 'market fundamentalism' (*On Globalisation*, New York: Norton, 2002).

6.   The 'Washington Consensus', as a name, was coined by John Williamson, with reference to the essence of IMF and World Bank's policies pursued in the last couple of decades.

7.   Joseph Stiglitz (1994, 2002) is the most notorious critic of the IMF, but the list includes Paul Krugman, Jeffrey Sachs, Jagdish Bhagwhati and others.

8.   James Wolfensohn himself has indicated that he is not insensitive to what is wrong with the World Bank.

9.   Easterly's results seem to contradict one of the main conclusions of the World Bank's *Global Economic Prospects for Developing Countries 2001*, which asserts that 'Developing countries as a group enjoyed accelerated economic growth over the past decade'(*World Bank Policy and Research Bulletin*, April–June 2001, p. 1). It is fair to say, however, that Easterly refers to per capita income growth.

10.   These countries achieved macroeconomic stabilisation via low budget deficits and tight monetary policies, but did not refrain from focusing on potential 'winners', through industrial and trade polices. A natural question arises whether such policies can be effective under the pressure of globalisation and when public administration is weak, or captured by vested interests, as is the case in many transition economies.

11.   William Easterly (2001a) manuscript. See also his *The Elusive Quest for Growth* (2001b).

12.   William Easterley (2001b, p. 291).

13.   See The World Bank's Annual Conference on Development Economics, proceedings of 1999 and 2000 meetings. As the World Bank economist P. Richard Agenor put it, 'the conventional neoclassical theory has proved incapable of explaining in a satisfactory manner the wide disparities in the rates of per capita output growth across countries' (2000, p. 392).

14.   Pioneered by Paul Romer and Robert Lucas. Lucas (1988, pp. 3–42) explains why divergence, instead of convergence, does happen.

15.   Dani Rodrik (2000a). Rodrik emphasises five functions that public institutions must serve for markets to work properly: protection of property rights, market regulation, macroeconomic stabilisation, social insurance and conflict management. He also underlines that 'there is in principle a large variety of institutional setups that could fulfill these functions' (p. 3).

16. Mauro F. Guillen (2001).
17. As the World Bank's *Global Economic Prospects and the Developing Countries 2001* report says, 'trade barriers in industrial countries represent a major roadblock for developing countries'(p. 2).
18. The preparations for the Doha WTO conference were quite telling in this respect, with the USA, the EU and Japan having basically set the agenda.
19. This is the message of George Soros (2002). Lord Dahrendorf is also very critical of the way in which the existing international institutions address these issues in his lecture delivered at the New Europe College, Bucharest, October 2001.
20. Larry Summers (2000, p. 1).
21. The 2002 annual report of the World Bank furthers the debate on the inadequacies of current policies for dealing with poverty reduction (*Financial Times*, 23 August, 2002).
22. Following these scandals the Anglo-American model has lost some of its lustre (see also Eric Orts, 'Law is never enough to guarantee fair practice', *Financial Times*, 23 August, 2002).
23. Think only of farm subsidies provided by both the USA and the EU, and steel protectionism on the part of the USA.
24. Paul Krugman developed the concept of 'strategic trade', which is rooted in the behaviour of large enterprises.
25. As Professor Tsumeaki Sato argued at the Zagreb conference, the 'market oriented regulatory state' gets an increasing profile.
26. Robert Gilpin (2001).
27. Michael Porter's use of clusters in explaining competitive advantages makes a link with Gunar Myrdal's concept of cumulative causation.
28. Paul Rosenstein-Rodan (1943).
29. Karla Hoff (2000, p. 170).
30. For an excellent presentation of Japan's current economic pains and travails, see Bai Gao (2001).
31. One can see here some bad effects of the repeal of the Glass–Steagall legislation.
32. Deepak Lal talks about the importance of shame-based and guilt-based cement in explaining cultural traits of long run economic performance (1999).
33. Corner solutions refer to pegged exchange rates (like currency boards) or free floating rates.
34. P.N. Rosenstein-Rodan (1943, reprinted in H.S. Ellis, 1961).
35. It should be acknowledged, nonetheless, that much of this growing inequality is unavoidable, as a result of the change from a command (highly egalitarian) to a market-based economic system.
36. When a developing economy grows faster than a developed economy, owing to faster efficiency gains in the tradeable sector, real wages throughout the economy would also increase faster, which would create higher inflation in the non-tradeable sector.
37. Dariusz Rosati (2001). See also Laszlo Halpern and Charles Wiplosz (2001).
38. One can make an analogy with the current debate on the adequacy of some of the provisions of the Stability Act of the European Union: the 3 per cent budget deficit upper limit at a time of very slow growth in the Eurozone.

REFERENCES

Agenor, P. Richard (2000), *The Economics of Adjustment and Growth*, New York: Academic Press.

Blanchard, Olivier (1997), *The Economics of Post-communism*, Oxford: Clarendon Press.

Daianu, Daniel (2002), 'How possible is catching up in Europe?', TIGER Working Papers, Warsaw, May.

Ellis, H.S. (ed.) (1961), *Economic Development for Latin America*, New York: St. Martin's Press.

Easterly, William (2001a), 'The lost decades: developing countries' stagnation in spite of policy reform 1980–1998' (manuscript).

Easterly, William (2001b), *The Elusive Quest for Growth*, Cambridge, MA: MIT Press.

Gao, Bai, (2001), *Japan's Economic Dilemma*, Cambridge: Cambridge University Press

Giddens, Anthony (1998), *The Third Way. The Renewal of Social Democracy*, London: Polity Press.

Gilpin, Robert, (2001), *Global Political Economy*, Princeton: Princeton University Press.

Guillen, Mauro F. (2001), *The Limits of Convergence. Globalization and Organizational Change in Argentina, South Korea and Spain*, Princeton: Princeton University Press.

Halpern, Laszlo and Charles Wiplosz (2001), 'Economic transformation and real exchange rates in the 2000s: the Balassa–Samuelson connection', *Economic Survey of Europe 2001*, Geneva: UN/ECE, pp. 227–40.

Hoff, Karla (2000), 'Beyond Rosenstein-Rodan: the modern theory of coordination problems in development' *Annual World Bank Conference on Development Economics. Proceedings*, Washington, DC: World Bank.

Kolodko, Grzegorz W. (2002), *Globalization and Catching-up in Transition Economies*, Rochester, NY and Woodbridge, UK: University of Rochester Press.

Krugman, Paul (1994), *Geography and Trade*, Cambridge, MA: MIT Press.

Lal, Deepak (1999), *Unintended Consequences. The Impact of Factor Endowments, Culture and Politics on Long-Run Performance*, Cambridge, MA: MIT Press.

Lucas, Robert (1988), 'On the mechanics of economic development', *Journal of Monetary Economics*, **22** (July), 3–42.

Ohmae, Kenichi, (1995), *The End of the Nation State. The Rise of the Regional Economies*, New York: The Free Press.

Rodrik, Dani, (1996), 'Understanding economic policy reform', *Journal of Economic Literature*, **XXXIV**, 9–41.

Rodrik, Dani (2000a), 'Development strategies for the next century', manuscript, Harvard University, February.

Rodrik, Dani, (2000b), *The New Global Economy and Developing Countries. Making Openness Work*, Washington, DC: Overseas Development Council.

Romer, Paul (1986), 'Increasing returns and long term growth', *Journal of Political Economy*, **94**, 1002–37.

Rosati, Dariusz (2001), 'The Balassa–Samuelson effect among the CEEC', paper presented at the Balassa Commemoration Conference, Budapest, 18–19 October.

Rosen, Sherwin (2002), 'Markets and diversity', *American Economic Review*, **92**(1), March, 1–16.

Rosenstein-Rodan, Paul (1943), 'Problems of industrialization of Eastern and South-Eastern Europe', *Economic Journal*, **53** (June–September), 202–11, reprinted in H.S. Ellis (1961).

Soros, George (2002), *On Globalisation*, New York: Norton.

Stiglitz, Joseph (1994), *Whither Socialism?* Cambridge, MA: MIT Press.

Stiglitz, Joseph (2002), *Globalisation and its Discontents*, New York: Norton.

Summers, Larry (2000), 'International financial crises: causes, prevention and cures', *American Economic Review*, Papers and Proceedings, May.

Williamson, John (1994), *The Political Economy of Policy Reform*, Washington, DC: The Institute of International Economics.

World Bank (2000), *Progress Toward the Unification of Europe*, Washington, DC: World Bank.

11. International institutions and financial market stability

Klaus Liebscher

INTRODUCTION

Today's liberalised and universal character of financial markets and capital flows has made it impossible for even the strongest national states to handle the governance of global finance on their own. Thus various networks of intergovernmental consultation and cooperation have developed in parallel with the accelerated globalisation of finance during recent decades.

Ensuring financial market stability can, therefore, be regarded as a global public good. This rests on the simple observation that banks and other financial institutions operate in many different jurisdictions, very often without due cognisance of the consequences they may create. This requires that international agreements, cooperation and coordination ensure international public control, so that negative externalities such as systemic risk or the possible negative impact on economic growth due to financial instability are prevented as far as possible. In addition, international cooperation helps to ensure that a regulatory 'level playing-field' exists such that the possibility of regulatory arbitrage is avoided. International financial integration and its governance thus implies that central banks and other national authorities have to develop policies that foster financial stability not only on a domestic but also on an international level. Let me give you an example to underline my point by referring to the tragic events of 9/11. Without cooperation between the Eurosystem of Central Banks, the Federal Reserve and other international central banks, we might, indeed, have had a very negative impact upon the international financial system and even worse repercussions on global growth.

In the past decades, an impressing number of policy measures and initiatives have been made on the European and the international level to govern issues of financial market stability and – in a broader context – of economic policy. On an international level we witnessed efforts to achieve global convergence in what are considered 'good economic policy measures'; on a European level Monetary Union represents a very successful model of (inter alia) instilling stability into the financial system; hard work has been put into forward-looking measures to prevent crisis in the financial system like Basle II or the IMF's Financial Sector Assessment Programs (FSAPs).

Let me outline a few of these international efforts at coordination and cooperation in more detail.

CONVERGENCE OF ECONOMIC POLICY MEASURES

The meetings of international economic policy makers in the various institutions and fora have produced a remarkable convergence of ideas concerning domestic economic management. The general approach to economic management within developing, emerging and transition economies as well as within the industrial world can perhaps be summed up as 'macroeconomic stability and supply-side flexibility'. These objectives pertaining to both monetary and fiscal policy were agreed to at the 1994 Annual Meeting of the IMF in Madrid.

The emphasis since then is on price stability as the immediate goal of macroeconomic policy. This aim of macroeconomic stability brings into sharper focus the structural, supply side, of the economy. Here, too, there has been a strengthening international presumption in favour of open markets and free competition, both domestically and internationally, with a continuing strong presumption against predatory trade or the use of competitive devaluation. The justification is that undistorted competition contributes to potential global economic growth through increased efficiency and the more effective allocation of productive resources. Faster growth in turn provides a more favourable context for addressing social concerns, including the issue of poverty.

MONETARY UNION: THE EUROPEAN DIMENSION

With the introduction of the Euro, the economic weight of the single market has risen to a level matching that of the USA. And the single currency has gained an important international dimension: the Euro segment of the global money market has risen to about 25 per cent. In the bond market, too, the Euro plays a crucial role in fostering a deeper and more liquid market. The introduction of the Euro paved the way for issuers to gain access to a broader base of investors. Investors too have gained access to a wider spectrum of investment opportunities. The Euro's share in net issuance currently amounts to 39 per cent. Regarding its use as an official reserve currency, the Euro has already attained the same weight as its predecessors.

Within the Euro area, monetary union has kept member countries from being exposed to harmful intra-European exchange rate tensions of the type that many countries used to suffer when external shocks occurred. It has become quite obvious that Austria's inclusion in the stability-oriented economic and monetary union has protected the country from negative shocks much more adequately than was possible under past regimes. Moreover, the almost four years of EMU bear impressive testimony to the fact that the stability-oriented interplay between monetary and fiscal policy provides a solid foundation which was well suited to weathering the economic policy challenges of this period.

With the Euro the EU successfully supplies an important international public good in the form of a stability anchor with deep and attractive financial markets. This is especially relevant with a view to enlargement of the EU. European integration will only be truly successful if it reaches out to the whole of Europe. If the EU manages the enlargement process successfully, this will also be conducive to the Eurosystem's goal of guaranteeing stability for the whole Euro area. Such a mutual improvement is desirable in a very broad sense: political stability, financial market stability, macroeconomic and, in the particular interest of the Eurosystem, price stability.

Already today, the Euro is a key currency in Central and Eastern Europe. In most of the CEECs' monetary policy strategies, exchange rates play a vital role and, wherever they are not a formal or informal intermediate target, they are at least a key monetary policy indicator. It is the Euro upon which the CEECs' currencies are oriented, or to which they are formally linked. Thus EMU and the Euro are already an anchor for stability for CEECs. Moreover enlargement will extend the zone of stability in Europe, strengthen Europe's international competitive position and will contribute substantially to prosperity, security and peace in the long term.

INTEGRATION OF FINANCIAL SERVICES MARKETS IN THE EU

Beyond monetary union a huge amount of work has been undertaken in the EU to improve the functioning of the single market and the international financial system. By abolishing national boundaries and harmonising different legislations, European integration has fostered the development of a single financial market in Europe, but the current regulatory and supervisory framework still strongly relies on national responsibilities.

The EU's Brouwer Report found that there is a need to enhance arrangements for cross-border and cross-sectional cooperation, to improve the alignment of supervisory practices and to reinforce the collaboration between supervisory and central banking functions. The EU's regulatory roadmap to integration is the Financial Services Action Plan, which contains more than

40 legislative and non-legislative measures. The deadline agreed by the European Council for implementing the entire plan is 2005, with an earlier deadline of 2003 for the securities and risk capital markets. Moreover considerable progress has been made in recent attempts to implement the Lamfalussy recommendations in the field of security market regulation.

These two examples illustrate that initiatives are under way and debate is going on. However, not all of the recommendations of the Brouwer Report have been implemented and many other issues still need further investigation and debate. But developments show that we are heading in the right direction.

At the national level we have been observing various proposals to reorganise and restructure financial markets supervision. In Austria, the legal foundations as well as the practice of supervision have been evolving rapidly to respond to developments in the financial sector, to implement the EU financial sector directives and to introduce continuing improvements in international best practice. The most visible change in supervision and regulation has been the establishment of a single financial supervisory agency. Since 1 April 2002, the Financial Market Authority (FMA) has been performing banking, securities, insurance and pension fund supervision.

The Financial Market Authority is autonomous. It operates independently and is not bound by any instructions. The restructuring was aimed at establishing a high-quality, effective and at the same time cost-efficient supervisory regime. Given the Oesterreichische Nationalbank's far-reaching operational integration in banking and financial market supervision, the Austrian central bank can fulfil its manifold macroprudential tasks also within the Eurosystem and can thus contribute to safeguarding financial stability.

The close involvement of central banks in the supervisory process has various advantages. It gives the central bank a much clearer picture of the economic reality that is behind the numbers visible in the books of banks. This information facilitates its role in safeguarding financial stability and creates a special advantage in spotting early warning indicators of financial crises and potential situations of economy-wide financial distress. Moreover, as a part of the Eurosystem, central banks are integrated into an already functioning network of national and supranational institutions. Such a network is of decisive importance in the light of the structural change in European financial markets that has already taken place or is likely to come in the near future.

INTERNATIONAL FINANCIAL SYSTEM: TRANSPARENCY AND CRISIS PREVENTION

The integration of international financial markets is not a new phenomenon. What is unprecedented is its short-term nature, the high turnover and the many financial market agents. This evolution has been actively encouraged by public policy makers and academics alike. In addition to an improved international allocation of capital, internationally integrated markets are thought to provide domestic policymakers with a welcome discipline.

The stability of the financial market rests, in essence, on three pillars: institutions, market participants and infrastructure. A financial system is only as strong as its governing practices, the financial soundness of its institutions and the efficiency of its market infrastructure. Installing and using sound governance practices is a shared responsibility of the market participants and the regulatory agencies. Indeed recent experiences with systemic or significant financial sector crises have underlined the importance of good governance on the part of regulatory agencies. In nearly all financial crises of the past decade (Venezuela, Mexico, East Asia, Russia, Ecuador and Turkey) political interference in the regulatory and supervisory process, weak regulations, inefficient supervision and lack of public sector accountability and transparency have been identified as contributing factors to the depth and size of the systemic crises.

Many of the major initiatives the international community had been taking occurred in reaction to financial crises in the 1990s. On this basis, policy makers have been trying to become more forward-looking to avoid potential difficulties. In particular, three areas of concern have emerged. First, many of the international fora are issuing internationally applicable 'core principles' or 'standards of best practice'. These should encourage improved practices in the economic and financial policies not only of emerging markets but also of industrial countries. Some noteworthy progress has been made in this area and many initiatives are emanating from the IMF.

The main vehicle for evaluating regulatory governance practices in the overall context of macroeconomic stability is the joint IMF–World Bank Financial Sector Assessment Program (FSAP). Aimed at identifying the risks, vulnerabilities and development needs in the financial system, one of the main principles underlying the FSAP is that quality and efficiency of regulatory governance have an impact on the overall governance practices within a financial system, and hence on its functioning and stability.

The FSAP provides an assessment framework that offers 'peer review' of national financial systems, and a common platform for policy advice and technical assistance from the Bank and the Fund. The main instrument through which regulatory governance practices are assessed under the FSAP is through the assessment of the key international financial sector standards. Since the inception of the FSAP in 1999, public sector governance issues have been assessed in almost 45 countries, through over 200 standards assessments. Given the positive impact FSAPs have had and the changes within Austrian supervisory structures with the establishment of the FMA, the Austrian authorities decided to apply for such an assessment themselves.

Second, transparency on the part of all economic agents is deemed to improve the functioning of international markets and lead to greater financial stability. Much has been said and, more importantly, achieved in the area of transparency in recent years. Indeed there has been an explosion of codes and standards on different aspects of economic and financial policy. So much so that some countries are claiming that the process needs to slow down. We should realise that standards and codes cannot be universal to a certain extent since some of them may not be appropriate for countries at a certain stage of development. Therefore standards and codes should reflect different stages of development. The IMF's initiative on Reports on the Observance of Standards and Codes (ROSCs) is a welcome step in this direction. I deem it critical that monitoring of the observance of standards and codes be fully integrated into IMF surveillance under Article IV.

Third, and most important, is how to turn principles of good behaviour into good practice. The international fora and institutions that I have mentioned do not have the power to enforce those principles. Only the IMF has some leverage in monitoring compliance, given its legitimacy and the Article IV consultation process, but it only has real bite in programme countries. Peer pressure, internationally accepted codes and market discipline seem viable ways forward. Yet in the end, enforcement and compliance are still at the discretion of nation states.

INTERNATIONAL INSTITUTIONS AND FORA GEARED TOWARDS FINANCIAL MARKET STABILITY

The institutional architecture of the current governance of global finance is both multi-layered and dispersed. It involves complex networks of state, suprastate, substate and private sector actors. The challenge ahead is certainly to coordinate this network more efficiently. Let me give you a few examples.

The IMF, thanks to its near universal membership of (currently) 184 countries, is probably the only true international organisation with legitimacy. Its mandate encompasses the promotion of macroeconomic stability and sustained non-inflationary growth among its members. The Fund contributes to good governance through its policy advice, technical assistance and programme conditionality. It does so within its areas of expertise which cover the effective and transparent management of public resources and the maintenance of a stable, economic, regulatory and legal environment. The Fund took a leading role in the management of the Third World debt crisis in the 1980s and the emerging market financial crises of the 1990s. Since 1996 the IMF has promoted data standards (the SDDS or Special Data Dissemination Standard) that aim to make information on and for financial markets more reliable and accessible. Recently the Fund's International Monetary and Financial Committee (IMFC) has served as an important forum for intergovernmental consultations regarding the international financial architecture, drawing upon discussions in the Financial Stability Forum (FSF) and the G20. At present, the IMFC is engaged, for example in drawing up the fundamentals for a sovereign debt restructuring mechanism (SDRM) which should allow for a better resolution of external sovereign debt crises.

Central bank governors of the Group of Ten (G10) advanced industrial countries have met regularly at Basle at the Bank for International Settlements (BIS) since 1962 to discuss monetary and financial matters of mutual concern. Unfortunately Austria is not a direct member of this group, but has certainly profited from their initiatives. Most important for international financial governance has been the Group of Seven (G7) summits, held annually since 1975. From time to time, G7 leaders have given orientation to important policy initiatives.

The G10 and the G7 have from time to time set up working parties to explore specific issues related to global finance. The best-known example is the Basle Committee on Banking Supervision (BCBS), formed as a standing group of the G10 in 1975. Most significantly, the BCBS has formulated the Basle Capital Accord, a framework first issued in 1988 for assessing the capital position of international banks, which is now under revision (Basle II), and Core Principles for Effective Banking Supervision, published in 1997.

On a more specific problem, the G7 created the Financial Action Task Force (FATF) in 1989 to combat drug-related money laundering and more recently has been involved in the fight against the financing of terrorism. After the Asian and Russian financial crises, the G7 promoted the establishment of the Financial Stability Forum (FSF), which first convened in April 1999.

While we greatly welcome the work of these important committees, we are not completely satisfied with the trend of moving important discussions out of the main international financial institutions, where all countries are represented, into special fora with a selective membership.

PRIVATE SECTOR INITIATIVES

The financial sector presents an outstanding example of another major trend in current governance, namely, the turn to non-official mechanisms of regulation. A number of national securities and exchange commissions have lain in the private sector for some time, of course, and the International Organisation of Securities Commission (IOSCO) also includes over 50 securities exchanges and dealers' associations as affiliate members. Meanwhile several industry associations have promoted the international harmonisation of standards and devised a number of self-regulatory instruments for bond and equity business in global financial markets.

These bodies include the International Council of Securities Associations (ICSA), the International Federation of Stock Exchanges (FIBV), the International Primary Market Association (IPMA) and the International Securities Market Association (ISMA). The ISMA, indeed, describes its task as 'regulation by the market, for the market'. In addition, private bond-rating agencies like Moody's Investors Service and Standard & Poor's – and the financial markets whose sentiments they reflect – have come to exercise considerable disciplining authority over many national governments.

Private industry plays an important role as a disciplining device in the specific area of conduct of business in securities markets. This is probably due to the ability shown by the securities industry, until recently, to discipline itself effectively and in line with public objectives. However, this ability is being called into question by the increasing complexity of financial markets and instruments, as the Enron case shows. Indeed a tendency to reinforce public authorities vis-à-vis self-regulatory organisations can be observed in Anglo-Saxon countries, in response to this concern.

Both the private and the public sector have a stake in the healthy functioning of financial markets. Therefore we have to foster a new public/private partnership in the governance of financial markets. Moreover we also need international public partnerships to avoid arbitrage of 'standards'.

CONCLUSION

First, standard-setters have, by and large, passed the initial stage of establishing continuity and have created mutual recognition and trust among their members. There are, however, clear differences in the level of ambition across the standard setters.

Second, whenever market forces fail to remove relevant obstacles to integration, public authorities have to intervene either to remove the obstacles or to act as a catalyst to complete the integration process. Moreover they have to act to provide genuine public goods. Hence public agents need to have a broad view of the necessary policies in support of integration, focusing, not just on lifting the remaining regulatory obstacles, but also on the cooperative arrangements among private agents, and maintaining effective competition to the benefit of market participants.

Third, the achievement of a public good can involve the national jurisdiction of the public authorities, while the overall global optimum may not be achieved. Thus national authorities have to take into account the externalities of their actions on an international level.

Fourth, the euro and the European integration process have greatly enhanced our capacity to absorb shocks and to react quickly in situations of financial turmoil. There are still tasks and room for improvement ahead of us, but we have done a lot in recent years constantly to optimise our financial infrastructure. In this way we have kept our own European style and still have worked successfully on gaining a strong voice in international fora, which are proliferating all around in the process of constant build-up of an international financial governance system.

A great deal of progress has already been made in strengthening the central pillars of the international financial system: institutions, markets and infrastructure. What is also clear is that further progress remains to be made in implementing internationally many practices already recognised as being desirable. Many years of effort, both at the domestic and at the international level, will be required on the part of central bankers, as well as many others, to ensure that the international financial system demonstrates the proper balance between efficiency and stability.

Index